BONUS MATERIAL

www.brainrules.net

**Videos guide you through
parenting concepts**

John Medina hosts fun videos on speaking
in parentese, the cookie experiment, dealing with temper tantrums, and more. Plus,
take our parenting quiz.

Film featuring John Medina

Take a lively, 45-minute tour of the
12 original Brain Rules for home, work,
and school—from "Exercise boosts
brain power" to "Sleep well, think well."

brin
rules

for

How to Raise a Smart and Happy Child
from Zero to Five

JOHN MEDINA

Pear
Press

Pear Press
P.O. Box 70525
Seattle, WA 98127-0525
U.S.A.

This book may be purchased for educational, business,
or sales promotional use. For information, please visit
www.pearpress.com.

SECOND EDITION

Edited by Tracy Cutchlow
Designed by Greg Pearson

Library of Congress Cataloging-in-Publication has been applied for.

ISBN-13: 978-0-9832633-8-8

10 9 8 7 6 5 4 3 2 1

Printed in the United States of America.

To my amazing kids
and their even more amazing mother,
for teaching me that when confronted with a choice
between two equally plausible theories,
it is always best to take the one
that is funnier.

contents

brain rules

pregnancy
Healthy mom, healthy baby

relationship
Start with empathy

smart baby
Feeling safe enables learning
Face time, not screen time

happy baby
Make new friends but keep the old
Labeling emotions calms big feelings

moral baby
Firm discipline with a warm heart

sleepy baby
Test before you invest

introduction

Every time I lectured to a group of parents-to-be about baby brain development, I made a mistake. The parents, I thought, had come for a tasty helping of science about the brain in utero—a little neural crest biology here, a little axonal migration there. But in the question-and-answer session after each lecture, the questions were always the same. A very pregnant woman, one rainy night in Seattle, asked, "What can my baby learn while she is still in my womb?" Another woman wondered, "What's going to happen to my marriage after we bring our baby home?" A dad delivered his question with some intensity: "How do I get my kid into Harvard?" An anxious mom asked, "How can I make sure my little girl is going to be happy?" One grandmother had taken over parenting responsibilities from a drug-addicted daughter. "How do I make my grandchild *good*?" she asked. And again and again, new parents pleaded, "How do I get my baby to sleep through the night?"

No matter how many times I tried to steer the conversation toward the esoteric world of neural differentiation, parents asked variations on these same six questions—over and over again. Finally, I realized my mistake. I was giving parents Ivory Tower when they needed Ivory Soap. So this book will not be concerned with the nature of gene regulation in the developing rhombencephalon. *Brain Rules for Baby* instead will be guided by the practical questions my audiences keep asking.

"Brain Rules" are what I call the things we know for sure about how the early-childhood brain works. Each one is quarried from the larger seams of behavioral psychology, cellular biology, and molecular biology. Each was selected for its ability to assist newly minted moms and dads in the daunting task of caring for a helpless little human.

I certainly understand the need for answers. Having a first child is like swallowing an intoxicating drink made of equal parts joy and terror, chased with a bucketful of transitions nobody ever tells you about. I know firsthand: I have two boys, both of whom came with bewildering questions, behavioral issues, and no instructions. I soon learned that's not all they came with. They possessed a gravitational pull that could wrest from me a ferocious love and a tenacious loyalty. They were magnetic: I could not help staring at their perfect finger-nails, clear eyes, and dramatic shocks of hair. By the time my second child was born, I understood that it is possible to split up love ad infi-nitum and not decrease any single portion of it. With parenting, it is truly possible to multiply by dividing.

As a scientist, I was very aware that watching a baby's brain develop feels as if you have a front-row seat to a biological Big Bang. The brain starts out as a single cell in the womb, quiet as a secret. Within a few weeks, it is pumping out nerve cells at the astonishing rate of 8,000 *per second*. Within a few months, it is on its way to becoming the world's finest thinking machine. These mysteries fueled not only wonder and love but, as a rookie parent, I remember, anxiety and questions.

Too many myths

Parents need facts, not just advice, about raising their children. Unfortunately, those facts are difficult to find in the ever-growing mountain of parenting books. And blogs. And message boards, and podcasts, and mother-in-laws, and every relative who's ever had a child. There's plenty of information out there. It's just hard for parents to know what to believe.

The great thing about science is that it takes no sides—and no prisoners. Once you know which research to trust, the big picture emerges and myths fade away. To gain my trust, research must pass my "grump factor." To make it into this book, studies must first have been published in the refereed literature and then successfully replicated. Some results have been confirmed dozens of times. Where I make an exception for cutting-edge research, reliable but not yet fully vetted by the passage of time, I will note it.

To me, parenting is about brain development. That's not surprising, given what I do for a living. I am a developmental molecular biologist, with strong interests in the genetics of psychiatric disorders. My research life has been spent mostly as a private consultant, a for-hire troubleshooter, to industries and public research institutions in need of a geneticist with mental-health expertise. I also founded the Talaris Institute, located in Seattle next to the University of Washington, whose original mission involved studying how infants process information at the molecular, cellular, and behavioral levels. That is how I came to talk to groups of parents from time to time, like on that rainy Seattle night.

Scientists certainly don't know everything about the brain. But what we do know gives us our best chance at raising smart, happy children. And it is relevant whether you just discovered you are pregnant, already have a toddler, or find yourself needing to raise grandchildren. So it will be my pleasure in this book to answer the big questions parents have asked me—and debunk their big myths, too.

Here are some of my favorites:

Myth: Playing Mozart to your womb will improve your baby's future math scores.

Truth: Your baby will simply remember Mozart after birth—along with many other things she hears, smells, and tastes in the womb (see "Babies remember," page 31). If you want her to do well in math in her later years, the greatest thing you can do is to teach her impulse control in her early years (see "Self-control," page 103).

Myth: Exposing your infant or toddler to language DVDs will boost his vocabulary.

Truth: Some DVDs can actually reduce a toddler's vocabulary (see page 146). It is true that the number and variety of words you use when talking to your baby boost both his vocabulary and his IQ (see "Talk to your baby—a lot," page 125). But the words have to come from *you*— a real, live human being.

Myth: To boost their brain power, children need French lessons by age 3 and a room piled with "brain-friendly" toys and a library of educational DVDs.

Truth: The greatest pediatric brain-boosting technology in the world is probably a plain cardboard box, a fresh box of crayons, and two hours. The worst is probably your new flat-screen TV. (See "Hurray for play!" on page 129.)

Myth: Continually telling your children they are smart will boost their confidence.

Truth: They'll become *less* willing to work on challenging problems (see "What happens when you say, 'You're so smart,'" page 138). If you want your baby to get into a great college, praise his or her effort instead.

Myth: Children somehow find their own happiness.

Truth: The greatest predictor of happiness is having friends. How do you make and keep friends? By being good at deciphering nonverbal communication. (See "Helping your child make friends," page 165.) Learning a musical instrument (see page 207) boosts the ability by 50 percent. Text messaging (see page 149) may destroy it.

Research like this is continually published in respected scientific journals. But unless you have a subscription to the *Journal of Experimental Child Psychology,* this rich procession of findings may pass you by. This book is meant to let you know what scientists know—without having a Ph.D. to understand it.

What brain science can't do

I am convinced that not having a robust-enough scientific filter is one of the reasons so many parenting books come to such opposing conclusions. Just try to find a consensus from parenting experts about how to get your baby to sleep through the night. I can't imagine anything more frustrating for first-time parents.

This underscores the fact that brain science can't solve every single parenting situation. It can give us overarching rules, but it is not always good at the specifics. Consider the story one parent posted on *TruuConfessions.com,* a source I use throughout the book:

> *Took dear son's door off last night. No yelling or anything. Warned him if he shut it again after I told him not to, then I was taking it off. Walked down the hall to find it shut again, came back with a power drill and the door went to the garage for the night. Put it back up today, but I'll take it right back down again if I need to.*

Can brain science weigh in on this situation? Not really. Research tells us that parents must have clear rules and swift consequences for rule violations. It can't tell us whether you should take off a door. In truth, we are just starting to learn what good parenting looks like. Parenting research is tough to do, for four reasons:

1. Every kid is different

Every brain is literally wired differently. No two kids are going to react to the same situation in an identical manner. So there is no such thing as one-size-fits-all parenting advice. Because of this individuality, I appeal to you to get to know your children. That means spending a lot of time with them. Knowing how they behave and how their behaviors change over time is the only way to discover what will and will not work in raising them.

From a researcher's perspective, the brain's willingness to respond to its external environment is pretty frustrating. Individual complexity is muddled in cultural differences, complete with their very own value systems. On top of that, families in poverty have very different problems from those of upper-middle-class families. The brain responds to all of this (poverty can influence IQ, for one). No wonder this stuff is so hard to research.

2. Every parent is different

Kids raised in two-parent households are confronted with not one parenting style but two. Moms and dads often hold different parenting priorities, a source of great conflict in some relationships. A *combination* of the two styles guides the child.

Here's one example:

> *I go nuts watching my brother and sister-in-law with their kids. She parents occasionally, from the couch. So he overcompensates by yelling at them for EVERYTHING. From the outside perspective, it looks like the reason the kids don't behave is that they have NO IDEA what the rules are; they just know they'll get in trouble no matter what they do and they stop trying to behave.*

Two styles indeed. This argues for 100 percent cooperation between father and mother about how their children will be raised. That, of course, is impossible. Child rearing in two-parent households will always be a hybrid proposition. Eventually, the children begin responding back to the parents, which will influence future parenting behavior. All of these changes complicate the research.

3. Kids are influenced by others

Life gets even more complex as a child grows up. School and peer interactions play an increasingly powerful role in shaping children. (Anybody out there have a horrible high-school experience you still think about?) One researcher has gone on record saying that peers—especially of the same sex—shape a child's behavior much more than parents do. As you might suspect, this idea has met with a great deal of skepticism. But not outright rejection. Children do not live in an exclusive social ecology dominated by parents and nobody else.

4. We can say "linked to" but not "causes"

Even if all brains were wired identically and all parents behaved in a cookie-cutter fashion, a great deal of current research would still be flawed (or, at best, preliminary). Most of the data we have are associative, not causal. Why is that a problem? Two things can be associated without one causing the other. For example, it is true that all children who throw temper tantrums also urinate—the association is 100 percent—but that doesn't mean urination leads to temper tantrums.

The ideal research project would be to (a) find the behavioral secret sauce that makes smart or happy or moral kids who they are, (b) discover parents who were missing the secret sauce and give it to them, and (c) measure the kids 20 years later to see how they turned out. That sounds not only expensive but impossible. This is why most research we have about parenting is associative, not causal. But these data will be shared in the spirit that the perfect should not be the enemy of the good. The other frustrating and wondrous thing is this:

Human behavior is complicated!

We can look simple and calm on the surface, like a glassy sea, but below that you find craggy canyons of emotion, murky ruminations, and floating, barely rational motivations. Occasionally, these characteristics—different ones for each person—will bubble to the surface. Consider one common emotional reaction to a toddler:

> *Well that's it, it's official. I have not one drop of patience left. The well is dry. My two-year-old son has managed to use up my life- time supply of patience, all before the age of 3. It's gone, and I don't see how it might be replenished to its original depths without concentrated effort … i.e., a week in the Caribbean w/ an endless supply of mai tais.*

As a brain scientist, I can count at least eight separate behavioral research issues in this woman's short paragraph. She is responding to stress, and the way her body does that was carved out long ago on the plains of the Serengeti. How she loses her patience depends in part on her genes, events while she was in the womb, and how she was raised as a little girl. Hormones are involved too, as are the neuro- logical signals she uses to perceive her recalcitrant toddler. A memory of relief is also apparent—perhaps she is recalling a cruise?—as is her desire to escape. In only five sentences, she has taken us from the African savannah to the 21st century.

And brain researchers, from evolutionary theorists to memory specialists, study all of it.

So there *are* some solid things researchers can say about raising kids. Otherwise, I would not have plopped down my own contribu- tion to the pile of 40 gazillion books for parents. It has taken many good researchers many years to mine these nuggets of information.

Relevant for kids through age 5

Brain Rules for Baby encompasses brain development in children ages 0 to 5. I know you're likely to inhale parenting information when you're pregnant, and you're less likely to return later for more. So the title of the book is intended to catch your attention early on. But what you do in your child's first five years of life—not just the first year—profoundly influences how he or she will behave as an adult. We know this because a group of researchers had the patience to follow 123 low-income, at-risk preschoolers for four decades, until their 40th birthdays. Welcome to the HighScope Perry Preschool Study, one of the most extraordinary studies of its kind.

In 1962, researchers wanted to test the effects of an early-childhood training program they had designed. Kids in Ypsilanti, Michigan, were randomly assigned to one of two groups. The first attended the preschool program (which eventually became a model for other preschool programs nationwide, including Head Start). The second group did not. The differences between the two groups powerfully illustrate the importance of a child's early years.

The kids in the program academically outperformed the controls in virtually every way you can measure performance, from IQ and language tests in the early years to standardized achievement assessments and literacy exams in the later years. To cite just one example (performance on the 1970 California Achievement Test), kids in the program scored far better than the controls: a whopping 49 percent vs. 15 percent. Among girls, though not boys, more graduated from high school (84 percent vs. 32 percent).

As adults, those who had been in the program were less likely to commit crimes and more likely to hold steady jobs. They made more money, more often had a savings account, and were more likely to own a home. Economists calculated that the return on society's investment in such a program was 7 to 10 percent, higher than what you'd historically get in the stock market. If each tax dollar was invested from age 4 through 65, it would return "in present-value terms $7 to $12 back to society," one analysis said.

Seed and soil

The HighScope study is a prime example of the importance of environment in raising children. But nature plays just as large a role. Often, they are tough to separate, as in this old joke: A third-grade boy comes home and hands his father his report card. His father looks at it and says, "How do you explain these D's and F's?" The boy looks up at him and says, "You tell me: Is it nature or nurture?"

I was once at a lively, noisy science fair with my own third-grade son, and we were touring some of his classmates' efforts. Several experiments involved seeds, soil, and growth curves. One memorable little girl took great pains to explain to us that her seeds had started with identical DNA. She had planted one in a nutrient-rich soil and watered it carefully. She had planted the other in a nutrient-poor soil and watered it carefully, too. Time passed. The seed nurtured with terrific soil made a terrific plant, which she proudly let me hold in my hands. The seed nurtured in poor soil made a pitiful, withered plant. She let me hold that, too. Her point was that the seed material provided identical growth opportunities for both plants, but that an equal start was not enough. "You need both seed and soil," she explained to me—nature and nurture—to get the desired results.

She's right, of course, and it's a metaphor I use in this book to organize the research on raising smart and happy kids. There are some factors parents can't control and some they can. There's seed, and there's soil. All of the nurture in the world won't change the fact that 50 percent of your child's potential is genetic. Good news: As a parent, you can only do your best. That said, even as a professional geneticist, I am convinced we can exert far more influence over our kids' behavior than is popularly imagined. It's a very, very big job that takes a lot of work. The reason has deep evolutionary roots.

Why do we need parenting, anyway?

It's a question that bothers many evolutionary scientists: How come it takes so long to raise a human child? Aside from perhaps a whale or two, we have the longest childhood on the planet. Where did this decades-long sojourn come from, and why don't other animals have to go through what we do? Just a couple of delightful things we human parents endure:

> *I feel so drained. JJ pooped in his diaper right after I got him off the potty, he threw up on the carpet, tipped his potty over and got pee on the carpet again, then he peed on the carpet AGAIN at bath time. I've come so far and feel like I can't do this mommy thing, then I realize—I'm doing it …*

> *Both my husband and I have rather colorful vocabularies. We never swear at our dear daughter, and try to watch our language around her, but we're obviously failing miserably—my mom asked her what her baby's name is, and she responded, "Asshole." Oops.*

Yes, you have to teach children *everything*—even how to regulate their body fluids. And they are built to learn, which means you have to watch even your most cavalier behaviors. Both take a tremendous amount of energy. So evolutionary biologists have to wonder: Why would anyone willingly take on this line of work?

The interview for the job, that single act of sex, is certainly fun. But then you get hired to *raise a child*. There are wonderful moments, but the essence of the contract is simply: They take. You give. You never get a paycheck with this job, only an invoice, and you'd better be prepared for some sticker shock. You'll be out more than $220,000—before the college loans. This career comes with no sick days or vacation time, and it puts you permanently on call nights and weekends. Its successful execution will probably turn you into a lifelong worrywart. Yet thousands of people every day say yes to this job. There must be some compelling reason.

Survival, first and foremost

Of course, there is. The brain's chief job description—yours, mine, and your hopelessly adorable children's—is to help our bodies survive another day. The reason for survival is as old as Darwin and as young as sexting: so we can project our genes into the next generation. Will a human willingly overcome self-interest to ensure the survival of his or her genes into the next generation? Apparently, yes. Enough of us did hundreds of thousands of years ago that we grew up to take over the Serengeti, then take over the world. Taking care of a baby is a sophisticated way of taking care of ourselves.

But why does it take so much time and effort?

Blame our big, fat, gold-plated, nothing-else-like-it brains. We evolved to have larger brains with higher IQs, which allowed us to move from leopard food to Masters of the Universe in 10 million very short years. We gained big brains through the energy savings of walking on two legs instead of four. But attaining the balance necessary to walk upright required the narrowing of the *Homo sapiens* pelvic canal. For females, that meant one thing: excruciatingly painful, often fatal births. An arms race quickly developed, evolutionary biologists theorized, between the width of the birth canal and the size of the brain. If the baby's head were too small, the baby would die (without extraordinary and immediate medical intervention, premature infants wouldn't last five minutes). If the baby's head were too big, the mother would die. The solution? Give birth to babies before their skulls become too big to kill mom. The consequence? Kids come into the world before their brains are fully developed. The result? *Parenthood.*

Because the bun is forced to come out of the oven before it is done, the child needs instruction from veteran brains for years. The relatives are the ones who get the job, as they brought the child into the world in the first place. You don't have to dig deep into the Darwinian playbook to find a cogent explanation for parenting behavior.

That's not the entire mystery of parenting, but it underscores its importance. We survived because enough of us became parents good enough to shepherd our pooping, peeing, swearing, breathtakingly vulnerable offspring into adulthood. And we have no real say in the matter. A baby's brain simply isn't ready to survive the world.

Clearly, childhood is a vulnerable time. More than a decade passes between the birth of a baby and its ability to reproduce—an eternity compared with other species. This gap shows not only the depth of the brain's developmental immaturity but also the evolutionary need for unflinchingly attentive parenting. As we evolved, adults who formed protective and continuous teaching relationships with the next generation were at a distinct advantage over those who either could not or would not. In fact, some evolutionary theorists believe that language developed in all its richness just so that this instruction between parent and child could occur with greater depth and efficiency. Relationships among adults were crucial to our survival as well—and they still are, despite ourselves.

We are social beings

Modern society is doing its level best to shred deep social connections. We move constantly. Our relatives are often scattered across hundreds, even thousands, of miles. These days we make and maintain our friendships electronically. One of the chief complaints new parents have in the transition to parenthood is the great isolation they feel from their social circle. To their relatives, baby is often a stranger. To their friends, baby is often a four-letter word. That's not how it was supposed to be. Take a moment to mark all of the times the writer of this story references her friends and family:

I moved back home with my grandparents to save money for school. I grew up here. My roots run deep. One of our dearest neighbors died and his family is getting the house together to sell. Tonight, a bunch of us, including his son, congregated in the garage, drank wine and reminisced about so many of the neighbors and family who are no longer with us. There was laughter and tears, but there was such a precious feeling [that] the ones who had gone before us were there, and laughing too. It was so amazing!

We are so darn social. Understanding this about the brain is fundamental to understanding many of the themes in this book, from empathy to language to the effects of social isolation. Because the brain is a biological organ, the reasons are evolutionary. Most scientists believe we survived because we formed cooperative social groups. This forced us to spend lots of time in the land of relationships, getting to know one another's motivations, psychological interiors, and systems of reward and punishment.

Two benefits emerged. One was the ability to work as a team—useful for hunting, finding shelter, and defending against predators. The other was the ability to help raise one another's children. The battle between birth-canal size and baby-skull size meant females needed time to recover from giving birth. Somebody had to take care of the kids. Or take over the nurturing if she died. The task fell mostly to females (males can't lactate, after all), though many scientists believe the most successful groups were ones where males played an active role in supporting the females. That communal need was so strong, and so critical to our survival, that researchers have given the phenomenon its own name: alloparenting. If as a parent you feel as though you can't do it alone, that's because you were never meant to.

Though no direct knowledge exists of how our hunter-gatherer ancestors raised their kids, evidence for these tendencies abounds today. We know babies come into this world wired with a deep desire to form relationships with other people. Since birth parents are the first humans that infants encounter, their natural first targets are family. But that soon extends to others. One mother reported watching *American Idol* with her son, age 2. As the host interviewed the crying contestants who didn't make it, the boy jumped up, patted the screen, and said, "Oh no, don't cry." This skill requires deep relational skills, illustrating as much a biological process as it does a sweet kid. All of us have natural connecting abilities.

If you understand that the brain has a deep need for relating to others, and that the brain is interested foremost in survival, the information in this book—the things that best develop your baby's brain—will make sense.

A few notes before we begin

Defining family

Maybe you saw this soft-drink commercial. The camera follows a pleasant-looking, college age young man at a social event in a large house. It's the holidays, and he is busy introducing you to his various friends and family, singing a song, and passing out soft drinks. There's his mom, his sis, his brother, his "surprisingly cool stepmother," and the two kids his stepmom had before meeting his dad, plus aunts, cousins, office mates, his best friend, his judo coach, his allergist, even his Twitter fans. It was the clearest example I have seen that the definition of the American family is changing. Rapidly.

It never was stable. The definition of a nuclear family—one man, one woman, and 2.8 kids—has been around only since Victorian times. With a divorce rate of 40 percent to 50 percent circling like a vulture over American marriages for more than three decades and remarriage common, the "blended" family is now the more typical family experience. So is the single-parent household, with more than 40 percent of all American births occurring to unmarried women. More than 4.5 million kids are being raised not by their biological parents but by their biological grandparents. One in five gay couples is now raising children.

Many of these social changes have moved too quickly for the scientific community to adequately study them. You can't do a 20-year study, for example, on gay marriages that have only recently been made legal. Over the years, the best parenting data have been mined from heterosexual relationships in a traditional 20th-century marriage. Until researchers have had a chance to investigate the dynamics of more modern families, we simply won't know if the insights described here directly apply to other situations. That's why I use the terms "marriage" and "spouse" instead of "partner."

The sources of the stories

Many of the first-person stories in this book come from *TruuConfessions.com*, a website where parents can post anonymously to get things off their chests, seek advice, or share their parenting experiences with the world.

Other stories come from experiences my wife and I have had parenting our two sons, Josh and Noah, who are teenagers at this writing. We have kept a diary of their growing-up years, writing down fragments of observations, scavenging our memories of a holiday, a trip, or some wonderful thing our kids taught us that day. Both boys reviewed every story in which they were involved, and I asked their permission to put each one in the book. Only the ones they said yes to made it into these pages. I applaud both their courage and their sense of humor for letting dear old Dad share slivers of their early lives.

The sources of the data

In these pages, there are places where virtually every sentence is referenced. But for readability of the book, the references have migrated online to *www.brainrules.net/references*. The Brain Rules website, *www.brainrules.net*, is chock-full of additional supporting material, including dozens of videos. Certain subjects I leave out altogether: some to keep the book at a reasonable length; others because there is just not enough supporting documentation.

My wife's kitchen

We're just about ready to get started. Given the tremendous amount of information in this book, I wanted a metaphor to help organize it. The solution comes from my wife, who, among countless talents, is a gifted cook. Our kitchen is stocked with many things, from mundane items like oatmeal (yes, our family eats "porridge") to bottles of exotic wine. She makes lots of comfort food, so there are ingredients for beef stew and spice rubs for chicken. Kari also keeps a garden of fruits and vegetables outside the kitchen door, and she uses a variety of natural fertilizers to enrich the soil. A three-legged stool in the kitchen helps our boys reach the cabinets and participate in the cooking. You'll recognize these items throughout the chapters, including the seeds and soil of the garden. I hope that visualizing my wife's garden and kitchen will render these many ideas in a friendly, accessible form.

Ready to grow a smart, happy baby? Pull up a chair. You are going to read about a truly magical world. The most important job you've ever signed up for may also be the most interesting thing you'll ever do.

pregnancy

brain rule

Healthy mom, healthy baby

pregnancy

 One day I gave a lecture to a group of expecting couples. A woman and her husband came up to me afterward, looking anxious. "My father is a ham radio operator," the wife said. "He told my husband that he should start tapping on my belly. Is that a good thing?" She looked puzzled. So did I. "Why tapping?" I asked. The husband said, "Not just any tapping. He wants me to learn Morse code. He wants me to start tapping messages into the kid's brain, so the little guy will be smart. Maybe we could teach him to tap back!" The wife interjected, "Will that make him smart? My belly is really sore, and I don't like it."

I remember this being a funny moment; we had a good laugh. But it was also sincere. I could see the questioning look in their eyes.

Whenever I lecture on the extraordinary mental life of the developing fetus, I can almost feel a wave of panic ripple across the room. Pregnant couples in the audience become concerned, then start furiously scribbling down notes, often talking in excited whispers to their neighbors. Parents with grown children sometimes seem satisfied, sometimes regretful; a few even look guilty. There is skepticism, wonder, and, above all, lots of questions. Can a baby really learn Morse code in the latter stages of pregnancy? And if he could, would it do him any good?

Scientists have uncovered many new insights about a baby's mental life in the womb. In this chapter, we'll delve into the magnificent mystery of how brains develop—all starting from a handful of tiny cells. We'll talk about what that means for Morse code, detailing the things proven to aid in utero brain development. Hint: There are only four. And we will explode a few myths along the way; for one, you can put away your Mozart CDs.

Quiet, please: Baby in progress

If I were to give a single sentence of advice based on what we know about in utero development during the first half of pregnancy, it would be this: The baby wants to be left alone.

At least at first. From the baby's point of view, the best feature of life in the womb is its relative *lack* of stimulation. The uterus is dark, moist, warm, as sturdy as a bomb shelter, and much quieter than the outside world. And it needs to be. Once things get going, your little embryo's pre-brain will pump out neurons at the astonishing rate of 500,000 cells a minute. That's more than 8,000 cells per second, a pace it will sustain for weeks on end. This is readily observable three weeks after conception, and it continues until about the midpoint in your pregnancy. The kid has a great deal to accomplish in a very short time! A peaceful lack of interference from amateur parents is just what you'd expect the baby to need.

In fact, some evolutionary biologists believe this is why morning sickness still persists in human pregnancies. Morning sickness, which can last the entire day (and, for some women, the entire pregnancy), makes a woman stick to a bland, boring diet—if she eats much at all. This avoidance strategy would have kept our maternal ancestors away from the natural toxins in exotic or spoiled foods in the wild, unregulated menu of the Pleistocene diet. The accompanying fatigue would keep women from engaging in physical activity risky enough to harm the baby.

Researchers now think it could make the baby smarter, too. One study, yet to be replicated, looked at children whose mothers suffered from major nausea and vomiting during pregnancy. When the children reached school age, 21 percent scored 130 or more points on a standard IQ test, a level considered gifted. If their mothers had no morning sickness, only 7 percent of kids did that well. The researchers have a theory—still to be proved—about why. Two hormones that stimulate a woman to vomit may also act like neural fertilizer for the developing brain. The more vomiting, the more fertilizer; hence, the greater effect on IQ.

Whatever the reasons, the baby seems to be going to great lengths to get you to leave it alone.

How good are we at leaving baby alone—at this stage or any other in the womb? Not very. Most parents have a gnawing desire to do *something* to help baby, especially when it comes to baby's brain. Fueling that drive is an enormous sector of the toy economy whose sole strategy is, I am convinced, to play off the fears of well-meaning parents. Pay close attention, for I am about to save you a ton of money.

Pregaphones and prodigies

Shopping in a toy store several years ago, I came across an ad for a DVD designed for newborns and toddlers, called *Baby Prodigy*. The flier stated: "Did you know that you can actually help to enhance the development of your baby's brain? The first 30 months of life is the period when a child's brain undergoes its most critical stages of evolution…. Together we can help to make your child the next Baby Prodigy!" It made me so angry, I crushed the flier and threw it in the garbage can.

These outlandish claims have a long history. The late 1970s saw the creation of Prenatal University, a for-purchase curriculum that claimed to boost a baby's attention span, cognitive performance, and vocabulary, all before labor. The kid actually received a degree declaring him or her "Baby Superior" after birth. The late '80s introduced the Pregaphone, a glorified funnel-and-speaker system designed to pump into a pregnant woman's belly the mother's voice or classical music or whatever other IQ-boosting noise du jour. More products soon followed, complete with some extraordinary advertising hype: "Teach your baby to spell in the womb!" "Teach your child a second language before birth!" "Improve your baby's math scores by playing classical music!" Mozart was a particular favorite, culminating in something you may have heard before: the Mozart Effect. Things did not get better in the 1990s. Books published in that decade outlined short, daily activities for pregnant couples claiming to "raise your baby's IQ as much as 27 to 30 points" and increase your baby's attention span "as much as 10 to 45 minutes."

> No commercial product has ever been shown to do anything to improve the brain performance of a developing fetus.

If you walk into any toy store today, you are bound to find products making similar claims. Almost none of their assertions are backed up by in-house testing, let alone backed up by independent, peer-reviewed research.

Crinkle. Toss.

Believe it or not, *no* commercial product has ever been shown in a scientifically responsible manner (or even in an irresponsible non-scientific manner) to do *anything* to improve the brain performance of a developing fetus. There have been no double-blind, randomized experiments whose independent variable was the presence or absence of the gadget. No rigorous studies showing that an in utero education curriculum produced long-term academic benefits when the child entered high school. No twins-separated-at-birth studies attempting to tease out nature and nurture components of a given product's effects. That includes the in utero university. And the in utero Mozart.

Sadly, myths rush in when facts are few, and they have a way of snaring people. Even after all these years, many of these products are still out there, functioning like untethered gill nets, trapping unsuspecting parents into parting with their hard-earned dollars.

The rush to create marketable products is appalling to us in the research community. Their spuriousness is also counter-productive. These products generate so much attention, they can obscure the reporting of some truly meaningful findings. There *are* activities that expecting parents can do to aid the cognitive development of their baby-under-construction. They've been tested and evaluated, with the results hashed out in refereed scientific literature. To understand their value, you need to know a few facts about the developing infant brain. Once you get a peek at what's really going on in there, it will be easy to see why so many products are just hype.

Let's get it on

The opening cast members of the baby-making play are simply a sperm and an egg and a saucy Marvin Gaye song. Once these two cells are joined, they begin producing lots of cells in a small space. The human embryo soon looks like a tiny mulberry. (Indeed, one early development stage is called the morula, Latin for mulberry.) Your mulberry's first decision is practical: It has to decide what part becomes baby's body and what part becomes baby's shelter. This happens quickly. Certain cells are assigned to housing construction, creating the placenta and the water balloon in which the embryo will float, the amniotic sac. Certain cells are assigned the duties of constructing the embryo, creating a knot of internal tissues termed the inner cell mass.

We need to stop right here and contemplate something: The inner cell mass at this stage possesses a cell whose entire offspring will form the human brain. The most complex information-processing device ever constructed is on its way. And it starts out a fraction of the size of the period at the end of this sentence.

I have been studying this stuff for more than 20 years, and I still find it amazing. As scientist Lewis Thomas put it in *The Medusa and the Snail*: "The mere existence of such a cell should be one of the great astonishments of the earth. People ought to be walking around all day, all through their waking hours, calling to each other in endless wonderment, talking of nothing except that cell." Go ahead, call your neighbor; I'll wait.

The miracle continues. If you could see it in action, this embryo floating in seawater, you would notice that the inner cell mass is actually swarming with cells, scurrying around like busy short-order cooks at the county fair. The cells arrange themselves into three living layers, looking for all the world like a cheeseburger. The bottom bun, called the endoderm, will form most of the cell systems that line your baby's organs and vessels. The burger layer, the mesoderm, forms your baby's bones, muscles, blood, and various connective tissues, amongst other systems. The top bun is the ectoderm. It will create your baby's skin, hair, nails, and nervous systems. It is within the ectoderm that the miraculous little pre-brain cell resides.

Looking closer, you would see the tiniest line of cells forming atop the bun's center. Below, a log-shaped cylinder begins to form and elongate itself, using the overhead line as a guide. This cylinder is the neural tube. It will give rise to the spinal column—the far end of the log becoming your baby's butt, the near end becoming baby's brain.

When something goes wrong

It's vital that this neural tube develop properly. If it doesn't, the baby could have a protruding spinal cord or a tumor near his lower back, a condition known as spina bifida. Or the baby could grow without a complete head, a rare condition known as anencephaly. This is why every pregnancy book strongly recommends taking the B-complex vitamin folic acid: It helps shape the proper neural tube— both the near and far ends. Women who take folic acid around conception and during the first few weeks of pregnancy are 76 percent less likely to create a fetus with neural tube defects than those who don't take the supplement. It is the first thing you can do to aid brain development.

Parents-to-be throughout history have worried about whether their babies are developing properly. In 1573, French surgeon Ambroise Paré catalogued the events to which prudent young pregnant couples should be alerted to avoid a child with birth defects. "There are several things that cause monsters," he wrote in *On Monsters and Marvels*. "The first is the glory of God. The second, His wrath. The third, too great a quantity of seed [sperm]. The fourth, too little a quantity." Paré hypothesized that a birth defect could be caused by indecent posturing of mom (she sat too long with her legs crossed). Or it could be due to the narrowness of the uterus, demons and devils, or the wicked spittle of beggars.

We can perhaps forgive Paré's pre-scientific misunderstanding of in utero brain development. Even to the modern mind, it is scary, hopelessly complex, and mostly mysterious. Researchers today are at a complete loss to explain nearly two-thirds of all birth defects. Indeed, only a quarter of all known birth defects have been tied to an isolable DNA problem. One of the reasons we know so little is that mom's body appears to have a fail-safe mechanism. If something goes wrong during development, her body often senses trouble and deliberately induces a miscarriage. About 20 percent of pregnancies end in spontaneous abortion. Known environmental toxins, things you can actually monitor, account for only 10 percent of the birth defects observed in the lab.

A delicate web of cells, crackling with electricity

Fortunately, most babies' brains form just fine. The brain end of the neural tube continues its construction project by creating bulges of cells that look like complex coral formations. These eventually form the large structures of the brain. Before the first month, the baby's tiny pre-brain cell has grown into a hefty army, millions of cells strong.

The brain does not develop in isolation, of course. The early embryo temporarily displays gill arches around the fourth week, for example, much like the ones fish have. These soon convert into face muscles and the throat structures that will allow your baby to speak. Your embryo next gets the stub of a tail but soon reverses course and resorbs the structure. There are strong evolutionary roots to our development, and we share this miracle with every other mammal on the planet. Except for one thing.

Those bulges at the end of your embryo's neural tube will turn into a great big, fat, super-smart brain—about the heaviest brain-per-body mass that exists on the planet. This massive structure is composed of a delicate spider web of cells, crackling with tiny bolts of electricity. Two types of cells are important here. The first type, glial cells, make up 90 percent of the brain cells inside your child's head. They give the brain its structure and help the neurons correctly process information. It's a good name; glial is a Greek word for glue. The second type of cell is the familiar neuron. Though they do a lot of your child's thinking, neurons make up only about 10 percent of the total number of brain cells. That's probably where we get the myth that you use only 10 percent of your brain.

One neuron, 15,000 connections

So how do cells turn into brains? Embryonic cells are manufactured into neurons in a process called neurogenesis. This is when the baby would like to be left alone, in the first half of pregnancy. Then, in the second half of pregnancy, the neurons migrate to the region they eventually will call home and start wiring together. This is called synaptogenesis.

Cell migration reminds me of when tracking bloodhounds are suddenly loosed from the sheriff's truck to pick up the scent of a criminal. Neurons bolt out of their ectodermal cages, crawling over one another, sniffing out molecular cues, pausing, trying out different pathways, slithering helter-skelter throughout the developing brain. Eventually they stop, having arrived at a destination that may be pre-programmed into their cellular heads. They look around their new cellular digs and try to hook up with the neighbors. When they do, tiny, lively gaps between neural cells are created, called synapses (hence, the term synaptogenesis). Electrical signals jump between the naked spaces to allow neural communication. This final step is the real business of brain development.

Synaptogenesis is a prolonged process, for an easily understood reason: It is ridiculously complex. A single neuron has to make an average of 15,000 connections with the locals before its wiring job is done. Some neurons have to make more than 100,000 connections. That means your baby's brain has to lash together an astonishing 1.8 million new connections per second to make a complete brain. Many of the neurons never complete the process. Like post-sex salmon, they simply die off.

Even given this incredible speed, baby brains never make the birth deadline. About 83 percent of synaptogenesis continues *after* birth. Surprisingly, your baby girl's brain will not completely finish its wiring until she is in her early 20s. Boys' brains may take even longer. In humans, the brain is the last organ to finish developing.

When can baby hear you, smell you?

The purpose of that furiously fast (then frustratingly slow) production is to build a functioning brain, one that can receive and respond to inputs. So the questions for prying parents become: What do fetuses know, and when do they know it? When is your baby capable of sensing, say, taps on your belly?

The developmental principle to remember is this: The brain spends the first half of pregnancy setting up its neuroanatomical shop, *blissfully ignoring most parental involvement.* (I am referring to well-intentioned interference. Drugs, including alcohol and nicotine, clearly can damage a baby's brain during pregnancy.) The second half of pregnancy is a different story. As brain development moves from mostly neurogenesis to mostly synaptogenesis, the fetus begins to exhibit much greater sensitivity to the outer world. The wiring of cells is much more subject to outside influences—including you— than the act of creating them in the first place.

The senses develop strategically

What is baby's approach to constructing the brain's sensory systems? Ask paratroop commanders. They will tell you that successfully fighting a war involves three steps: parachuting into enemy territory, securing hostile real estate, and communicating back to home base. This process gives central command both knowledge about progress and "situational awareness" of what to do next. Something similar happens to sensory systems in the brain as they develop in utero.

Like parachutists securing enemy territory, neurons invade a given region of the brain and establish various sensory bases. Neurons that hook up to the eyes will eventually be used for vision, ears for hearing, nose for smelling. Once their areas are secured, these cells will establish linkages that help them reach out to the perceptual command-and-control structures also growing up within the brain. (In the real world of the brain, there are many central commands.) These CEO-like structures, which give us perceptual abilities, are busily capturing territory just like the paratroopers. And they are some of the last areas in utero to wire up properly. This means neurons hooked up to the eyes or ears or nose might receive a busy signal when they try to report back to their home base. Because of this odd timing, parts of a baby's brain can respond to sensory stimulation before a baby can actually perceive being stimulated.

But once babies can perceive inputs like sounds and smells, starting around the second half of the pregnancy, they become precisely attuned to them. And they subconsciously remember. Sometimes it's spooky, as legendary conductor Boris Brott discovered one day.

Babies remember

"It just jumped out at me!" Brott exclaimed to his mother. Brott had been at the podium of a symphony orchestra, conducting a piece of music for the first time, when the cellist began to play. He instantly *knew* he'd heard this piece before. This was no casual reminder of some similar but forgotten work: Brott could predict exactly what musical phrase was coming next. He could anticipate the flow of the entire work during the course of the rehearsal; he knew how to conduct it even when he lost his place in the score.

Freaking out, he called his mother, a professional cellist. She asked for the name of the piece of music, then burst out laughing. *It was the piece she had been rehearsing when she was pregnant with him.* The cello was up against her late-pregnancy mid-abdomen, a structure filled with sound-conducting fluids, fully capable of relaying musical information to her unborn son. His developing brain was sensitive enough to record the musical memories. "All the scores I knew by sight were the ones she had played while she was pregnant with me," Brott later said in an interview. Incredible stuff for an organ not even 0 years old.

This is but one of many examples of how babies in the womb can pick up information from the outer world. As we'll see, what you eat and smell can influence your infant's perceptions, too. For a newborn, these things are the familiar comforts of home.

Let's look at when your baby's senses—touch, sight, hearing, smell, balance, taste—start to function as you transit through pregnancy.

Touch

One of the earliest senses to come on line is touch. Embryos about 1 month old can sense touch to their noses and lips. The ability spreads quickly, and nearly the entire surface of the skin is sensitive to touch by 12 weeks of age.

I swear I could detect this by the time my wife was in the middle of her third trimester with our youngest son. He was quite a mover, and at times I could see what looked like a bulging shark's fin move across my wife's belly, swelling, then submerging. Creepy. And cool. Thinking it might be the little guy's foot, I tried touching the bulge when it appeared one morning. The bulge immediately "kicked" back (!), causing us both to yelp with excitement.

If you try this in the first half of pregnancy, you won't get any results. Not until about the fifth month after conception can babies truly experience touch in the way you and I might perceive it. That's when your baby's brain develops "body maps"—tiny neurological representations of his entire body.

By the beginning of the third trimester, a fetus readily displays avoidance behaviors (trying to swim away, for example, when a needle comes near for biopsy). From this we conclude that babies can feel pain, though it is impossible to measure this directly.

The fetus appears to possess sensitivity to temperature by this time, too. But it's possible that the wiring diagrams for temperature sensation aren't fully completed at birth and that they require experience with the outside world to fully develop. In two unrelated child-abuse cases, a French boy and an American girl were kept in isolation for years. Both children had an eerie inability to distinguish between hot and cold. The little girl never dressed appropriately for the weather, even when it was freezing outdoors. The little boy regularly pulled potatoes out of a roaring fire with his bare hands, oblivious to the temperature difference. We don't know exactly why. We do know that touch remains very important for a baby's development after birth.

Sight

Can babies see in the womb? That's a tough question to answer, mostly because vision is our most complex sense.

Vision begins developing about four weeks after conception, the fetus forming little eye-dots on either side of her tiny head. Cup-shaped structures within these dots soon emerge, which will form, in part, the lens of the eye. Retinal nerves then snake out from behind these primitive eyes, trying to reach the back of the head and connect to regions that will eventually form the visual cortex. The cells in this cortex have themselves been busy, getting ready to greet these neural travelers and form partnerships. The second and third trimesters are filled with massive neural meet and greets in these regions, a fair bit of cell death, and lots of chattering connectivity. At this point, the brain is forming about 10 billion new synapses per day. You'd think a baby would get a migraine!

One result of all this activity is that the neural circuitry necessary to control blinking, dilation of pupils, or tracking moving objects is present before birth. Experiments show that infants just entering the third trimester will move or alter their heart rate, or both, in response to a strong light beamed at the womb. But it takes so long to build adequately functioning circuits that the baby needs more than nine months to finish the job. The brain will continue forming 10 billion synapses a day for almost a year after birth. During that interval, the brain uses external visual experiences to help it finish its internal construction projects.

Hearing

If you were to tell me that an important scientific fact was going to be discovered using a combination of mouth sucking and reading *The Cat in the Hat*, I would have suggested you change your brand of beer. But in the early 1980s, that's exactly what happened. During the final six weeks of pregnancy, women in a study were asked to read the Dr. Seuss book out loud twice a day. That's a lot: Total infant exposure was about five hours. When the babies were born, they were given a pacifier hooked up to a machine that could measure the strength and frequency of their sucking. Rates of strength and frequency can be used to assess whether an infant recognizes something (a form of pattern matching). The babies then heard tapes of their mothers reading *The Cat in the Hat* or a different story. Sucking rates and patterns were measured at all points.

What the researchers found was astonishing. The babies who had heard Dr. Seuss while in the womb appeared to recognize, and prefer, a tape of their mother reading *The Cat in the Hat*. They sucked their pacifiers in a pattern triggered by her reading that book, but not a different book. The babies recognized their previous in-womb auditory experience.

We now know that auditory perception begins at a much earlier age than that of the babies tested in this amazing result. Tissues involved in hearing can be observed just four weeks after conception. Hearing begins with the emergence of two structures that look like miniature saguaro cacti sprouting from either side of your baby's head. They are called primordial otocysts, and they will form a great deal of your child's hearing apparatus. Once this territory is established, the next weeks are devoted to setting up house, from internal hairs that look like tiny whiskers to the canals they line, which look just like snail shells.

When do these structures hook up to the rest of the brain, allowing babies to hear? The answer should be familiar by now: not until the beginning of the third trimester. At six months, you can supply a sound to a fetus in the womb (mostly clicks) and listen in astonishment as the brain weakly fires back electrical responses! In another month, this crackling call-and-response increases not only in intensity but in speed of reaction. Give it another month or so, and everything has changed. Now you have a preterm infant who can not only hear and respond but can discriminate between various speech sounds like "ah" and "ee," or "ba" and "bi." We once again see this paratrooper pattern of establishing the territory first, then hooking things up to central command.

Babies can hear mom's voice in the womb by the end of the second trimester, and they prefer it to other voices at birth. They respond especially strongly after birth if mom's voice is muffled, re-creating the sonic environment of the womb. Babies even respond to television shows their mothers watched while they were pregnant. One funny test exposed preterm infants to the opening jingle of a particular soap opera. When these babies were born, they would stop crying the moment they heard that jingle! Controls had no such distinguishing response.

Newborns have a powerful memory for sounds they encountered while still in the womb.

The point is not to panic over your reading or viewing habits. The point is simply that newborns have a powerful memory for sounds they encountered while still in the womb in the last part of gestation.

Smell

The same thing is true of smells. Just five weeks after fertilization, you can see the brain's complex wiring for smell. But, as with the other senses, the perception is not available simply because the machinery is there. At first, babies suffer from an acutely stuffy nose. The nasal cavity is filled with material that probably works like protective shrink-wrap, shielding the nose's delicate interior tissues until they are ready to become operational. Smelling, at least as we know it, is probably impossible.

All of that changes during the third trimester. The protective plug is replaced with snot (mucous membranes)—and lots of neurons hooked directly into the perceptual areas of the brain. Mom's placenta also becomes less picky, granting permission for more and more smell-mediating molecules (called odorants) to enter the womb. Because of these biological changes, the olfactory world of your baby becomes richer and more complex after the sixth month of gestational life. Smells don't have to be right under baby's nose. Your baby can detect the perfume you wear and even the garlic you ate.

As a newborn, your baby will actually prefer these smells. The preference is called "olfactory labeling." This is the basis for a piece of advice by neuroscientist Lise Eliot, in her book *What's Going On in There?*: Don't wash baby with soap and water immediately after she's born. The smell of amniotic fluid calms her down, studies show. Why? As with sounds, smells remind babies of the comfortable home they were inhabiting for the past nine months.

Balance

Here's something you can try at home if you are eight months pregnant or if you have a baby younger than 5 months old. If the infant has already arrived, place him on his back. Then gently lift up both of his legs, or both of his arms, and let them drop back to the bed of their own weight. His arms will usually fling out from the sides of his body, thumbs flexed, palms up, with a startled look on his face. This is called the Moro reflex.

At eight months of pregnancy, you can usually observe the Moro reflex internally. If you are reading this in your soft bed, go ahead and roll over; if you are seated, stand up. Feel anything dramatic? A fetus is capable of executing a full Moro while still in the womb. These actions often incite it.

The Moro reflex is normal and usually occurs if an infant is startled, especially if he senses he is falling. It is believed to be the only unlearned fear response humans possess. It's important that an infant has these reflexes. The absence of a good solid Moro can be a sign of a neurological disorder. Infants need to be able to do it within five months of birth. It is time limited, though; its persistence beyond five months is also a sign of a neurological disorder.

The Moro demonstrates that a great deal of motor (movement) and vestibular (balance) abilities have already been laid down by eight months. Vestibular abilities allow muscles to be in constant communication with the ears, all coordinated by the brain. You need a fairly sophisticated form of this communication in order to do a Moro.

Babies don't start off capable of doing full-tilt gymnastics, of course. But they are capable of "quickening," which is a flutter of embryonic limbs, at about six weeks post-conception, though the mother usually can't feel anything for another five weeks. This movement is also important. It must occur, or your baby's joints will not develop properly. By the middle of the third trimester, your baby is fully capable of deliberately commanding her body to perform a coordinated series of movements.

Taste

The tissues that mediate "gustatorial sensations" don't emerge from your embryo's tiny tongue until about eight weeks after conception. That doesn't mean your baby simultaneously acquires the ability to taste something, of course; that doesn't happen until the third trimester. Once again we see the reception-before-perception pattern of sensory development.

At that point, you can observe some behaviors familiar to all of us. Third-trimester babies change their swallowing patterns when mom eats something sweet: They gulp more. Flavorful compounds from a mother's diet cross the placenta into the amniotic fluid, which babies in the third trimester swallow at the rate of a quart a day. The effect is so powerful that what you eat during the last stages of pregnancy can influence the food preferences of your baby.

In one study, scientists injected apple juice into the wombs of pregnant rats. When the rat pups were born, they showed a dramatic preference for drinking apple juice. A similar taste preference happens with humans. Mothers who drank lots of carrot juice in the later stages of pregnancy had infants who preferred carrot-flavored cereal. This is called flavor programming, and you can do it soon after your baby is born, too. Lactating mothers who eat green beans and peaches while nursing produce weaned toddlers with the same preferences.

It's possible that anything that can cross the placenta can incite a preference.

Getting it just right

From touch and smell to hearing and vision, babies have an increasingly active mental life in the womb. What does this mean for parents eager to aid that development? If motor skills are so important, shouldn't moms-to-be do cartwheels every 10 minutes to induce the Moro reflex in their in utero partners? If food preferences are established in the womb, shouldn't moms-to-be become vegetarians in the last half of pregnancy if they want their kids to eat fruits and vegetables? And is there an effect, beyond creating potential preferences, of pumping Mozart or Dr. Seuss into your unborn baby's brain?

It is easy to start making assumptions. So a word of caution. These studies represent the edge of what is known, and it is very easy to over-interpret what the data mean. These are all interesting research questions. But today's data are not strong enough to solve the mystery of early mental life. They are just enough to reveal it.

The Goldilocks Effect

The biology of infant brain development reminds me of "Goldilocks and the Three Bears." The classic version of the story describes a young girl with blond hair breaking into and essentially vandalizing a bear family's vacant hut. She samples and renders judgments over their bowls of porridge, chairs, and beds. Goldilocks doesn't like Papa Bear's or Mama Bear's belongings; the physical characteristics are just too extreme. But Baby Bear's stuff is "just right," from temperature to sturdiness to the bed's cozy comfort. Like so many legendary children's stories, there are many renditions of this odd little tale. The first published version, by 19th-century poet Robert Southey, had an angry old woman breaking into the bears' hut and sampling the wares of three male bears. Some literary historians suggest Southey borrowed from the story of Snow White, who breaks into the dwarves' house, tastes their food, sits on their stools, and then falls asleep on one of their beds. In one early version of "Goldilocks," the intruder was a fox, not a woman; later she became a girl variously called Silver Hair, Silver-Locks, and Golden Hair. But the "just right" principle is preserved throughout.

So many creatures have this just-right characteristic embedded in their biology that scientists have given the phenomenon its own rather unscientific name: the Goldilocks Effect. It is so common because biological survival in this hostile world often calls for a balancing act between opposing forces. Too much or too little of something, such as heat or water, often hurts biological systems, most of which are obsessed with homeostasis. A full description of many biological processes involves this "just right" idea.

Four things proven to help baby's brain

The behaviors proven to aid and abet brain development in the womb—especially important in the second half of pregnancy—all follow the Goldilocks principle. We will look at four of these balancing acts:

- weight
- nutrition
- stress
- exercise

And there's not a pregaphone in sight.

1. Gain just the right weight

You're pregnant, so you need to eat more food. And if you don't overdo it, you will grow a smarter baby. Why? Your baby's IQ is a function of her brain volume. Brain size predicts about 20 percent of the variance in her IQ scores (her prefrontal cortex, just behind her forehead, is particularly prescient). Brain volume is related to birth weight, which means that, to a point, larger babies are smarter babies. The increase slows as baby reaches 6.5 pounds: There is only 1 IQ point difference between a 6.5-pounder and a 7.5-pounder.

The fuel of food helps grow a larger baby. Between four months and birth, the fetus becomes almost ridiculously sensitive to both the amount and the type of food you consume. We know this from malnutrition studies. Babies experiencing a critical lack of nutriment have fewer neurons, fewer and shorter connections between the neurons that exist, and less insulation all around in the second trimester. When they grow up, the kids carrying these brains exhibit more behavioral problems, show slower language growth, have lower IQs, get worse grades, and generally make poor athletes.

How much do you need to eat? That depends upon how fit you are going into the pregnancy. Unfortunately, 55 percent of women of childbearing age in the United States are already too fat. Their Body Mass Index, or BMI, which is a kind of a "gross domestic product" of how fat you are, is between 25 and 29.9. If that's you, then you need to gain only about 15 to 25 pounds to create a healthy baby, according to the Institute of Medicine. You want to add about half a pound a week in the critical second and third trimesters of pregnancy. If you are underweight, with a typical BMI of less than 18.5, you need to gain between 28 and 40 pounds to optimize your baby's brain development. That's about a pound a week in the critical last half of pregnancy. This is true for women of healthy weight, too.

So the amount of fuel is important. There is increasing evidence that the type of fuel you eat during the critical period also is important. The next balance comes between foods that a pregnant mom *wants* to eat and foods that are optimal for a baby's brain development. Unfortunately, they are not always the same thing.

2. Eat just the right foods

Women have strange experiences with food preferences during pregnancy, suddenly loathing foods they used to love and craving foods they used to loathe. It's not just pickles and ice cream, as any pregnant woman can tell you. One woman developed a craving for lemon juice on a burrito—a need that lasted for three months. Another wanted pickled okra. A surprising number crave crushed ice. Women can even desire to eat things that aren't food. Items that regularly make the Top 10 List of Weird Pregnancy Cravings include baby talcum powder and coal. One woman wanted to lick dust. Pica is a common disorder: a craving lasting longer than a month for eating things that aren't food, like dirt and clay.

Is there any evidence you should pay attention to these cravings? Is the baby telegraphing its nutritional needs? The answer is no. There is some evidence that iron deficiencies can be consciously detected, but the data are thin. Mostly it's a matter of how a person uses food in her daily life. An anxious person who is comforted by the chemicals in chocolate might grow to crave chocolate whenever she feels stressed—and a woman will feel stressed a lot during pregnancy. (This craving for chocolate reflects a learned response, not a biological need, though I think my wife would disagree.) We actually don't know why a pregnant woman's random cravings occur.

That doesn't mean the body doesn't have nutritional needs, of course. The pregnant woman is a ship with two passengers but only one galley, and we're looking to stock this kitchen with the right ingredients for brain growth. An infant's body needs 45 different nutrients for healthy growth. A whopping 38 of these are critically involved in the development of the nervous system. You can look on the back of most pregnancy-formulated vitamin supplements to see the list. We can look to our evolutionary history for some guidance on what to eat to get these nutrients. Since we know something of the climate in which we developed for millions of years—one that supported ever-increasing brain girth—we can speculate about the type of foods that helped it along.

Caveman cuisine

An old movie called *Quest for Fire* opens with our ancestors seated by a fire, munching on a variety of foods. Large insects buzz about the flames. All of a sudden, one of our relatives shoots out his arm, clumsily grabbing an insect out of thin air. He stuffs it into his mouth, munches heartily, and continues staring into the fire. His colleagues later dig around the soil for tuberous vegetables and scrounge for fruit in nearby trees. Welcome to the world of Pleistocene haute cuisine. Researchers believe that for hundreds of thousands of years, our daily diet consisted mostly of grasses, fruits, vegetables, small mammals, and insects. Occasionally we might fell a mammoth, so we would gorge on red meat for two or three consecutive days before the kill spoiled. Once or twice a year we might run into a beehive and get sugar, but even then only as unlinked glucose and fructose. Some biologists think we are susceptible to cavities now because sugar was not a regular part of our evolutionary experience, and we never developed a defense against it. Eating this way today (well, except for the insects) is called in some circles the paleo diet.

So it's a bit boring. And familiar. Eating a balanced meal, with a heavy emphasis on fruits and vegetables, is probably still *the* best advice for pregnant women. For the non-vegetarians in the crowd, a source of iron in the form of red meat is appropriate. Iron is necessary for proper brain development and normal functioning even in adults, vegetarian or not.

Miracle drugs

There is a lot of mythological thinking out there about what you should and should not eat—not just during pregnancy but your whole life long. I had an honors student at the University of Washington, the thoughtful type of kid who has to sit on his hands not to answer a question. One day he came up to me after class, breathless. He was taking an entrance exam for medical school and had just found out about a "miracle" drug. "It's a neurotonic!" he exclaimed. "It improves your memory. It'll make you think better. Should I take it?" He thrust in front of my face an advertisement for ginkgo root. Derived from the ginkgo tree, *ginkgo biloba* has been advertised for decades as a brain booster, improving memory in both young and old, even treating Alzheimer's. These claims are testable. A number of researchers began to study gingko as they would any promising pharmaceutical. Sorry, I told the student. *Ginkgo biloba* does not improve cognition of any kind in healthy adults—not memory, not visual-spatial construction, not language or psychomotor speed or executive function. "What about old people?" my student asked. Nope. It doesn't prevent or slow down Alzheimer's, dementia, or even normal age-related cognitive decline. Other botanicals, like St. John's wort (purported to treat depression) show similar impotence. My student left, crestfallen. "The best thing you could do is get a good night's sleep!" I hollered after him.

Why is it that these nutrition myths can fool even bright kids like my student? First, nutrition research is really, really hard to do, and it is shockingly underfunded. The types of long-term, rigorous, randomized trials needed to establish the effects of food often go undone. Second, most foods we consume are very complex at the molecular level; wines, for example, can have more than 300 ingredients. It is often tough to discern what part of a food product is actually giving the benefit or doing the harm.

The way our bodies handle food is even more complex. We don't all metabolize food exactly the same way. Some people can suck calories out of a piece of paper; some people wouldn't gain weight if they inhaled milkshakes. Some people use peanut butter as their primary source of protein; others will die of an allergic reaction if they smell it on an airplane. To the eternal frustration of just about every researcher in the field, no single diet is going to work the same way for all people, and that's because of this extraordinary individuality. This is especially true if you're pregnant.

Neurons need omega-3s

So you can see why only two supplements thus far have enough data behind them to support an influence on brain development in utero. One is the folic acid taken around conception. The other: omega-3 fatty acids. Omega-3s are a critical component of the membranes that make up a neuron; without it, neurons don't function very well. Humans have a hard time making omega-3s, so we have to outsource the materials to get them into our nerves. Eating fish, especially oily ones, is a good way to do it. Those of us who don't get enough omega-3s, studies show, are at much greater risk for dyslexia, attention-deficit disorders, depression, bipolar disorder, even schizophrenia. Most of us get enough of the fatty acids in our regular diet, so it's generally not a problem. But the data underscore a central fact: The brain needs omega-3 fatty acids for its neurons to function properly. Apparently, the Three Stooges knew this decades ago! (Larry: "You know, fish is great brain food." Moe: "You know, you should fish for a whale.")

If a moderate amount of omega-3s keeps you from being mentally disabled, does a whale-sized helping of it increase brain power, especially for the baby? Here the evidence is decidedly mixed, but a few studies indicate the question warrants further research. One Harvard study looked at 135 infants and the eating habits of their mothers during pregnancy. The researchers determined that mothers who ate more fish starting in the second trimester had smarter babies than those who didn't. By smarter, I mean that the babies performed better on cognitive tests that measure memory, recognition, and attention at six months post-birth. The effects weren't large, but they existed. As a result, researchers recommend that pregnant women eat at least 12 ounces of fish per week. What about the mercury in fish, which can hurt cognition? It appears that the benefits outweigh the harm. Researchers recommend that pregnant women eat those 12 ounces from sources possessing less concentrated mercury (salmon, cod, haddock, sardines, and canned light tuna) as opposed to longer-lived predatory fish (swordfish, mackerel, and albacore tuna).

My belly is evidence that I know how tough it is to eat properly, whether you are trying to control how much to eat, what to eat, or both. There's Goldilocks again: You need enough, but not too much, of the right types of food. And the third factor usually doesn't help.

3. Avoid too much stress

It was not a good idea to be in Quebec and pregnant around January 4, 1998. For more than 80 hours, freezing rain and drizzle fell relentlessly across eastern Canada—immediately followed by a steep drop in surface temperature. This meteorological one-two punch turned eastern Canada into ice hell. Under the weight of the freeze, more than a thousand towering metal power-line structures toppled like dominoes. Tunnels collapsed. Thirty people died. A state of emergency soon was declared; the army was called up. Even so, thousands of residents were without power for weeks, in freezing temperatures. If you were pregnant and could not get to a hospital for your regular checkups—God forbid if you went into labor—you were stressed out of your mind. And so, it turned out, was your infant. The effects of that storm could be seen on the children's brains *years* later.

How do we know that? A group of researchers decided to study the effects of this natural disaster on babies in the womb—then follow the children as they grew older and entered the school system. The result was scary. By the time these "ice storm" children were 5, their behaviors differed markedly from children whose mothers hadn't experienced the storm. Their verbal IQs and language development appeared stunted, even when the parents' education, occupation, and income were taken into account. Was the mother's stress the culprit? The answer turned out to be yes.

Maternal stress can profoundly influence prenatal development. We didn't always think so. For a while, we weren't even sure if mom's stress hormones could reach her baby. But they do, and that has long-lasting behavioral consequences, especially if the woman is severely or chronically stressed in those hypersensitive last months of pregnancy. What kind of consequences?

If you are severely stressed during pregnancy, it can:

- change the temperament of your child. Infants become more irritable, less consolable.
- lower your baby's IQ. The average decline is about 8 points in certain mental and motor inventories measured in a baby's first year of life. Using David Wechsler's 1944 schema, that spread can be the difference between "average IQ" and "bright normal."
- inhibit your baby's future motor skills, attentional states, and ability to concentrate—differences still observable at age 6.
- damage your baby's stress-response system.
- shrink the size of your baby's brain.

A review of more than 100 studies in various economically developed countries confirm that these powerful, negative effects on prenatal brain development are cross-cultural. David Laplante, lead author of the ice-storm study, said in a somewhat understated fashion: "We suspect that exposure to high levels of [stress] may have altered fetal neurodevelopment, thereby influencing the expression of the children's neurobehavioral abilities in early childhood."

Moderate vs. toxic stress

Is this stressing you out? Luckily, not all stresses are created equal. Moderate stress in small amounts, the type most women feel in a typical pregnancy, actually appears to be good for infants. Stress tends to get people moving, and we think that enriches the baby's environment. The womb is a surprisingly hearty structure, and both it and its tiny passenger are well equipped to ride out the typical stressors of pregnancy. It is just not prepared for a sustained assault. How can you tell the brain-damaging stress from the typical, benign, even mildly positive stress?

Most toxic stresses have one common characteristic: you feel out of control over the bad stuff coming at you. As stress moves from moderate to severe, and from acute to chronic, this loss of control turns catastrophic. That can affect baby. Bad types of stress seem obvious once you know where to look. They include major life events such as a divorce, death of spouse (or other loved one), job termination, or being a victim of a crime. Income is a big factor too, especially around the poverty line. Other factors may not seem so obvious: a lack of friends (social isolation), sustained dissatisfaction at work, or a long-term illness.

Of course, the story of stress reactivity isn't simple. Some people appear to weather stressful events better than others. Some are stress resistant; others are stress sensitive. There is increasing evidence that this sensitivity has a genetic component. Women under such a biological dictatorship need to keep stress to a minimum during pregnancy. The key issue, regardless of your background, is a loss of control.

Bull's-eye: Baby's stress-response system

Lots of research has gone into trying to understand *how* maternal stress affects brain development. And we have begun to answer this question at the most intimate level possible: that of cell and molecule. The important stress hormone is cortisol. It's the star player in a team of nasty molecules called glucocorticoids. These hormones control many of our most familiar stress responses, from making our hearts race like NASCAR autos to a sudden urge to pee and poop. Glucocorticoids are so powerful, the brain has developed a natural "braking" system to turn them off as soon as the stress has passed. A pea-sized piece of neural real estate in the middle of the brain, called the hypothalamus, controls the release and braking of these hormones.

A woman's stress hormones affect her baby by slipping through the placenta and entering the baby's brain, like cruise missiles programmed to hit two targets. The first target is the baby's limbic system, an area profoundly involved in emotional regulation and memory. This region develops more slowly in the presence of excess hormone, one of the reasons we think baby cognition is damaged if mom is severely or chronically stressed.

The second target is that braking system I mentioned, the one that's supposed to rein in glucocorticoid levels after the stress has passed. Excess hormone from mom can mean baby has a difficult time turning off her own stress hormone system. Her brain becomes marinated in glucocorticoids whose concentrations are no longer easily controllable. The baby can carry this damaged stress-response system into adulthood. The child may have a difficult time putting on the brakes whenever she gets stressed out; elevated levels of glucocorticoids thus become a regular part of her life. If she eventually gets pregnant, she bathes *her* developing infant with the excess toxic stuff. The fetus develops a partially confused hypothalamus, pumping out more glucocorticoids, and the next-generation brain shrinks further. The vicious cycle continues. Excessive stress is contagious: You can get it from your kids, and you can give it to them, too.

Take back control

Clearly, too much stress is not good for pregnant women or their babies. For optimal development of your baby's brain, you will want to exist in a less-stressed environment, especially in the last few months of pregnancy. You can't completely upend your life, of course, which could be stressful on its own. But you can reduce your stress, with your spouse's tender loving care. We'll say much more about that in the next chapter. You can also begin identifying the areas in your life where you feel out of control, then deliberately form strategies that will allow you to take back control. In some cases, that means exiting the situation that is causing the stress. A temporary helping of courage will translate to a lifetime of benefit for your baby's brain.

There are plenty of ways to actively practice general stress relief, too. At *www.brainrules.net*, we've listed a number of techniques known from the research literature to reduce stress. A big one is exercise, which has so many benefits that it is the subject of our fourth and final balancing act.

4. Exercise just the right amount

I am always amazed at the life cycle of wildebeests. They are best known for their spectacular annual migrations in the plains and open woodlands of Tanzania and Kenya, thousands upon thousands of them in hypnotic, constant motion. They move for two reasons. First and foremost, they are looking for new pastures. But wildebeests are also 600-pound steaks on legs; they have to keep moving because they are very popular with predators.

Given this urgency, the most interesting part of their life cycle is their pregnancy and birth. The gestation is nearly as long as a human's, about 260 days, but the similarities end as soon as labor begins. The mother gives birth quickly. Unless there are complications, she also recovers quickly. So do the calves, typically rising to their feet—well, hooves—an hour after they're born. They have to. Calves represent the herd's future, but they are also the herd's most vulnerable population, liable to become leopard food.

We, too, spent our evolutionary adolescence on these same savannahs, and we share many of the wildebeests' same predator/

prey problems. There are, you might imagine, major differences in birthing and parenting between wildebeests and humans. Women take a long time to recover from birth (it's that big, overweight brain again, evolution's secret weapon, forcing itself through a narrow birth canal), and their kids won't be walking for almost a year. Nonetheless, evolutionary echoes imply that exercise was very much a part of our lives, including during pregnancy. Anthropologists think we walked as many as 12 miles per day.

Fit women have to push less

Does that mean exercise should be a part of human pregnancies? Evidence suggests the answer is yes. There are many reasons to stay fit during pregnancy, but the first benefit is a practical one having to do with labor. Many women report that giving birth is both the most exhilarating experience of their lives and the most painful. Pushing, as you know, is usually the toughest part. Studies show that if you are not in shape, it takes you twice as long to transit through the "pushing phase" of labor than if you are fit. Not surprisingly, fit women perceive this stage as being far less painful.

Because the pushing phase is shorter, babies also are less likely to experience brain damage from oxygen deprivation. If you are afraid of labor, you owe it to yourself to become as fit as possible going into it. And the reasons are argued purely from the Serengeti.

Exercise buffers against stress

Fit mothers also tend to give birth to smarter babies than obese mothers do. There are two reasons for this. One may have to do with the direct effects of exercise—especially aerobic exercise—on a baby's developing brain. This notion needs more research. More powerful are the data linking aerobic exercise and stress reduction.

Certain types of exercise actually buffer a pregnant woman against the negative influence of stress. Remember those toxic glucocorticoids, the ones that invade neural tissue and cause brain damage? Aerobic exercise elevates a molecule in your brain that can specifically block the toxic effects of those nasty glucocorticoids. This heroic molecule is termed brain-derived neurotrophic factor. More BDNF means less stress, which means fewer glucocorticoids in your womb, which means better baby brain development.

It may sound strange to say, but a fit mom has a much better chance of having a smart baby—or at least one best able to mobilize his or her IQ—than an unfit mom.

Too strenuous, and baby overheats

As usual, though, there's a balance. A baby can feel and react to the mother's motion. When her heart rate goes up, so does baby's. When mom's breathing rate increases, so does baby's. But only if the exercise is moderate. During strenuous exercise, especially in the later stages of pregnancy, the baby's heart rate and breathing begin to decline. The concern is that overdoing it might increase the temperature of the womb or restrict baby's access to oxygen. As ever, your pediatrician can provide guidance about the amount of exercise you should be doing in these later stages. Your oxygen reserve levels are pretty low by the third trimester, so it's a good time to wind down strenuous activities in preparation for labor. Swimming is one of the best forms of exercise in later stages; the water helps transfer excess heat away from the womb.

What is the proper balance? Four words: moderate, regular aerobic exercise. For most women, that means keeping your heart rate below 70 percent of its maximal rate (which is 220 beats per minute minus your age), then slowing things down as the due date approaches. But you should exercise. As long as you don't have obstetric or other medical complications, the American College of Obstetricians recommends 30 minutes or more of moderate exercise *per day*.

Good advice, even though we are not wildebeests.

Every little bit counts

Maybe you're not in the habit of exercising every day. Maybe you're feeling guilty enough already for drinking that second cup of coffee while pregnant. If so, perhaps you will appreciate some reassurance from the research world: As a species, *Homo sapiens* have been successfully making babies for 250,000 years. We did very well without all this fancy knowledge, thank you, and with such success that we conquered the world. Your best intentions—Morse code belly tapping notwithstanding—will go a long way toward creating a great environment for your developing baby.

Key points

- In the first half of pregnancy, babies want to be left alone.
- Don't waste your money on products claiming to improve a preborn baby's IQ, temperament, or personality. None of them have been proved to work.
- In the second half of pregnancy, babies begin to perceive and process a great deal of sensory information. They can even smell the perfume you wear.
- Brain boosters at this stage: gaining the proper weight, eating a balanced diet, exercising moderately, and reducing stress.

relationship

brain rule

Start with empathy

relationship

I remember feeling almost completely overwhelmed when we brought our firstborn son, Joshua, home from the hospital. We placed our new baby in the car seat for the first time, praying that we were buckling him in correctly. I drove home from the hospital at a snail's pace—miraculous, for me. My wife was in the backseat, just to keep an eye on things. So far, so good.

When the little guy entered our house, his tiny face suddenly corrugated into annoyance. He started screaming. We changed his diaper. Still he screamed. My wife fed him. He took one or two gulps, then resumed screaming, tried to wiggle out of my wife's arms, tried to get away. This didn't happen in the hospital. Were we doing something wrong? I held him. My wife held him. Eventually, he calmed down. Then he seemed to go to sleep. We were so relieved. "We can do this," we kept telling ourselves. It was late, and we decided to follow his lead. No sooner did our heads hit the pillow than Joshua started crying again. My wife got up and fed him, then handed Josh to me. I burped him, changed him, laid him back down. He was calm and settled, and we went back to bed. I didn't even get to feel the warmth of the sheet before the crying and screaming resumed. My wife was exhausted, recovering from a 21-hour labor, in no shape to help. I got up, held the baby, then set him back into his crib. He calmed down. Success! I crept back to bed. I got only as far as the pillow before the crying began again. I tucked my head under the blankets, hoping it would stop. It didn't. What was I supposed to do?

This bewildering routine, and my reactions to them, recurred day after day. I had deep feelings for my son—always will—but I wondered at the time what ever made me decide to have a baby. I had no idea that something so wonderful was also going to be so hard. I learned a difficult but important lesson: Once a kid comes into the world, the calculus of daily living coughs up new equations. I am good at math, but I was no good at this. I had no idea how to solve these problems.

For most first-time moms and dads, the first shock is the overwhelmingly relentless nature of this new social contract. The baby *takes*. The parent *gives*. End of story. What startles many couples is the excruciating toll it can take on their quality of life—especially their marriages. The baby cries, the baby sleeps, the baby vomits, gets held, needs changing, must be fed, all before 4:00 a.m. Then you have to go to work. Or your spouse does. This is repeated day after day after ad nauseam day. Parents want just one square inch of silence, one small second to themselves, and they routinely get neither. You can't even go to the bathroom when you want. You're sleep deprived, you've lost friends, your household chores just tripled, your sex life is nonexistent, and you barely have the energy to ask about each other's day.

Is it any surprise that a couple's relationship suffers?

It's rarely talked about, but it's a fact: Couples' hostile interactions sharply increase in baby's first year. Sometimes the baby brings a hormone-soaked honeymoon period. (One couple I know constantly quoted Tagore to each other: "Every child comes with the message that God is not yet discouraged of man!") Even then, things quickly deteriorate. The hostility can be so severe that, in some marriages, having a baby is actually a risk factor for divorce.

Why do I bring this up in a book about baby brain development? Because it has serious consequences for the baby's brain. We learned in the Pregnancy chapter how exquisitely sensitive a baby in the womb is to outside stimuli. Once baby leaves his comfortable, watery incubator, his brain becomes even more vulnerable. Sustained exposure to hostility can erode a baby's IQ and ability to handle stress, sometimes dramatically. An infant's need for caregiver stability is so strong, he will *rewire* his developing nervous system depending upon the turbulence he perceives. If you want your child to be equipped with the best brain possible, you need to know about this before you bring home your bundle of joy.

When I lecture on the science of young brains, the dads (it's almost always the dads) demand to know how to get their kids into Harvard. The question invariably angers me. I bellow, "You want to get your kid into Harvard? You *really* want to know what the data say? I'll tell you what the data say! Go home and love your wife!" This chapter is about that retort: why marital hostility happens, how it alters a baby's developing brain, and how you can counteract the hos-tility and minimize its effects.

Most marriages suffer

Most couples don't imagine such marital turbulence when they get pregnant. Babies, after all, are supposed to bring endless, unremitting joy. That's the idealistic view many of us have, especially if our parents grew up in the late 1950s—an era steeped in a traditional view of marriages and families. TV programs like *Leave It to Beaver* and *Ozzie & Harriet* depicted working fathers as all-wise; stay-at-home mothers as all-nurturing; children as surprisingly obedient and, when not, creating small but manageable crises easily resolvable in 23 minutes.

The protagonists were mostly middle class, mostly white, and, it turns out, mostly wrong.

A bracingly cold glass of water was thrown on this Eisenhower-esque perception by famed sociologist E. E. LeMasters. Rather than babies bringing nirvana to marriages, he showed the opposite. In 1957, he published a paper showing that 83 percent of married couples experienced *more* turbulence in their relationships with the birth of a baby—some couples severely so. Not surprisingly, these findings were met with a great deal of skepticism.

Time, and further research, proved to be on the side of LeMasters. Armed with better methodologies and longer study periods, studies consistently show that having a baby stresses most couples' marriages. LeMasters, it turns out, was on to something.

By the late 1980s and '90s, investigations in 10 industrialized countries, including the United States, demonstrated that marital satisfaction for most men and women dropped after they had their first child—and continued to fall over the next 15 years. Things didn't improve for most couples until the kids left home.

We now know that this long-term erosion is a regular experience of married life, starting in the transition to parenthood. Marital quality, which peaks in the last trimester of a first pregnancy, decreases anywhere from 40 percent to 67 percent in the infant's first year. More recent studies, asking different questions, put the figure closer to 90 percent. During those 12 months, scores on hostility indices—measures of marital conflict—skyrocket. The risk for clinical depression, for both fathers and mothers, goes up. Indeed, one-third to one-half of new parents display as much marital distress as troubled couples already in therapy trying to save their relationship. The dissatisfaction usually starts with the mother, then migrates to the father. To quote an excerpt from a recent research paper published in the *Journal of Family Psychology*: "In sum, parenthood hastens marital decline—even among relatively satisfied couples who select themselves into this transition."

A British divorce lawyer recalled one illustrative case. Emma's husband was obsessed with soccer, particularly the Manchester United team, also called the Reds. This condition was made worse with the introduction of a child. Emma actually cited it as grounds for the divorce. Her husband responded, "I have to admit that nine times out of 10, I would rather watch the Reds than have sex, but that's no disrespect to Emma."

Given all of these findings, it seems any couple contemplating children should undergo a psychiatric evaluation, then choose voluntary sterilization. What are we going to do?

Seeds of hope

There is hope. We know four of the most important sources of marital conflict in the transition to parenthood: sleep loss, social isolation, unequal workload, and depression. We will examine each. Couples who make themselves aware of these can become vigilant about their behavior, and they tend to do better. We also know that not every marriage follows this depressing course of events.

Couples going into pregnancy with strong marital bonds withstand the gale forces of baby's first year better than those who don't. Those who carefully plan for their children prior to pregnancy do, too. In fact, one of the biggest predictors of marital bliss appears to be the agreement to have kids in the first place. One large study examined couples where both parties wanted kids versus couples where only one did. If both partners wanted the child, very few divorced, and marital happiness either stayed the same or increased in the baby's first year of life. *All* conflicted couples where one partner had caved (usually the man) were either separated or divorced by the time the child was 5.

The data behind this come from the *Journal of Family Psychology* study mentioned previously. The full quote gives much more hope: "In sum, parenthood hastens marital decline—even among relatively satisfied couples who select themselves into this transition—*but planning status and pre-pregnancy marital satisfaction generally protect marriages from these declines."*

Marriages do not suffer evenly in the transition to parenthood; some not at all. But as LeMasters and later researchers showed, that is not the majority experience. The social consequences were great enough to warrant investigation. Researchers began to ask: What do couples fight about when a baby comes home? And what does that conflict do to the baby?

Babies seek safety above all

What researchers found is that the emotional ecology into which a baby is born can profoundly influence how his or her nervous system develops. To understand this interaction, we have to address the almost unbelievable sensitivity a baby has to the environment in which he or she is being raised. It is a sensitivity with strong evolutionary roots.

Hints of this vulnerability first came from the lab of Harry Harlow, who was observing monkey baby behavior at the University of Wisconsin–Madison. That his findings apply to human infants illustrates how deep these evolutionary roots can go. Harlow looked like virtually every other scientist of the 1950s, complete with nerdy, Frisbee-sized glasses. By his own admission, he was preoccupied with "love," though he had a strange way of showing it—both professionally and personally. He married his first wife, who had been his student, divorced her after two children, married a psychologist, watched her die of cancer, and then, in his final years, remarried his former student.

Harlow also designed a series of groundbreaking experiments with rhesus monkeys that was so brutal, some scholars credit Harlow for inadvertently creating the animal rights movement. These experiments involved isolation chambers and metallic surrogate mothers. Harlow himself would use colorful language to describe his research, calling his chambers "pits of despair" and his surrogate mothers "iron maidens." But he almost single-handedly uncovered the idea of infant emotional attachment. This in turn laid the groundwork for understanding how parental stress influences a baby's behaviors.

Harlow's classic attachment experiments involved two of these iron maidens—doll-like structures serving as maternal stand-ins. One was made of harsh wire, the other of soft terry cloth. He took newly born rhesus monkeys, removed them from their biological mothers, and placed them into cages containing both dolls. There are many variations on this experiment, but the initial finding was striking. The cold wire doll provided food, delivered from an attached bottle. The soft terry-cloth doll did not. Nonetheless, the animals greatly preferred the cloth mom. The baby would feed from the wire mom, but do so while clinging tightly to the cloth mom. If the babies were placed in an unfamiliar room, they clung tightly to the cloth surrogate until they felt secure enough to explore the cage on their own. If placed in that same room without the cloth mother, the animals froze in terror, then went crying and screaming, running from one object to another, seemingly looking for their lost mother.

The preference was the same no matter how many times the experiment was done or in what variation. These experiments are heartbreaking to watch—I've seen old films of this stuff—and the conclusions are unforgettable. It wasn't the presence of food that telegraphed reassurance to these little ones, a behavioral idea prevalent at the time. It was the presence or absence of a safe harbor.

Human babies, complex as they are, are looking for the same thing.

Monkey see, monkey do

Babies are highly attuned to these perceptions of safety, though they may not look it. At first blush, babies seem mostly preoccupied with more mundane biological processes, like eating and pooping and spitting up on your shirt. This fooled a lot of researchers into believing that babies weren't thinking about anything at all. Scientists coined the term "tabula rasa"—blank slate—to describe these "empty" creatures. They regarded infants as merely helpless helpings of cute, controllable, human potential.

Modern research reveals a radically different point of view. We now know that a baby's greatest biological preoccupation involves the organ atop their necks. Infants come preloaded with lots of software in their neural hard drives, most of it having to do with learning. Want some startling examples?

In 1979, University of Washington psychologist Andy Meltzoff stuck out his tongue at a baby 42 minutes old, then sat back to see what happened. After some effort, the baby returned the favor, slowly rolling out his own tongue. Meltzoff stuck his tongue out again. The infant responded in kind. Meltzoff discovered that babies could imitate right from the start of their little lives (or, at least, 42 minutes from the start of their little lives). That's an extraordinary finding. Imitation involves many sophisticated realizations for babies, from discovering that other people exist in the world to realizing that they have operating body parts, and the same ones as you. That's not a blank slate. That's an amazing, fully operational cognitive slate.

Capitalizing on this finding, Meltzoff designed a series of experiments revealing just how much babies are prewired to learn—and how sensitive they are to outside influences in pursuit of that goal. Meltzoff constructed a wooden box, covered by an orange plastic panel, into which he inserted a light. If he touched the panel, the light turned on.

What happened next is described in the book *The Scientist in the Crib*: "[Andy] would show babies a completely unexpected way to use a new object—he would touch his forehead to the top of a box, and it would light up. The babies watched in fascination, but they weren't allowed to touch the box themselves." Mom and baby would then leave the lab, probably wondering what they'd just experienced.

But the experiment wasn't over: "A week later, the babies came back to the lab. This time Andy just gave them the box, without doing anything to it himself. But the babies immediately touched *their* foreheads to the top of the box."

The babies remembered! With only a single exposure to this event, eight out of 12 babies recalled it perfectly a week later. None of the 24 babies in the control group made the motion on their own.

Those are just two examples illustrating that infants come equipped with an amazing array of cognitive abilities—and are blessed with many intellectual gadgets capable of extending those abilities. They understand that size stays constant even when distance changes the appearance of size. They display velocity prediction. They understand the principle of common fate; for example, the reason the black lines on the basketball move when the ball bounces is because the lines are part of the basketball. Infants can discriminate human faces from nonhuman faces at birth and seem to prefer human ones. From an evolutionary perspective, this latter behavior represents a powerful safety feature. We will be preoccupied with faces most of our lives.

How did babies acquire all of this knowledge before being exposed to the planet? Nobody knows, but they have it, and they put it to good use with astonishing speed and insight. Babies create hypotheses, test them, and then relentlessly appraise their findings with the vigor of a seasoned scientist. This means infants are extraordinarily delightful, surprisingly aggressive learners. They pick up everything.

There's a funny example of this. A pediatrician was taking her 3-year-old daughter to day care. The good doctor had left her stethoscope in the backseat and noticed that the little girl began playing with it, even inserting the ear pieces correctly. The pediatrician got excited: Her daughter was following in her footsteps! The little girl grabbed the bell of the stethoscope, then put it to her mouth and declared in a loud voice: "Welcome to McDonald's. Can I take your order, please?"

Yes, your children are constantly observing you. They are profoundly influenced by what they record. And *that* can quickly turn from funny to serious, especially when mommy and daddy start fighting.

Limited time to establish perceptions of safety

If survival is the brain's most important priority, safety is the most important expression of that priority. This is the lesson Harlow's iron maidens teach us. Babies are completely at the mercy of the people who brought them into the world. This understanding has a behavioral blast radius in infants that obscures every other behavioral priority they have.

How do babies handle these concerns? By attempting to establish a productive relationship with the local power structures—you, in other words—as soon as possible. We call this attachment. During the attachment process, a baby's brain intensely monitors the caregiving it receives. It is essentially asking such things as "Am I being touched? Am I being fed? Who is safe?" If the baby's requirements are being fulfilled, the brain develops one way; if not, genetic instructions trigger it to develop in another way. It may be a bit disconcerting to realize, but infants have their parents' behaviors in their sights virtually from the moment they come into this world. It is in their evolutionary best interests to do so, of course, which is another way of saying that they can't help it. Babies have nowhere else to turn.

There's a window of several years during which babies strive to create these bonds and establish perceptions of safety. If it doesn't happen, they can suffer long-term emotional damage. In extreme cases, they can be scarred for life.

We know this because of a powerful and heartbreaking story from Communist Romania, discovered circa 1990 by Western reporters. In 1966, in an effort to boost the country's low birth rate, the dictator Nicolae Ceausescu banned both contraception and abortion and taxed those who were childless after age 25—whether married, single, or infertile. As the birth rate rose, so did poverty and homelessness. Children were often simply abandoned. Ceausescu's response was to create a gulag of state orphanages, with children warehoused by the thousands.

The orphanages soon were stripped of resources as Ceausescu began exporting most of Romania's food and industry to repay the country's crippling national debt. The scenes in these orphanages were shocking. Babies were seldom held or given deliberate sensory stimulation. Many were found tied to their beds, left alone for hours or days, with bottles of gruel propped haphazardly into their mouths. Many infants stared blankly into space. Indeed, you could walk into some of these hundred-bed orphanages and not hear a sound. Blankets were covered in urine, feces, and lice. The childhood mortality rate in these institutions was sickening, termed by some Westerners "pediatric Auschwitz." Horrible as these conditions were, they created a real opportunity to investigate—and perhaps treat—large groups of severely traumatized children.

One remarkable study involved Canadian families who adopted some of these infants and raised them back home. As the adopted children matured, researchers could easily divide them into two groups. One group seemed remarkably stable. Social behavior, stress responses, grades, medical issues—all were indistinguishable from healthy Canadian controls. The other group seemed just as remarkably troubled. They had more eating problems, got sick more often, and exhibited increasingly aggressive antisocial behaviors. The independent variable? The age of adoption.

If the children were adopted before the fourth month of life, they acted like every other happy kid you know. If they were adopted after the eighth month of life, they acted like gang members. The inability to find safety through bonding, by a specific age in infancy, clearly caused immense stress to their systems. And that stress affected these children's behavior years later. They may have been removed from the orphanages long ago, but they were never really free.

What stress does is kick into action our "fight or flight" responses. They really should just be called "flight," though. The typical human stress response is devoted to a single goal: getting enough blood into your muscles to get you out of harm's way. We generally lash out only when cornered. Even then, we usually engage in combat just long enough to escape. When threatened, the brain signals the release of two hormones, epinephrine (also known as adrenaline) and cortisol, from a class of molecules termed glucocorticoids.

These responses are complex enough that it takes time to properly tune every connection. That's what the first year of life is for. If the infant is marinated in safety—an emotionally stable home—the system will cook up beautifully. If not, normal stress-coping processes fail. The child is transformed into a state of high alert or a state of complete collapse. If the baby regularly experiences an angry, emotionally violent social environment, his vulnerable little stress responders turn hyperreactive, a condition known as hypercortosolism. If the baby is exposed to severe neglect, like the Romanian orphans, the system becomes under-reactive, a condition known as hypocortisolism (hence, the blank stares). Life, to quote Bruce Springsteen, can seem like one long emergency.

What happens when parents fight

You don't have to raise kids under death-camp conditions to see negative changes in baby brain development. All you need are parents who, on a regular basis, wake up wanting to throw emotional punches at each other. Marital conflict is fully capable of hurting a baby's brain development. The effects begin early and, though there is some controversy about this, may echo clear into adulthood.

Every parent knows children become stressed when their kids see them fighting. But the age at which they can react was completely unexpected by researchers. Infants younger than 6 months old can usually detect that something is wrong. They can experience physiological changes—such as increases in blood pressure, heart rate, and stress hormones—just like adults. Some researchers claim they can assess the amount of fighting in a marriage simply by taking a 24-hour urine sample of the baby. Babies and small children don't always understand the content of a fight, but they are very aware that something is wrong.

Difficulty regulating emotions and much more

The stress shows up behaviorally, too. Babies in emotionally unstable homes are much less able to positively respond to new stimuli, calm themselves, and recover from stress—in short, regulate their own emotions. Even their little legs sometimes won't develop properly, as stress hormones can interfere with bone mineralization. By the time these children are 4 years old, their stress hormone levels can be almost twice as high as children in emotionally stable homes.

And that's sad, because the effects are fully reversible. Even infants younger than 8 months who are taken from severely traumatized homes and placed in empathic, nurturing environments can show improvements in their stress-hormone regulation in as little as 10 weeks. All you have to do is put down the boxing gloves.

If marital hostility continues, the children show all the unfortunate behavioral signs of long-term stress. They are at greater risk for anxiety disorders and depression. They catch colds more often, because stress cripples the immune system. They're more antagonistic toward peers. They're less able to focus attention or regulate their emotions. Such children have IQs almost 8 points lower than children being raised in stable homes. Predictably, they don't complete high school as often as their peers and attain lower academic achievement when they do.

If we take the end point of this instability—divorce is a convenient target—we observe that kids are still paying for it years later.

Children from divorced households are 25 percent more likely to abuse drugs by the time they are 14. They are more likely to get pregnant out of wedlock. They are twice as likely to get divorced themselves. In school, they get worse grades than children in stable households. And they are much less likely to receive support for college. When marriages stay together, 88 percent of college-bound kids will receive consistent support for their college education. When marriages fall apart, that figure shrinks to 29 percent.

So much for Harvard.

Reconcile in front of your kids

Even in an emotionally stable home, one without regular marital hostility, there will be fights. Fortunately, research shows that the amount of fighting couples do in front of their children is less damaging than the lack of reconciliation the kids observe. Many couples will fight in front of their children but reconcile in private. This skews a child's perceptions, even at early ages, for the child always sees the wounding but never the bandaging. Parents who practice bandaging each other after a fight, deliberately and explicitly, allow their children to model both how to fight fair *and* how to make up.

The four biggest reasons you'll fight

Why will you fight? I mentioned four consistent sources of marital conflict in the transition to parenthood. Left to their own devices, all can profoundly influence the course of your marriage, and that makes them capable of affecting your child's developing brain. I'll call them the Four Grapes of Wrath. They are:

- sleep loss
- social isolation
- unequal workload
- depression

If you have a child, you are statistically likely to tramp on at least a few of these when your baby comes home. The battle begins in bed —and no, it's not about sex.

1. Sleep loss

If you know new parents, ask them if this complaint from "Emily" sounds familiar:

I am spiteful of my husband because he gets to sleep through the night. My daughter is 9 months old and still waking up 2–3 times per night. My husband sleeps right through, and then wakes up "so exhausted." I have not had more than 5–6 hours of sleep per night in the last 10 months, have an annoying toddler and a baby to deal with all day, and HE's tired???

We'll address the marital disparity in this behavioral snapshot, but first let's examine how little sleep Emily is getting and what it is doing to her marriage.

It is hard to overestimate the effect that sleep loss exerts over couples in the transition to parenthood. Most parents-to-be have a notion that something will change at night. Most don't realize how big it is going to be. Write this across your heart: *Babies have no sleep schedule when they are born.* The fact that *you* do does not occur to them. Sleep and eating times have no fixed pattern in the newborn brain; the behaviors are randomly distributed throughout a 24-hour period. There's that social contract again. They take. You give.

This can persist for months. A predictable schedule may not make itself visible for half a year, maybe longer, though most babies show some kind of organizing pattern by 3 months old. Between 25 percent and 40 percent of infants experience sleep problems in that time frame, a statistic observable around the world. Babies eventually acquire a sleep schedule; we think it is actually burned into their DNA. But there are many frequent disturbances in the dry, uncomfortable post-uterine world—some internal, some external—capable of keeping infants up at night. It just takes a while for their inexperienced brains to adjust. Even after a year, 50 percent still require some form of nighttime parental intervention. Because most adults require about half an hour to fall back asleep after they attend to an awakened child, moms and dads may go for weeks on end with only half the hours of sleep per night they need. That's not healthy for their bodies. Not for their marriages, either.

Sleep-deprived people become irritable—far more irritable—than people who are not. Subjects saddled with sleep debt typically suffer a 91 percent loss in their ability to regulate strong emotions compared with controls. The decline in general cognitive skill is equally dramatic (which is why chronically drowsy people don't perform as well at work, either). Problem-solving abilities typically plummet to 10 percent of their non-drowsy performances, and even motor skills become affected. You have to be moderately sleep deprived for only a week to start getting these numbers. Mood changes occur first; cognitive changes come next, followed by alterations in physical performance.

If you don't have a lot of energy, and you are called upon to give to your youngest several times a minute (preschoolers demand some form of attention 180 times per hour, behavioral psychologists say), you quickly exhaust your reservoir of good will toward your spouse. Sleep loss alone can predict most of the increases in hostile interactions between new parents.

2. Social isolation

This rarely happens in a visit to the pediatrician's office, but it should. The good doctor would ask you about the health of your baby and give your little bundle of joy a routine examination. Then she'd look you in the eyes and ask some truly intrusive questions about your social life. "Do you have many friends?" the pediatrician would inquire. "What social groups do you and your husband belong to? How important are these groups to you? How diverse are they? How much contact time do you and your husband have with them?" The doctor doesn't ask about these things because your social life is none of her business. The problem is, it is plenty of the infant's business.

Social isolation can lead to clinical depression in the parents, which can affect the parents' physical health, including an increased risk of infectious diseases and heart attacks. Social isolation is the lonely result of the energy crisis that faces most new parents. Studies show it is the main complaint of most marriages in the transition to parenthood. One mom wrote:

I have never felt more alone than I do right now. My kids are oblivious and my husband ignores me. All I do is housework, cooking, childcare ... I'm not a person anymore. I can't get a minute to myself, and yet, I am completely isolated.

Loneliness, painful and ubiquitous, is experienced by as many as 80 percent of new parents. After the birth of a child, couples have only about one-third as much time alone together as they had when they were childless. The thrill of having a child wears off, but the incessant job of parenting does not. Being a mom or dad becomes a duty, then a chore. Night after sleepless night depletes the family energy supply; increasing spousal conflicts exhaust the reserves.

These losses cause a couple's social activities to run out of gas. Mom and dad have trouble maintaining friendships with each other, let alone with acquaintances. Friends stop coming over. Parents find little energy to make new ones. Outside of their spouses, typical new parents have less than 90 minutes per day of contact time with another adult. A whopping 34 percent spend their entire days in isolation.

Not surprisingly, many new parents feel trapped. Said one stay-at-home mother, "Some days, I just want to shut myself in my bedroom and talk on the phone with my best friend all day instead of dealing with my children. I love them, but being a stay-at-home mom is not all I dreamt it would be." Another simply said of the loneliness: "I cry in my car. A lot."

Belonging to multiple social groups is a critical buffer. But those relationships are most likely to collapse in the transition to parenthood. Women experience a disproportionate amount of this isolation, and there are biological reasons why it may be particularly toxic for them. Here's the theory:

Birth—before the advent of modern medicine—often resulted in the mother's death. Though no one knows the true figure, estimates run as high as one in eight. Tribes with females who could quickly relate to and trust nearby females were more likely to survive. Older females, with the wisdom of their prior birthing experiences, could care for new mothers. Women with kids could provide precious milk to a new baby if the birth mother died. Sharing and its accompanying social interactions thus provided a survival advantage, says anthropologist Sarah Hrdy (no, there's no *a* in her last name). She calls it "alloparenting." Consistent with this notion is the finding that we are the only primates who regularly let others take care of our children.

One mother put this need for social connections succinctly: "Sometimes when I'm holding my beautiful baby in my arms and we're gazing lovingly at each other, I secretly wish that she would fall asleep so that I could check my email."

Why female neighborliness and not male? Part of the reason may be molecular. Females release oxytocin as part of their normal response to stress, a hormone that increases a suite of biological behaviors termed "tend and befriend." Men don't do this. Their resident testosterone provides too much hormonal signal-to-noise, blunting the effects of their endogenous oxytocin. The hormone, which also acts as a neurotransmitter in both sexes, mediates feelings of trust and calm, perfect if you need to cement relationships with someone who may have to become a foster parent. Astonishingly, conveniently, and completely consistent with this notion, oxytocin is also involved in stimulating lactation.

Social relationships, it turns out, have deep evolutionary roots. You will not escape the need in your lifetime. Psychotherapist Ruthellen Josselson, who has studied "tend and befriend" relationships, underscores their importance: "Every time we get overly busy with work and family, the first thing we do is let go of friendships with other women. We push them right to the back burner. That's really a mistake because women are such a source of strength to each other."

3. Unequal workload

The third Grape of Wrath is pointedly illustrated by the painful testimony of a new mom I'll call Melanie.

If my husband tells me one more time that he needs to rest because he "worked all day," I will throw all of his clothes on the front lawn, kick his car into neutral and watch it roll away and I'll sell all of his precious sports stuff on eBay for a dollar. And then I'll kill him. He seriously doesn't get it! Yes, he worked all day, but he worked with English speaking, potty trained, fully capable adults.

He didn't have to change their diapers, give them naps and clean their lunch from the wall. He didn't have to count to 10 to calm himself, he didn't have to watch Barney 303,243,243 times, and he didn't have to pop his boob out 6 times to feed a hungry baby and I KNOW he didn't have peanut butter and jelly crust for lunch. He DID get TWO 15-minute breaks to "stroll," an hour break to hit the gym, and a 1 hour train ride home to read or nap.

So maybe I don't get a paycheck, maybe I stay in my sweatpants most of the day, maybe I only shower every 2 or 3 days, maybe I get to "play" with our kids all day ... I still work a hell of a lot harder in one hour than he does all day. So take your paycheck, stick it in the bank and let me go get a freakin' pedicure once a month without hearing you say "Maybe if you got a job ... and had your own money."

Ouch. And, I might add, bull's-eye. I will give you fair warning: This next section is not going to be pleasant reading if you are a guy. But it may be the most important thing you read in this book.

Along with sleep loss and social isolation, there is a whopping disparity in who does the housework in the transition to parenthood. Simply put, women get saddled with most of it. It doesn't matter if the woman is also working or how many children the couple has. Even with 21st-century changes in attitudes, women still do more of virtually everything domestic. As civil-rights activist Florynce Kennedy once said, "Any woman who still thinks marriage is a fifty-fifty proposition is only proving that she doesn't understand either men or percentages."

Melanie's complaint illustrates that this imbalance has a corrosive effect on the quality of a marriage. Which means it is fully capable of negatively affecting a baby's brain development. I told you this would not be pleasant reading. Here are the numbers: Women with families do 70 percent of all household tasks. Dishes, dirt, diapers, minor household repairs, all of it. These data are often couched as good news, for 30 years ago the figure was 85 percent. But it doesn't take a math major to know these figures aren't equal. Household duties increase three times as much for women as for men when baby comes home. The lack of contribution is so great that having a husband around actually creates an *extra* seven hours of work per week for women. That's not true the other way around. A wife *saves* her husband about an hour of housework per week. Says one young mother, "I sometimes fantasize about getting divorced just so I can have every other weekend off."

Women spend twice as much time as men do physically caring for their kids: 66 minutes versus 26 minutes per day. The 2013 report, from the US Bureau of Labor Statistics, looked at households with children younger than 6. This is more than double the amount of time guys spent with kids in 1985, so it's usually couched as good news. Yet no one would call this equal, either.

This imbalance in workload—along with financial conflicts, which may be related—is one of the most frequently cited sources of marital conflict. It plays a significant factor in a woman's opinion of the man she married, especially if he pulls the "I am the bread-winner card" as Melanie's husband did. The financials speak loudly here. A typical stay-at-home mom works 94.4 hours per week. If she were paid for her efforts, she would earn about $117,000 per year. (This is a calculation of hourly compensation and time spent per task for the 10 job titles moms typically perform in American households, including housekeeper, van driver, day-care provider, staff psycholo-gist, and chief executive officer.) Most guys do not spend 94.4 hours a week at their jobs. And 99 percent of them earn less than $117,000 per year.

This may explain why, in the vast majority of cases, the increase in hostile interactions usually starts with the woman and spreads to the man.

Which brings us to a little book that may provide a clue to the cure. My wife got it as a gift from a friend. It is titled *Porn for Women*. It's a picture book of hunks, photographed in all their chiseled, muscle-bound, testosterone-marinated, PG-rated glory. Lots of naked chests and low-cut jeans, complete with tousled hair and beckoning eyes. And they are ALL doing housework. A well-cut Adonis loads the washing machine; the caption reads: "As soon as I finish the laundry, I'll do the grocery shopping. And I'll take the kids with me so you can relax." Another hunk, the cover guy, vacuums the floor. A par-ticularly athletic-looking man peers up from the sports section and declares, "Ooh, look, the NFL play-offs are today. I bet we'll have no trouble parking at the crafts fair."

Porn for Women. Available at a marriage near you.

4. Depression

What to make of the transition to parenthood? We have so far outlined an experience that requires a "giving response" three times per minute, allows half the sleep you need, provides little energy for friendships, and turns issues like who takes out the garbage into divorce risks. If these aren't perfect conditions from which to ferment our final Grape of Wrath, I don't know what are. Our fourth subject is depression. Fortunately, the majority of you won't experience it, but it is serious enough to warrant attention.

About half of all new mothers experience a transient postpartum sadness that vanishes within a few days. These baby blues are typical. But another 10 percent to 20 percent of mothers experience something much deeper and infinitely more troubling. These women are dogged by feelings of deepening despair, sorrow, and worthlessness, even if their marriages are doing well. Such painful, bewildering feelings last for weeks and months. Afflicted mothers cry all the time or simply stare out the window. They may stop eating. They may eat too much. These mothers are becoming clinically depressed, a condition known as postpartum depression. Though plenty of controversy rages about its sources and the criteria used to diagnose it, there is no controversy about the solution.

Women experiencing overwhelming anxiety, moodiness, or sadness require intervention. Left untreated, the consequences of postpartum depression can be tragic, ranging from a severe drop in quality of life to infanticide and suicide. Left untreated, postpartum depression also will debilitate the lively, interactive bonds that are supposed to develop between parent and child in the earliest months. Instead, the baby begins mirroring the mother's depressive actions. It's called reciprocal withdrawal. These children become more insecure, socially inhibited, timid, and passive—about twice as fearful on average as children raised by mothers who aren't depressed. The damage is still observable 14 months after birth.

It's not just the woman who's at risk for depression. Between one-tenth and one-quarter of all new dads become depressed when baby is born. If the woman is also depressed, that figure goes up to 50 percent. Not a pretty picture of bringing a baby home, is it?

Happily, this is not the complete picture.

The good news

A common comment I hear from parents when I lecture on brain development is "Nobody told me it was going to be so hard." I do not wish to minimize the difficulty of the transition to parenthood, but I wish to offer some perspective on it:

One of the reasons veteran parents don't focus on the hardness of having babies is that "hard" is not the whole story. It's not even the major part. The time you will actually spend with your kids is breathtakingly short. They will change very quickly. Eventually, your child will find a sleep schedule, turn to you for comfort, and learn from you both what to do and what not to do. Then your child will leave you and start an independent life.

What you will take away from the experience will not be how hard having a baby was but how vulnerable to it you became. Author Elizabeth Stone once said, "Making a decision to have a child—it's momentous. It is to decide forever to have your heart go walking around outside your body."

Veteran parents have experienced the sleepless nights, but they've also experienced the exhilaration of a first bike ride, a first graduation, and, for some, a first grandchild. They've experienced the rest of the story. They know it's worth it.

There's more good news.

How to protect your relationship

Couples who know about the Four Grapes of Wrath and who begin preparing in advance are much less likely to trample on them once baby comes home. When conflicts occur for these couples, the effects are usually much milder.

I can attest to that. I grew up in a military household in the 1950s. Whenever we took a car ride, my mother scrambled to prepare two kids under 3 years of age for the excursion, assembling blankets, bottles, diapers, and clean clothes. My father never assisted and actually grew impatient if preparations took too long. Storming out of the house, he would plunk down in the driver's seat and gun the engine to announce his irritation. Lots of strong feelings there, about as useful as a heart attack.

I only dimly recalled this behavior as an adult. But six months into my own marriage, my wife and I were late to a grad school meet-and-greet dinner. She was taking an especially long time to get ready, and I grew impatient. I stormed out of the house, got into the car, and put the key into the ignition. All of a sudden it hit me what I was doing. I remember taking a long breath, marveling at how deeply parents can *still* influence their kids, and then recalling novelist James Baldwin's quote: "Children have never been good at listening to their parents, but they have never failed to imitate them." Slowly, I removed the keys from the ignition, returned to my new bride, and apologized. I never pulled that stunt again. Years later, getting ready for a trip with two kids of our own, I was putting our youngest in the car seat when suddenly his diaper exploded. I grinned as I felt my car keys in my pocket and repaired to the changing table, humming. There would be no gunning of an engine. The lesson was long-lasting, the change surprisingly easy to maintain.

There is nothing particularly heroic about this story. Nothing really changed except a specific awareness. But it is this awareness that I want to share, for its inner workings have very powerful positive consequences. Researchers know how to make the transition to parenting easier on couples, and I wish not only to tell you how but to testify that it really works. As long as you are willing to put in some effort, babies are not some terminal disease from which no marriage safely recovers. As of this writing, I am into my 30th year of marriage, and my children are near teenagers. These have been the best years of my life.

What is obvious to you is obvious to you

The story of the car keys involves a change in perspective, which I like to describe as "What is obvious to you is obvious to you." My father did not see what needed to be done to get the kids ready (and may not have wanted to help even if he did). But my mother saw very clearly what needed to be done. There was a "perceptual asymmetry" in their points of view. It led to some really nasty fights.

In 1972, sociologists Richard Nisbett and Edward Jones hypothesized that perceptual asymmetry lay at the heart of most conflicts. They further suggested that bridging this asymmetry would assist in most conflict resolutions. They were right. Their key observation was this: People view their own behaviors as originating from situations beyond their control, but they view other people's behaviors as originating from inherent personality traits. Say a guy arrives late for a date. He is likely to ascribe his tardiness to external factors (being caught in traffic). She is likely to ascribe his tardiness to being a careless person (not taking traffic into account). One invokes a situational constraint to explain being late. The other invokes an insult.

Nisbett and colleagues have been cataloguing these asymmetries for decades. Nisbett found that people tend to have inflated views of themselves and their futures. They think they're more likely than they actually are to become wealthy and to have a brighter occupational future, and are somehow less likely to contract infectious diseases (one reason illnesses like cancer can be so emotionally devastating is that people never think it will happen to them, only to the "other guy"). People overestimate how much they can learn about others from short encounters. When fighting, people believe *they* are perfectly unbiased, informed, and objective, while simultaneously thinking their *opponents* are hopelessly prejudiced, clueless, and subjective.

These asymmetries originate from a phenomenon well established in the cognitive neurosciences. Any human behavior has many moving parts, roughly divisible into background and foreground elements. Background components involve our evolutionary history, genetic makeup, and fetal environment. Foreground components involve acute hormones, prior experiences, and immediate environmental triggers. Alone in our skulls, we have privileged access to both sets of components, providing detailed knowledge of our psychological interiors, motivations, and intentions. Formally called introspection, we know what we intend to mean or to communicate on a minute-to-minute basis. The problem is, nobody else does. Other people can't read our minds. The only information others have about our interior states and our motives is what our words say and how our faces and bodies appear. This is formally called extrospection.

We are amazingly blind to the limits of extrospective information. We know when our actions fail to match our inner thoughts and feelings, but we often forget that this knowledge is not available to others. The disparity can leave us bewildered or surprised at how we come across to other people. As poet Robert Burns wrote, "Oh that God the gift would give us / to see ourselves as others see us."

Introspective knowledge clashing with extrospective information is the Big Bang of most human conflicts. It has been directly observed between people trying to give directions to a lost soul and between warring nations trying to negotiate a peace agreement. It forms the basis of most breakdowns in communication, including conflicts in marriage.

Would you win an empathy contest?

If asymmetry lies at the heart of most struggles, it follows that more symmetry would produce less hostility. Hard to believe that a 4-year-old boy in a cheesy empathy contest could illustrate this insight to be essentially correct, but he did. The late author Leo Buscaglia tells of being asked to judge a contest to find the most caring child. The boy who won related a story about his elderly next-door neighbor. The man had just lost his wife of many decades. The 4-year-old heard him sobbing in his backyard and decided to investigate. The boy crawled onto the neighbor's lap and just sat there while the man grieved. It was strangely comforting to the gentleman. The boy's mom later asked her son what he had said to the neighbor. "Nothing," the little guy said. "I just helped him cry."

There are many layers to this story, but its essence is distillable: This is a response to an asymmetrical relationship. The old man was sad. The little boy was not. Yet the willingness of this inadvertent counselor to enter the emotional space of the old man, to *empathize*, changed the equilibrium of the relationship.

Choosing to empathize—at its heart it is simply a choice—is so powerful, it can change the developing nervous systems of infants whose parents regularly practice it.

Defining empathy

I used to think that squishy topics like empathy had as much neuroscientific support as the psychic hotline. If 10 years ago someone had told me that empathy was going to be as empirically well described as, say, Parkinson's disease, I would have laughed out loud. I'm not laughing now. Growing and robust research literature describes empathy, defining it with three key ingredients:

- *Affect detection.* First, a person must detect a change in the emotional disposition of someone else. In the behavioral sciences, "affect" means the external expression of an emotion or mood, generally associated with an idea or an action. Kids who are autistic usually don't get to this step; as a result, they rarely behave with empathy.

- *Imaginative transposition.* Once a person detects an emotional change, he transposes what he observes onto his own psychological interiors. He "tries on" the perceived feelings as if they were clothes, then observes how he would react given similar circumstances. For those of you in the theater, this is the heart of Stanislavski's Method acting. For those of you about to have children, you have just begun to learn how to have a fair fight with them, not to mention your spouse.

- *Boundary formation.* The person who is empathizing realizes at all times that the emotion is happening to the other person, never to the observer. Empathy is powerful, but it also has boundaries.

Make empathy a reflex: Two simple steps

Couples who regularly practice empathy see stunning results. It is the independent variable that predicts a successful marriage, according to behaviorist John Gottman, who, post hoc criticisms notwithstanding, forecasts divorce probabilities with accuracy rates approaching 90 percent. In Gottman's studies, if the wife felt she was being heard by her husband—to the point that he accepted her good influence on his behavior—the marriage was essentially divorce-proof. (Interestingly, whether the husband felt heard was not a factor in divorce rates.) If that empathy trafficking was absent, the marriage foundered.

Research shows that 70 percent of marital conflicts are not resolvable; the disagreement remains. As long as the participants learn to live with their differences—one of the biggest challenges in marriage—this is not necessarily bad news. But differences must be grasped, even if no problems are solved. One of the reasons empathy works so well is because it does not require a solution. It requires only understanding. That's extremely important to recognize. If there is wiggle room for negotiation only 30 percent of the time, empathy becomes the premier exercise in any couple's conflict-management workout. That's probably why its absence is such a powerful predictor of divorce. Gottman, among other researchers, discovered a similar effect in child rearing. He has said, "Empathy not only matters; it is the foundation of effective parenting."

What must you do to get the kind of marital successes Gottman reported? You need to close that gap I described, the imbalance between what you know about your inner feelings and what you deduce about your spouse's. The way to do that is to create an "empathy reflex"—your first response to any emotional situation. Researchers defined the empathy reflex while attempting to socialize high-functioning autistic children. It's surprisingly simple and surprisingly effective, something akin to the little boy crawling up onto the old man's lap. When you first encounter somebody's "hot" feelings, execute two simple steps:

1. Describe the emotional changes you think you see.

2. Make a guess as to where those emotional changes came from.

Then you can engage in whatever nasty, reactive bad habits are normal for you. I give you fair warning, however. If the empathy reflex becomes an active part of the way you manage conflicts, it will be difficult for you to stay nasty and reactive. Here's a real-life example taken from one of my research files.

A woman's 15-year-old daughter was allowed to go out on Saturdays but had to obey a strict midnight curfew. She ignored this curfew one weekend, not returning until 2:00 a.m. The daughter crept into the house and saw the dreaded living room lamp still on, with a visibly angry mother waiting in the chair. The kid was scared out of her wits, of course. She also seemed troubled. Mom perceived she'd had a tough night. This scene would normally signal the opening rounds of an emotional smackdown, a familiar and draining event for both. But Mom had heard from a friend about the empathy reflex and chose to deploy it instead.

Beginning with a simple affective description, she commented, "You look scared out of your mind." The teenager paused, nodded slightly. "You not only look scared," she continued, "you look upset. Really upset. In fact, you look humiliated." The teenager paused again. This was not what she was expecting. The mom then deployed step 2, guessing at the origin.

"You had a bad time tonight, didn't you?" The daughter grew wide-eyed. A tough night indeed. Tears suddenly sprang into her eyes. Mom guessed what probably occurred, and her voice softened. "You had a fight with your boyfriend." The teenager burst out crying. "He broke up with me! I had to get another ride home! That's why I was late!" The daughter collapsed into her mother's loving arms, and both of them cried. There would be no smackdown that evening. There seldom is in the arms of an empathy reflex—whether in parenting or in marriage.

Mom still punished her daughter; rules are rules, and she was grounded for a week. But the complexion of the relationship changed. Her daughter even began imitating the empathy reflex, a common research finding in households where it is actively practiced. Early the next week, the daughter saw her mother scrambling to make a late dinner, visibly upset after a long day at work. Instead of asking what was on the menu, the daughter said, "You look really upset, Mom. Is it because it's late and you're tired and you don't want to make dinner?"

The mother couldn't believe it.

An ounce of prevention

Couples who have solid relationships defined by empathy and who prepare for the transition to parenthood avoid the worst of the Four

Grapes of Wrath. Such preparation creates the best domestic ecology for the child's healthy brain development.

These parents may or may not get their kid into Harvard, but they will not get their kid into a custody battle. They enjoy the highest probability for raising smart, happy, morally aware kids.

Key points

- More than 80 percent of couples experience a huge drop in marital quality during the transition to parenthood.
- Hostility between parents can harm a newborn's developing brain and nervous system.
- The four most common sources of marital turbulence are: sleep loss, social isolation, unequal distribution of household workload, and depression. Awareness of these allows couples to create a buffer against them.
- Regularly practice the empathy reflex. As your first response to any emotional situation, describe the emotional changes you think you see, and then make a guess as to their origins.

reminder: references at www.brainrules.net/references

smart baby: seeds

brain rule

Feeling safe enables learning

smart baby: seeds

 Nothing in President Theodore Roosevelt's early life suggested even a whiff of future greatness. He was a sickly child, nervous and timid, and so asthmatic that he had to sleep upright in bed to keep from asphyxiating. He was too ill to attend formal classes, forcing his parents to school him at home. Because of a serious heart condition, his doctors suggested he find a line of work that would tether him to a desk and by all means avoid strenuous physical activity.

Fortunately, Roosevelt's mind did not cooperate with either his body or his doctor. Possessed of a voracious intellect, a photographic memory, and a ceaseless need to achieve, he wrote his first scientific paper ("The Natural History of Insects") at the age of 9. He was accepted to Harvard at the age of 16, graduated Phi Beta Kappa, ran for the state legislature at age 23, and published his first scholarly book, a history of the War of 1812, the next year. He gained a reputation as a thought-provoking historian and, eventually, an able politician. And zoologist. And philosopher, geographer, warrior, and diplomat. Roosevelt became commander in chief at the age of 42, the youngest ever. He remains the only president awarded the Congressional Medal of Honor, and he was the first American to win the Nobel Peace Prize.

What made Roosevelt so darn smart, given his less than auspicious start? Clearly, genetics helped our 26th president. For all of us, nature controls about 50 percent of our intellectual horsepower, and environment determines the rest. This means two things for parents: First, no matter how hard your child tries, there will be limits to what his brain can do. Second, that's only half of the story. Aspects of your child's intelligence will be deeply influenced by his environment, especially by what you do as parents. We'll look at both the seed and the soil. This chapter discusses the biological basis of a child's intelligence. The next chapter explains what you can do to optimize it.

What a smart brain looks like

If you could peer inside your baby's brain, would there be clues to her future intellectual greatness? What does intelligence look like in the twists and folds of the brain's convoluted architecture? One obvious, if ghoulish, way to answer these questions is to look at the brains of smart people after they have died and seek clues to intelligence in their neural architecture. Scientists have done this with a variety of famous brains, from the mathematical German Carl Gauss to the not-so-mathematical Russian Vladimir Lenin. They've studied Albert Einstein's brain, too, with surprising results.

Just your average genius

Einstein died in New Jersey in 1955. His autopsy was performed by Thomas Stoltz Harvey, who must go down as the most possessive pathologist in history. He excised the famous physicist's brain and photographed it from many angles. Then he chopped the brain into tiny blocks. Then he got into trouble. Harvey apparently did not secure permission from Einstein or his family to pixellate the physicist's famous brain. Princeton Hospital administrators demanded that Harvey surrender Einstein's brain. Harvey refused, forfeited his job, fled to Kansas, and held the preserved samples for more than 20 years. From time to time, Harvey would send researchers tantalizing bits of Einstein's brain for analysis. Finally, Harvey decided to give Einstein's brain, or at least what was left of it, back to the chief of pathology at Princeton Hospital. Now the tissues could be subject to more systematic study, with scientists looking for clues that would reveal Einstein's genius.

What did they discover? The most surprising finding was that there was nothing surprising. Einstein had a fairly average brain. The organ had a standard internal architecture, with a few structural anomalies. The regions responsible for visuospatial cognition and math processing were a bit larger, 15 percent fatter than average. He was also missing some sections that less agile brains possess, accompanied with a few more glial cells than most people carry (glial cells help give the brain its structure and assist with information processing). None of these results are very instructive, unfortunately. Most brains possess structural abnormalities: some regions more shrunken than others, some more swollen. Because of this individuality, it is currently impossible to demonstrate that certain physical differences in brain structure lead to genius. Einstein's brain certainly was smart, but not one of its dice-sized pieces would definitively tell us why.

What about looking at live, functioning brains? These days, you don't have to wait until someone is dead to determine structure-function relationships. You can use noninvasive imaging technologies to look in on the brain while it is performing some task. Can we detect smartness in people by observing an organ caught in the act of being itself? The answer, once again, is no. Or at least not yet. When you examine living geniuses solving some tough problem, you do not find reassuring similarities; you find disconcerting individualities. Problem solving and sensory processing do not look the same in *any* two brains.

This has led to great confusion and contradictory findings. Some studies purport to show that "smart" people have more efficient brains (they use less energy to solve tough problems), but other researchers have found exactly the opposite. Gray matter is thicker in some smart people, white matter thicker in others. Scientists have found 14 separate regions responsible for various aspects of human intelligence, sprinkled throughout the brain like cognitive pixie dust. These magical regions are nestled into an idea called P-FIT, short for Parieto-Frontal Integration Theory. When P-FIT regions are examined as people think deep thoughts, researchers again find that, frustratingly, overarching patterns are few. Different people use varying combinations of these regions to solve complex problems. These combinations probably explain the wide variety of intellectual abilities we can observe in people.

We have even less information about a baby's intelligence. It is very difficult to do noninvasive imaging experiments with the diaper-and-pull-up crowd. To do a functional MRI, for example, the head needs to stay perfectly still for long stretches of time. Good luck trying to do that with a wiggly 6-month-old! Even if you could, given our current understanding, brain architecture cannot successfully predict whether your child is going to be smart.

In search of a "smart gene"

How about at the level of DNA? Have researchers uncovered a "smart gene"? A lot of people are looking. Variants of one famous gene, called COMT (catechol-O-methyl transferase, since you asked), appear to be associated with higher short-term-memory scores in some people, though not in others. Another gene, cathepsin D, also was linked to high intelligence. So was a variant of a dopamine receptor gene, from a family of genes usually involved in feeling pleasure. The problem with most of these findings is that they have been difficult to replicate. Even when they have been successfully confirmed, the presence of the variant usually accounted for a boost of only 3 or 4 IQ points. To date, no intelligence gene has been isolated. Given the complexity of intelligence, I highly doubt there is one.

Bingo: A baby IQ test

If cells and genes aren't any help, what about behaviors? Here, researchers have struck gold. We now have in hand a series of tests for infants that can predict their IQs as adults. In one test, preverbal infants are allowed to feel an object hidden from their view in a box. If the infants can then correctly identify the object by sight—called cross-modal transfer—they will score higher on later IQ tests than infants who can't. In another test, measuring something researchers call visual recognition memory, infants are set in front of a checkerboard square. This is an oversimplification, but the longer the infants stare, the higher their IQ is likely to be. Sound unlikely? These measurements, taken between 2 and 8 months of age, correctly predicted IQ scores at age 18!

What does that really mean? For one thing, it means that when these children reach school age, they will do well on an IQ test.

The intelligence of IQ

IQ matters a lot to some people, such as the admissions officers of elite private kindergarten and elementary schools. They often demand that children take intelligence tests; the WISC-IV, short for Wechsler Intelligence Scale for Children, Version Four, is common. Many schools accept only those kids who score in the ridiculously high 97th percentile. These $500 tests are sometimes administered to 6-year-olds, or kids even younger, serving as an entrance exam to kindergarten!

Here are two typical questions on IQ tests:

1. Which one of the five is least like the other four? Cow, tiger, snake, bear, dog.

Did you say snake? Congratulations. The testers who designed the question agree with you (all the other animals have legs; all the others are mammals).

2. Take 1000 and add 40 to it. Now add another 1000. Now add 30. And another 1000. Now add 20. Now add another 1000. Now add 10. What is the total?

Did you say 5,000? If so, you're in good company. Research shows that 98 percent of people who tackle this question get that answer. But it is wrong. The correct answer is 4,100.

IQ tests are filled with questions like these. If you get them right, does that mean you are smart? Maybe. But maybe not. Some researchers believe IQ tests measure nothing more than your ability to take IQ tests. The fact is, researchers don't agree on *what* an IQ test measures. Given the range of intellectual abilities that exist, it is probably smart to reject a one-number-fits-all notion as the final word on your baby's brain power. Armed with a little history on these inventories, you can decide for yourself.

The birth of the IQ test

Many sharp folks have investigated the definition of human intelligence, often in an attempt to figure out their own unique gifts. One of the first was Francis Galton (1822–1911), half cousin to Charles Darwin. Possessed with enormous and fashionable pork-chop sideburns but otherwise balding, Sir Francis was stern, brilliant, and probably a little crazy. He came from a famous line of pacifist Quakers whose family business was, oddly enough, the manufacture of guns.

Galton was a prodigy, reading and quoting Shakespeare by the time he was 6, and speaking both Greek and Latin at an early age. He seemed to be interested in everything, as an adult making contributions to meteorology, psychology, photography, and even criminal justice (he advocated for the scientific analysis of fingerprints to identify criminals). Along the way, he invented the statistical concepts of standard deviation and linear regression, and he used them to study human behavior.

One of his chief fascinations concerned the engines that power human intellect—especially inheritance. Galton was the first to realize that intelligence both had heritable characteristics and was powerfully influenced by environment. He's the one who coined the phrase "nature versus nurture." Because of these insights, Galton is probably the man most responsible for inspiring scientists to consider the definable roots of human intelligence. But as researchers began to investigate the matter systematically, they developed a curious compulsion to describe human intelligence with a single number. Tests were used—and are still used today—to yield such numbers. The first one is our oft-mentioned IQ test, short for intelligence quotient.

IQ tests originally were designed by a group of French psychologists, among them Alfred Binet, innocently attempting to identify children who might need help in school. The group devised 30 tasks that ranged from touching one's nose to drawing patterns from memory. The design of these tests had very little empirical support in the real world, and Binet consistently warned against interpreting these tests literally. He felt presciently that intelligence was quite plastic and that his tests had real margins for errors. But German psychologist William Stern began using the tests to measure children's intelligence, quantifying the scores with the term "IQ." The score was the ratio of a child's mental age to his or her chronological age, multiplied by 100. So a 10-year-old who could solve problems normally solved only by 15-year-olds had an IQ of 150: (15/10) x 100. The tests became very popular in Europe, then floated across the Atlantic.

In 1916, Stanford professor Lewis Terman removed some of the questions and added new ones—also without many empirical reasons to do so. The configuration has been christened the Stanford-Binet test ever since. Eventually, the ratio was changed to a number distributed along a bell curve, setting the average to 100. A second test, developed in 1923 by British Army officer-turned-psychologist Charles Spearman, measured what he called "general cognition," now simply referred to as "g." Spearman observed that people who scored above average on one subcategory of pencil-and-paper tests tended to do well on the rest of them. This test measures the tendency of performance on a large number of cognitive tasks to be intercorrelated.

Battles have been raging for decades about what these test scores mean and how they should be used. That's a good thing, because intelligence measures are more plastic than many people realize.

Gaining and losing a pound of IQ

I remember the first time I saw the actress Kirstie Alley on-screen, playing a smart, sexy character in a *Star Trek* movie. A former cheerleader, Kirstie went on to star in a number of television shows, including the role for which she won two Emmys, the legendary sitcom *Cheers*. But she may be better known for her issues with weight. In 2005, Kirstie reportedly weighed more than 200 pounds, mostly because of poor eating habits. She became a spokesperson for a weight-loss program and at one point starred in a television show about an overweight actress attempting to get work in Hollywood. She eventually lost 75 pounds. Since then, however, her weight has continued to fluctuate.

What does this unstable number have to do with our discussion of intelligence? Like Kirstie's dress size, IQ is malleable. IQ has been shown to vary over one's life span, and it is surprisingly vulnerable to environmental influences. It can change if one is stressed, old, or living in a different culture from the testing majority. A child's IQ is influenced by his or her family, too. Growing up in the same household tends to increase IQ similarities between siblings, for example. Poor people tend to have significantly lower IQs than rich people. And if you earn below a certain income level, economic factors will have a much greater influence on your child's IQ than if your child is middle class. A child born in poverty but adopted into a middle-class family will on average gain 12 to 18 points in IQ.

There are people who don't want to believe IQ is so malleable. They think numbers like IQ and "g" are permanent, like a date of birth instead of a dress size. The media often cast our intellectual prowess in such permanent terms, and our own experience seems to agree. Some people are born smart, like Theodore Roosevelt, and some people are not. The assumption is reassuringly simplistic. But intelligence isn't simple, and neither is our ability to measure it.

You'd be smart to reject a one-number-fits-all notion as the final word on your baby's brain power.

Smarter every year

One damning piece of evidence is the fact that somehow IQs have been increasing for decades. From 1947 to 2002, the collective IQ of American kids went up 18 points. James Flynn, a crusty, wild-haired old philosopher from New Zealand, discovered this phenomenon (a controversial finding cheerfully christened the "Flynn Effect"). Flynn set up the following thought experiment. He took the average American IQ of 100, then ran the numbers backward from the year 2009 at the observed rate. He found that the average IQ of Americans in 1900 would have been between 50 and 70. This is the same score of most people with Down syndrome, a classification termed "mild mental retardation." Most of our citizens at the turn of the century did not have Down syndrome. So is there something wrong with the people or something wrong with the metric? Clearly, the notion of IQ permanence needs some retooling.

I certainly believe in the concept of intelligence, and I think IQ and "g" assess some aspect of it. So do many of my colleagues, who signed a 1997 editorial in the research journal *Intelligence* declaring that "IQ is strongly related, probably more so than any other single measurable human trait, to many important educational, occupational, economic and social outcomes." I agree. I just wish I knew what was actually being measured.

What does it mean to be smart?

The variability of these IQ tests can be frustrating. Parents want to know if their kid is smart. And they want their kid to *be* smart. Given our knowledge-based 21st-century economy, that makes sense. When you drill down on the subject, however, many parents really mean that they want their kids to be academically successful, which is a better guarantee of their future. Are "smart" and "grade-point average" related? They are, but they are not the same thing, and the link is not as strong as one might think.

Single numbers—or even correlations between single numbers— simply do not have enough flexibility to describe the many complexities of human intelligence. Harvard psychologist Howard Gardner, who published his latest theory of multiple intelligences in 1993, put it this way: Strong evidence exists "that the mind is a multifaceted, multicomponent instrument, which cannot in any legitimate way be captured in a single paper-and-pencil-style instrument." Ready to cry uncle? Is intelligence going to be the province of comments like "I don't know what it is, but I know when I see it"? No, but to see the issue more clearly, we are going to have to replace this one-number-fits-all notion.

Human intelligence is more like ingredients in a stew than numbers in a spreadsheet.

Mom's beef stew: Five ingredients of intelligence

The smell of my mother's beef stew simmering in the kitchen on a cold winter's day is easily the best comfort-food memory I have. The crackling sounds of braised beef; the sweet, stinging smell of chopped onions; the delightful sight of quarter-sized medallions of carrots floating in a Crock-Pot … Mom's stew was like a warm hug in a bowl.

She once marched me into the kitchen to teach me how to make her famous beef stew. No easy task, this, for she had the annoying habit of changing the recipe almost every time she made it. "It depends on who's coming over for dinner," Mom would explain, "or whatever we have lying around the house." According to her, only two elements were critical to pull off her masterpiece. One was the quality of the beef. The other was the quality of the gravy surrounding the meat. If those issues were settled, the stew was going to be a success, regardless of what else went into the pot.

Like Mom's stew, human intelligence has two essential components, both fundamentally linked to our evolutionary need to survive. The first is the ability to record information. This is sometimes called "crystallized intelligence." It involves the various memory systems of the brain, which combine to create a richly structured database.

The second component is the capacity to adapt that information to unique situations. This involves the ability to improvise, based in part on the ability to recall and recombine specific parts of the database. This capacity for reasoning and problem solving is termed "fluid intelligence." From an evolutionary perspective, the potent combination of memorization and extemporization conferred on us two survival-rich behaviors: the ability to learn rapidly from our mistakes and the ability to apply that learning in unique combinations to the ever-changing, ever-brutal world of our East African cradle.

Intelligence, seen through this evolutionary lens, is simply the ability to do these activities better than someone else.

Mandatory as memory and fluid intelligence are, though, they are not the entire recipe for human smarts. Just like my mother's shifting recipe, different families have different combinations of talents stewing in their cerebral Crock-Pots. One son might have a poor memory but dynamite quantitative skills. One daughter might display an extraordinary penchant for language yet remain mystified by even simple division. How can we say one child is less intelligent than the other?

Many ingredients make up the human intelligence stew, and I'd like to describe five that I think you would do well to consider as you contemplate your child's intellectual gifts. They are:

- The desire to explore
- Self-control
- Creativity
- Verbal communication
- Interpreting nonverbal communication

Most of these characteristics fall outside the spectrum of the usual IQ suspects. We believe many have genetic roots; most can be seen in newborns. Rooted as these five ingredients may be in our evolutionary history, however, they do not exist in isolation from the outside world. Nurture—even for Teddy Roosevelt—plays an important role in whether a child is able to maximize his or her intelligence.

I. The desire to explore

This is one of my favorite examples of an infant's penchant for exploration. I was attending the Presbyterian baptism of a 9-month-old. Things started out well enough. The infant was nestled quietly in his dad's arms, waiting for his turn to be sprinkled in front of the congregation. As the parents turned to face the pastor, the baby spied the handheld microphone. He quickly tried to wrest the mike out of the pastor's grip, flicking his tongue out at the ball of the microphone.

The little guy seemed to think that the mike was some kind of ice cream cone, and he decided to test his hypothesis.

This was highly inappropriate Presbyterian behavior. The pastor swung the microphone out of reach and immediately realized his mistake: Even in the preverbal crowd, hell hath no fury like a scientist denied his data. The baby howled, tried to wiggle free, and clawed at the microphone, all while licking at the air. He was exploring, darn it, and he did not appreciate being interrupted in the pursuit of knowledge. Especially if it involved sugar.

I'm not sure about the parents, but I was delighted to see such a fine example of pediatric research enthusiasm. Parents have known that children were natural scientists long before there were microphones. But it wasn't until the last half of the 20th century that we could isolate components of their wonderful exploratory behaviors.

Thousands of experiments confirm that babies learn about their environment through a series of increasingly self-corrected ideas. They experience sensory observations, make predictions about what they observe, design and deploy experiments capable of testing their predictions, evaluate their tests, and add that knowledge to a self-generated, growing database. The style is naturally aggressive, wonderfully flexible, and annoyingly persistent. They use fluid intelligence to extract information, then crystallize it into memory. Nobody teaches infants how to do this, yet they do it all over the world. This hints at the behavior's strong evolutionary roots. They are *scientists*, as their parents suspected all along. And their laboratory is the whole world, including microphones in church.

An innovator's DNA

Exploratory behavior—the willingness to experiment, to ask extraordinary questions of ordinary things—is a talent highly prized in the working world, too. Good ideas tend to make money. The trait seems to be as valuable a survival strategy today as it was on the plains of the Serengeti.

What traits separate creative, visionary people who consistently conjure up financially successful ideas from less imaginative, managerial types who carry them out? Two business researchers explored that simple question. They conducted a whopping six-year study with more than 3,000 innovative executives, from chemists to software engineers. After being published in 2009, the study won an award from *Harvard Business Review.*

Visionaries had in common five characteristics, which the researchers termed "Innovator's DNA." Here are the first three:

- **An unusual ability to associate.** They could see connections between concepts, problems, or questions not obvious to others.

- **An annoying habit of consistently asking "what if."** And "why not" and "how come you're doing it this way." These visionaries scoured out the limits of the status quo, poking it, prodding it, shooting upward to the 40,000-foot view of something to see if it made any sense and then plummeting back to earth with suggestions.

- **An unquenchable desire to tinker and experiment.** The entrepreneurs might land on an idea, but their first inclination would be to tear it apart, even if it was self-generated. They displayed an incessant need to test things: to find the ceiling of things, the basement of things, the surface area, the tolerance, the perimeters of ideas—theirs, yours, mine, *anybody's.* They were on a mission, and the mission was discovery.

The biggest common denominator of these characteristics? A willingness to explore. The biggest enemy was the non-exploration-oriented system in which the innovators often found themselves. Hal Gregersen, one of the lead authors of the study, said in *Harvard Business Review:* "You can summarize all of the skills we've noted in one word: 'inquisitiveness.' I spent 20 years studying great global leaders, and that was the big common denominator." He then went on to talk about children: "If you look at 4-year-olds, they are constantly asking questions. But by the time they are 6½ years old, they stop asking questions because they quickly learn that teachers value the right answers more than provocative questions. High-school students rarely show inquisitiveness. And by the time they're grown up and are in corporate settings, they have already had the curiosity drummed out of them. Eighty percent of executives spend less than 20 percent of their time on discovering new ideas."

That's a heartbreaker. Why we've designed our schools and workplaces this way has never made sense to me. But you, as a parent, can encourage your child's natural desire to explore—starting with understanding how inquisitiveness contributes to your child's intellectual success.

2. Self-control

A healthy, well-adjusted preschooler sits down at a table in front of two giant, freshly baked chocolate-chip cookies. It's not a kitchen table—it's Walter Mischel's Stanford lab during the late 1960s. The smell is heavenly. "You see these cookies?" Mischel says. "You can eat just one of them right now if you want, but if you wait, you can eat both. I have to go away for five minutes. If I return and you have not eaten anything, I will let you have *both* cookies. If you eat one while I'm gone, the bargain is off and you don't get the second one. Do we have a deal?" The child nods. The researcher leaves.

What does the child do? Mischel has the most charming, funny films of children's reactions. They squirm in their seat. They turn their back to the cookies (or marshmallows or other assorted caloric confections, depending on the day). They sit on their hands. They close one eye, then both, then sneak a peek. They are trying to get both cookies, but the going is tough. If the children are kindergartners, 72 percent cave in and gobble up the cookie. If they're in fourth grade, however, only 49 percent yield to the temptation. By sixth grade, the number is 38 percent, about half the rate of the preschoolers.

Welcome to the interesting world of impulse control. It is part of a suite of behaviors under the collective term "executive function." Executive function controls planning, foresight, problem solving, and goal setting. It engages many parts of the brain, including a short-term form of memory called working memory. Mischel and his many colleagues discovered that a child's executive function is a critical component of intellectual prowess.

Executive function is a better predictor of academic success than IQ.

We now know that it is actually a *better* predictor of academic success than IQ. It's not a small difference, either: Mischel found that children who could delay gratification for 15 minutes scored 210 points higher on their SATs than children who lasted one minute.

Why? Executive function relies on a child's ability to filter out distracting (in this case, tempting) thoughts, which is critical in environments that are oversaturated with sensory stimuli and myriad on-demand choices. That's our world, as you have undoubtedly noticed, and it will be your children's, too. Once the brain has chosen relevant stimuli from a noisy pile of irrelevant choices, executive function allows the brain to stay on task and say no to unproductive distractions.

At the neurobiological level, self-control comes from "common value signals" (measures of neural activity) generated by a specific area of the brain behind your forehead. It is called—brain jargon alert—the ventromedial prefrontal cortex. Another area of the brain, the dorsolateral prefrontal cortex, throws out bolts of electricity to this ventromedial cousin. The more practice a child has in delaying gratification, the better aimed the jolt becomes, and the more control it can exert over behavior. Researchers originally discovered this while having diet-conscious adults look at pictures of carrots, then switching the picture to candy bars. Their brains exerted powerful

"I-don't-care-if-it's-sugar-you-can't-have-any" signals when the choco-late appeared.

A child's brain can be trained to enhance self-control and other aspects of executive function. But genes are undoubtedly involved. There seems to be an innate schedule of development, which explains why the cookie experiment shows a difference in scores between kin-dergartners and sixth graders. Some kids display the behaviors earlier, some later. Some struggle with it their entire lives. It's one more way every brain is wired differently. But children who are able to filter out distractions, the data show, do far better in school.

3. Creativity

My mother's favorite artist in the world was Rembrandt. She was enraptured by his use of light and space, which transported her effort-lessly into his 17th-century world. She was much less enamored of 20th-century art. I remember her railing about Marcel Duchamp's *Fountain*—simply a urinal—being placed in the same artistic firma-ment as her beloved van Rijn. Toilets as art? And she *hated* it? For me as an 11-year-old boy, that was artistic Valhalla!

Mom, to whom I owe every atom of curiosity I possess, reacted with her typical parental insight and grace: She set aside her own pref-erences and followed my curiosity. She brought home two pictures wrapped in brown paper and sat me down. "Imagine," she began, with just a hint of eye rolling, "that you tried to express in two dimen-sions all the information of a three-dimensional object. How would you do it?" I stumbled around trying to get the right answer, or any answer, but made no progress. Mom interrupted. "Perhaps you would come up with something like this!" With the flourish of an actress, which she briefly was, Mom ripped off the wrapping, revealing prints of Picasso masterpieces: *Three Musicians* and *Violin and Guitar*. It was love at first cube. Not to take anything away from Rembrandt, but *Three Musicians* was a revelation to me, as was the creative mind that conceived it.

Why did I think that? How does anyone recognize creativity? It is a tough question, saturated in cultural subjectivity and individual experience, as the differences between me and my mother showed. Researchers do believe that creativity has a few core components, however. These include the ability to perceive new relationships between old things, to conjure up ideas or things or *whatever* that do not currently exist. (Attempts to depict 3-D in a 2-D world come to mind.) Creativity also must evoke emotions, positive or negative, in someone else. Something—a product, a result—has to come of the process. And it involves a healthy dose of risk taking. It took a lot of guts to make a painting of musicians that looked as if they had exploded. It took a lot of guts to plop down a urinal in a 1917 New York show and call it art.

Human creativity involves many groups of cognitive gadgets, including episodic memory and autobiographical memory systems. Like a TiVo recording a sitcom, these systems permit the brain to keep track of events happening to you, allowing you a reference to your personal experiences in both time and space. You can recall going to the grocery store and what you bought there, not to mention the idiot who stubbed your heel with a grocery cart, because of these episodic memory systems. They are separate from the memory systems that allow you to calculate the sales tax of your purchase, or even remember what a sales tax is. But that's not all episodic systems do.

Scientist Nancy Andreasen found that these TiVos are recruited when innovative people start associating connectively—making the insightful connections across seemingly unrelated notions that allow them to *create*. The TiVos reside in brain regions called association cortices, which are huge in humans—the biggest of any primate—stretching out like cobwebs across the frontal, parietal, and temporal lobes.

A second set of findings associates creativity with risk taking. This is not the kind of foolishness where you as an undergraduate ate two 16-inch pizzas in one sitting because someone named Tom-Tom dared you (don't ask). Abnormal risk taking, which is also associated more with substance abuse and bipolar mania, does not make you more creative. There is a type of risk taking that does, however, and the research community calls it "functional impulsivity." Researchers uncovered two separate neural processing systems that manage functional impulsivity. One governs low-risk, or "cold," decision-making behaviors; the other governs high-risk, or "hot," decision-making behaviors. A cold decision might involve a child agreeing to go to a favorite restaurant with a friend. A hot decision might involve ordering the nuclear inferno chili appetizer on the friend's dare.

With all the crazy things children do, how can we tell functional impulsivity from abnormal risk taking? Unfortunately, there is no test that can distinguish "productive" from "stupid" in kids (or adults, for that matter).

Research on risk shows some sex-based differences. Boys are less cautious, for example. The difference starts showing up in the second year of life, and then things really ramp up: Boys are 73 percent more likely than girls to die from accidents between birth and puberty, and they break rules more often. But in recent decades, the sex-based differences have begun to shrink, perhaps because of changing expectations. Separating nature from nurture is darned hard with issues like these.

Whatever their gender, creative entrepreneurs have functional-impulsivity instincts in spades. They score atmospherically high on tests that measure risk taking, and they have a strong ability to cope with ambiguity. When their brains are caught in the act of being creative, the medial and orbital sectors of the prefrontal cortex, regions just behind the eyes, light up like crazy on an fMRI. More "managerial types" (that's actually what researchers call them) don't have these scores—or these neural activities.

Can you predict creativity in kids? Psychologist Paul Torrance created a 90-minute exam called the Torrance Tests of Creative

Thinking. The tests are composed of some truly delightful problems. Children might be presented with a picture of a stuffed rabbit, then told they have three minutes to improve upon the design to make it more fun to play with. They might be presented with a scribble, then told to make a narrative from it. Torrance first administered the exam in 1958 to several hundred children, then followed their lives into adulthood, assessing their creative output throughout: things like patents filed, books written, papers published, grants awarded, and businesses started. The study is still ongoing, the participants christened "Torrance's Kids." Torrance died in 2003, and the study is now supervised by colleagues.

As a research tool, the exam has been formally evaluated many times. Though the test is not without its critics, the most amazing finding remains how well a child's scores predict his or her future creative output. Indeed, the scores predict lifetime creative output with a correlation three times stronger than native IQ can predict. The test has been translated into 50 languages and taken by millions of people. It is the go-to standard for evaluating creativity in children.

4. Verbal communication

The most memorable experience in my rookie year of parenting our younger son, Noah, was the moment he said his first multisyllable word. Noah's first six months had been a fountain of joy for our family. He is a glass-half-full kind of kid, with a smile as effervescent as root beer and a laugh like bubble bath, and Noah approached his language skills with the same joy. He possessed a particular preoccupation with sea creatures, which I blame in equal parts on *Finding Nemo* and *National Geographic*. We put pictures of sea animals on the ceiling above his changing table, including a cartoon of a giant red Pacific octopus. He had not yet said any full words at the half-year mark, but he was about to.

One morning I was busy changing his diaper, just before work. Noah suddenly stopped smiling and just stared straight at the ceiling as I cleaned him up. Slowly, deliberately, he pointed his finger upward, turned his gaze from the ceiling, looked me straight in the eye, and said in a clear voice: "Oct-o-pus." Then he laughed out loud. He pointed at it again, said it louder: "OCT-O-PUS," and giggled. I almost had a heart attack. "Yes!" I cried, "OCTOPUS!" He replied, "Octo, octo, octopus," laughing now. We both chanted it. I forgot what I was doing the rest of that morning—I think I called in sick for work—and we had a dance that day, celebrating all things eight-legged. Other words came in rapid succession in the days following. (So did my absenteeism.)

You can't argue with the fact that verbal skills are important in human intelligence. They even make it into IQ tests. One of the seminal joys for any parent is to watch a child grapple with this unique human talent in the first months of life. What happened in Noah's brain that made so many things come together at once on that changing table—or in any other child's brain as language dawns on her like a sunrise? We don't really know. Many theories abound about how we acquire language. Famed linguist Noam Chomsky believes we are born with language software preloaded into our heads, a package he calls universal grammar.

Once language acquisition gets going, it tends to develop quickly. Within a year and a half, most kids can pronounce 50 words and understand about 100 more. That figure explodes to 1,000 words by a child's third birthday and to 6,000 just before the sixth birthday. Calculated from birth, we acquire new words at the rate of three per day. This project takes a long time to finish. English will require the mastery of about 50,000 words, and that doesn't even include idioms and fixed expressions like "hitting a home run" or "pot of gold." It's pretty complex stuff. On top of vocabulary, children have to learn the sounds of the language (phonemes) and the social meaning of the words (affective intent).

Infants track these characteristics of language at an astonishingly early age. At birth, your baby can distinguish between the sounds of every language that has ever been invented. Professor Patricia Kuhl, co-director of the Institute for Learning and Brain Sciences at the University of Washington, discovered this phenomenon. She calls kids at this age "citizens of the world." Chomsky puts it this way: We are not born with the capacity to speak a specific language. We are born with the capacity to speak *any* language.

Foreign languages

That doesn't last. By their first birthday, Kuhl found, babies can no longer distinguish between the sounds of every language on the planet. They can distinguish only between those to which they have been exposed in the past six months. A Japanese baby not exposed to "rake" and "lake" during her second six months of life cannot distinguish between those two sounds by the time she is 1 year old. As always, there are exceptions. Adults with training can still learn to distinguish speech sounds in other languages. But in general, the brain appears to have a limited window of opportunity in an astonishingly early time frame. The cognitive door begins swinging shut at 6 months old, and then, unless something pushes against it, the door closes. By 12 months, your baby's brain has made decisions that affect her the rest of her life.

What is strong enough, Kuhl and other researchers wondered, to keep that door from closing? Say you expose your baby, in the critical period, to a tape of someone speaking a foreign language. Does the brain stay open for phonemic business? The answer is no. How about a DVD of someone speaking the foreign language? The door continues to shut. Only one thing keeps that door open to another language. You have to deliver the words through a social interaction. A real live person has to come into the room and speak the language directly to the child. If the child's brain detects this social interaction, its neurons will begin recording the second language, phonemes and all. To perform these cognitive tasks, the brain needs the information-rich, give-and-take stimulation that another human being provides.

Tucked into these data is a bombshell of an idea, one with empirical support across the developmental sciences. *Human learning in its most native state is primarily a relational exercise.* Intelligence is not developed in the electronic crucibles of cold, lifeless machines but in the arms of warm, loving people. You can literally rewire a child's brain through exposure to *relationships.*

Hear that laughter? That's the sound of my son Noah, demonstrating to his old man how important honest-to-God active parenting is in teaching him how to do something as wonderful, and as human, as learning languages.

> **Intelligence is not developed in the crucibles of machines but in the arms of warm, loving people.**

5. Interpreting nonverbal communication

Though speech is a uniquely human trait, it is nestled inside a vast world of communication behaviors, many of which are used by other animals, too. But we aren't always communicating the same thing, as legendary dog whisperer Cesar Millan points out.

If you've ever seen National Geographic's *Dog Whisperer*, you know Millan is a world-champion dog handler. His secret is that he thinks like a dog, not like a person, when he's interacting with a dog. Millan told *Men's Health*, "A lot of people who meet a new dog want to go over to him, touch him, and talk to him." That is, of course, the custom when people meet a new person. But, Millan says, "in the language of dogs, this is very aggressive and confusing." Instead, Millan says, when you meet a new dog, ignore the animal like an aloof, jilted lover. Don't make eye contact. Let the dog come over and inspect you, sniff you. Once the dog gives you cues that he doesn't find you a threat—like backing away or rubbing against you—then you can talk, touch, or make eye contact. When dogs attack people, they may in some cases simply be acting upon an ancient behavioral reflex involving a reaction to, of all things, somebody's face.

Face-to-face communication in the animal world has many meanings, most of them not very nice. Extracting social information by examining the face is a powerful slice of mammalian evolutionary history. But we humans use our faces, including eye-to-eye contact, for many reasons besides communicating threats. We have the most sophisticated nonverbal message systems on the planet. From babies on up, we constantly communicate social information with our bodies in coordination with our smiles and frowns. Together they constitute the crown jewels of extrospective information—remember that term?—which is a potent way to get a point across quite quickly.

Though much mythology surrounds the meaning of body language (sometimes people cross and uncross their legs simply because their legs get tired), real findings have emerged from the study of it, some relevant to parenting. Two of the more intriguing studies involve how body language and gestures interact with human speech.

Learning sign language may boost cognition by 50 percent

Gestures and speech used similar neural circuits as they developed in our evolutionary history. University of Chicago psycholinguist David McNeill was the first to suggest this. He thought nonverbal and verbal skills might retain their strong ties even though they've diverged into separate behavioral spheres. He was right. Studies confirmed it with a puzzling finding: People who could no longer move their limbs after a brain injury also increasingly lost their ability to communicate verbally. Studies of babies showed the same direct association. We now know that infants do not gain a more sophisticated vocabulary until their fine-motor finger control improves. That's a remarkable finding. Gestures are "windows into thought processes," McNeill says.

Could learning physical gestures improve other cognitive skills? One study hints that it could, though more work needs to be done. Kids with normal hearing took an American Sign Language class for nine months, in the first grade, then were administered a series of cognitive tests. Their attentional focus, spatial abilities, memory, and visual discrimination scores improved dramatically—by as much as 50 percent—compared with controls who had no formal instruction.

Babies need face time

An important subset of gestures, you might guess, are facial expressions. Babies love to gaze at human faces. Mom's is best of all— but they prefer any human face over any monkey face, llama face, cat face, or dog face. What are they looking for in your face? Emotional information. Are you happy, sad, threatened?

We all spend a great deal of time reading faces. A person's non-verbal communication can confirm his or her verbal communication, undermine it, or even contradict it. Our relationships depend on our ability to interpret it. So humans read faces reflexively, and you can observe this even in an infant's earliest hour. The skill develops over time, with the most sophisticated behavior observable about five to seven months after birth. Some people are born better at it than others. But we sometimes get it wrong. Researchers call it Othello's Error.

In Shakespeare's tragic play, the Moor Othello believes his wife is fooling around on him. Othello is enraged as he confronts her in their bedroom. She is naturally scared out of her mind. Seeing her panicked face, he interprets this fear as guilt, all the evidence of infidelity that he needs. Before he smothers her in bed, out come these famous love-hate words:

> *Ay, let her rot, and perish, and be damned to-night;*
> *for she shall not live: no, my heart is turned to*
> *stone; I strike it, and it hurts my hand. O, the*
> *world hath not a sweeter creature: she might lie by*
> *an emperor's side and command him tasks.*

Competently decoding another person's face can take years of experience; like Othello, adults sometimes make mistakes. The only way to improve this accuracy is by interacting with other people. That's why babies need human time in their earliest years. Not computer time. Not television time. Your baby's brain needs interaction with you, in person, on a consistent basis.

Either that, or training by psychologist Paul Ekman.

What's in a face

Paul Ekman, professor emeritus from the University of California– San Francisco, seldom misinterprets people's faces. He has cataloged more than 10,000 possible combinations of facial expressions, creating an inventory called the Facial Action Coding System (FACS). This research instrument allows a trained observer to dissect an expression in terms of all the muscular actions that produced it.

Using this tool, Ekman has found several surprising things about human facial recognition. First, people all over the world express similar emotions using similar facial muscles. These universal basic emotions are happiness, sadness, surprise, disgust, anger, and fear. (The finding was originally quite startling; research at the time chalked up facial expressions mostly to cultural mores.) Second, the conscious control we can exert over our facial features is limited, which means we give away a lot of free information. The muscles that surround our eyes, for example, are not under conscious management. This may be why we tend to believe them more.

One of Ekman's research videotapes shows an interaction between a psychiatrist and "Jane," his very troubled patient. Jane had been suffering from such severe depression that she was hospitalized and under suicide watch. When she seemed to show real signs of improvement, she asked her physician to let her go home for the weekend. The camera is on Jane's face, full view, when the doctor asks about her plans for the future. As Ekman slows the tape, examining it frame by frame, a sudden flash of deep desperation arcs across Jane's face. She doesn't seem to be able to control it. It turns out Jane was planning to kill herself when she got home, which fortunately she admitted before she was discharged. Ekman uses the tape to train police officers and mental-health professionals. He stops the tape and asks the students if they can see the flash of desperation, only a twelfth of a second long. Once they know what to look for, they can.

These flashes are called micro-expressions, facial gestures that last a fraction of a second but tend to reveal our truest feelings in response to rapid-fire questioning. Ekman found that some people could detect and interpret these micro-expressions better than others. People lie a lot, and those who could pick up these micro-expressions were terrific at detecting falsehoods. Ekman found that he could train people to read these micro-expressions, improving their ability to pick up nonverbal cues.

How can we tell that face-reading abilities are so important? In part because the brain devotes a tremendous amount of neural real estate, including an important region called the fusiform gyrus, to the single task of processing faces. Neural acreage of this size is expensive; the brain doesn't fence off one area for such a restricted function unless it has a darn good reason.

We know the brain has face-specific regions because a person can damage them and lose the ability to recognize the people to whom the faces belong. The disorder is called prosopagnosia, or face blindness. Parents of face-blind kids have to provide them with instructions like "Remember, Drew is the one with the orange T-shirt; Madison is wearing a red dress." Otherwise, they lose track of the kids they're playing with. Nothing is wrong with the children's eyes, just their brains.

Team player

Being able to correctly interpret gestures and facial expressions would have been highly prized in the merciless Serengeti. That's because social coordination is a great survival skill, useful whether you are hunting animals bigger than you or just trying to get along with the neighbors. Among many other gifts, social coordination allows the concept of teamwork. Most researchers believe the ability to work as a team allowed us to pole-vault over our otherwise debilitating physical wimpiness.

How does interpreting faces help with teamwork? The ability to cooperate in a high-risk setting requires an intimate, moment-by-moment knowledge of another's intentions and motivations. Knowing the forward progress of somebody's psychological interior allows a more accurate prediction of his or her behavior (just ask any quarterback in the NFL). Reading the emotional information in someone's face is one of the quickest ways to get these insights. And those who could do it accurately functioned better on Team Serengeti. Today, when people have a difficult time reading the emotional information embedded in faces, we call it autism. Teamwork is tough for these kids.

Innovators are nonverbal experts

Could your child's ability to read faces and gestures predict her success in our 21st-century workforce? The investigators who studied successful entrepreneurs think so. We've already explored three of the five characteristics in the Innovator's DNA study. The other two are incredibly social in origin:

- **They were great at a specific kind of networking.** Successful entrepreneurs were attracted to smart people whose educational backgrounds were very different from their own. This allowed them to acquire knowledge about things they would not otherwise learn. From a social perspective, this behavioral pirouette is not easy to execute. How did they manage to do it consistently? Using insights generated by the final common trait.

- **They closely observed the details of other people's behaviors.** The entrepreneurs were natural experts in the art of interpreting extrospective cues: gestures and facial expressions. Consistently and accurately interpreting these nonverbal signals is probably how they were able to extract information from sources whose academic resources were so different from their own.

Want your baby to grow up to be a successful innovator? Make sure she has nonverbal skills down cold—and an inquisitiveness to match.

Not on IQ tests

From exploration, self-control, and creativity to verbal and nonverbal ability, it is clear that the intelligence stew has many ingredients. Standard IQ tests are not capable of measuring most of these elements, even though they play a powerful role in the future success of your children. Given their uniqueness, that's not surprising. Some are so unexpected as to defy belief (your kid's chances of being a great entrepreneur are linked to her ability to decode *faces*?). So you need not be discouraged if your kid isn't in the 97th percentile on certain tests. She may have many other intellectual aspects in abundance that IQ tests are inherently incapable of detecting.

That's not to say that everyone is a potential Einstein. These gifts are unevenly sprinkled among our children, and most have genetic components. Your autistic child may never have the warmth of a pastor, for example, no matter how hard you try. But as you know, there's more to intelligence than just seeds.

Time to get our hands a little dirty, tilling some truly remarkable findings about the soil that makes our kids as smart as their seeds will allow them to be.

Key points

- There are aspects of your child's intelligence about which you can do nothing; the genetic contribution is about 50 percent.
- IQ is related to several important childhood outcomes, but it is only one measure of intellectual ability.
- Intelligence has many ingredients, including self-control, creativity, communication skills, and a desire to explore.

smart baby: soil

brain rule

Face time, not screen time

smart baby: soil

Theodore Roosevelt was so sick as a child, his parents had to instruct him at home. That was probably the best thing that ever happened to him. Young Teddy's illness put him in constant contact with arguably the most loving dad a future president could have; if there were ever a hall of fame for fathers of vulnerable children, Theodore Sr. should be its founding member. Writing in his diary, Teddy Roosevelt remembers as a child being regularly scooped up into his daddy's big arms. Up and down the hallways the elder Roosevelt would pace, carrying his bright son upright for hours, ensuring that the boy could breathe. They explored the great outdoors when weather permitted, libraries when it did not. Gradually, the son grew stronger. At every precious point, Dad would encourage Teddy to try hard. Then harder. Then hardest. Said the president in a diary decades later:

> *He not only took great and untiring care of me ... he also most wisely refused to coddle me, and made me feel that I must force*

myself to hold my own with other boys and prepare to do the rough
work of the world.

The senior Roosevelt could not know this, but he was exercising some pretty solid cognitive neuroscience in the nurturing of his famous child. Teddy was born smart and born into wealth, two factors not every parent is capable of providing. But Teddy was also born into love and attentive guidance, two things *every* parent is capable of providing. Indeed, there are plenty of behaviors over which you, like Roosevelt Sr., can exert enormous authority. Regardless of their genes, you can help your children mobilize their intelligence as fully as Theodore Roosevelt, Albert Einstein, or the most successful innovators working today. Just how do you grow a smart baby?

We're thinking in terms of soil, so it makes sense to formulate a fertilizer. What you put in is as important as what you leave out. There are four nutrients you will want in your behavioral formula, adjusting them as your baby gets older: breast-feeding, talking to your baby, guided play, and praising effort rather than accomplishment. Brain research tells us there are also several toxins: pushing your child to perform tasks his brain is not developmentally ready to take on; stressing your child to the point of a psychological state termed "learned helplessness"; and, for the under-2 set, television. A few additives, hawked by marketers, are optional to irrelevant. What we'll discover is the profound need to strike a balance between intellectual freedom and well-disciplined rigor.

The brain's day job is not learning

First, I need to correct a misconception. Many well-meaning moms and dads think their child's brain is interested in learning. That is not accurate. The brain is not interested in learning. The brain is interested in *surviving*. Every ability in our intellectual tool kit was engineered to escape extinction. Learning exists only to serve the requirements of this primal goal. It is a happy coincidence that our intellectual tools can do double duty in the classroom, conferring on us the ability to create spreadsheets and speak French. But that's not the brain's day job. That is an incidental by-product of a much deeper force: the gnawing, clawing desire to live to the next day. We do not survive so that we can learn. We learn so that we can survive.

This overarching goal predicts many things, and here's the most important: If you want a well-educated child, you must create an environment of safety. When the brain's safety needs are met, it will allow its neurons to moonlight in algebra classes. When safety needs are not met, algebra goes out the window. Roosevelt's dad held him first, which made his son feel safe, which meant the future president could luxuriate in geography.

A laser focus on safety

One simple example of the brain's fixation on safety occurs during an assault. It's called "weapon focus." Victims of an assault often suffer from amnesia or confusion; they usually can't recall the facial features of the criminal. But they often can completely recall the details of the weapon used. "It was a Saturday night special, held in the left hand, wood handle," a witness might exclaim. Why remember the perp's gun, which is not always helpful to the police, and not the perp's face, which almost always is? The answer reveals the brain's familiar priority: safety. The weapon holds the biggest potential threat, and the brain focuses on it because the brain is built to concentrate on survival. The brain is learning under these hostile conditions (stress can marvelously focus the mind); it is just concentrating on the source of the threat.

A former fighter pilot, teaching at an aeronautics university, discovered how this works in the classroom. One of his students had been a star in ground school but was having trouble in the air. During a training flight, she misinterpreted an instrument reading, and he yelled at her, thinking it would force her to concentrate. Instead, she started crying, and though she tried to continue reading the instruments, she couldn't focus. He landed the plane, lesson over. What was wrong? From the brain's perspective, nothing was wrong. The student's mind was focusing on the source of the threat, just as it had been molded to do over the past few million years. The teacher's anger could not direct the student to the instrument to be learned because the instrument was not the source of danger. The teacher was the source of danger. This is weapon focus, merely replacing "Saturday Night Special" with "ex–fighter pilot."

The same is true if you are a parenting a child rather than teaching a student. The brain will never outgrow its preoccupation with survival.

Four brain boosters

Now we can dig into our fertilizer, starting with four ingredients you want in your developmental soil.

1. Breast-feed for a year

I remember meeting up for lunch with a long-time friend who had just become a mother. Upon entering the restaurant, baby in tow, she insisted on sitting at a private booth. After five minutes, I discovered why: Mom knew that once her baby smelled food, he'd become hungry. When he did, she discreetly unbuttoned her blouse, adjusted her bra, and began breast-feeding. The baby latched on for dear life. Mom had to go through all kinds of contortions to hide this activity. "I've been thrown out of other places because I did this," she explained. Though shrouded in an oversize sweater, she was visibly nervous as the waiter took her order.

If America knew what breast milk can do for the brains of its youngest citizens, lactating mothers across the nation would be enshrined, not embarrassed. Though the topic is much debated, there's little controversy about it in the scientific community. Breast milk is the nutritional equivalent of a magic bullet for a developing baby. It has important salts and even more important vitamins. Its immune-friendly properties prevent ear, respiratory, and gastrointestinal infections. And in a result that surprised just about everybody, studies around the world confirmed that breast-feeding, in short, makes babies smarter. Breast-fed babies in America score on average 8 points higher than formula-fed kids when given cognitive tests, an effect still observable nearly a decade after the breast-feeding has stopped. They get better grades, too, especially in reading and writing.

How does that work? We're not really sure, though we have some ideas. Breast milk has ingredients a baby's brain needs to grow postnatally but can't make on its own very well. One of these is taurine, an amino acid essential for neural development. Breast milk also contains omega-3 fatty acids, whose benefits on pediatric cognition we discussed in the Pregnancy chapter ("Eat just the right foods"). The American Academy of Pediatrics recommends that all mothers breast-feed exclusively for the first six months of their babies' lives, continue breast-feeding as their kids start taking on solids, and wean them after a year. If we as a country wanted a smarter population, we would insist on lactation rooms in every public establishment. A sign would hang from the door of these rooms: "Quiet, please. Brain development in progress."

2. Talk to your baby—a lot

For the longest time, we couldn't figure out the words coming from our 9-month-old son. Whenever he took a car ride, he would start saying the word "dah," repeating it over and over again as we strapped him into his car seat, "Dah dah dah, goo, dah dah, big-dah, big-dah." It often sounded like a child's version of an old Police song. We couldn't decode it and would just respond, a bit sheepishly, "Dah?" He would emphatically reply, "Dah." Sometimes our response made him happy. Sometimes it didn't do anything at all. It wasn't until we were tooling down the interstate one fine sunny day, moon-roof wide open to the clouds, that we finally figured it out.

Josh saw an airplane flying overhead and shouted excitedly, "Sky-dah! Sky-dah!" My wife suddenly understood. "I think he means airplane!" she said. She asked him, pointing to the sky, "*Sky*-dah?" Josh cheerily replied, "Sky-dah!" Just then a big noisy semi-truck passed us, and Josh pointed to it with concern. "Big-dah, Big-dah," he said. My wife pointed at the truck too, now shrinking in the distance. "*Big*-dah?" she asked, and he responded excitedly, "Big-dah!" Then "dah, dah, dah." We got it. For whatever reason, "dah" had become Joshua's word for "vehicle." Later, Josh and I watched a ship cross Puget Sound. I pointed to the container vessel and guessed, "*Water*-dah?" He sat up, staring at me like I was from Mars. "*Wet*-dah," he declared, like a mildly impatient professor addressing a slow student.

Few interactions with children are as much fun as learning to speak their language. As they learn to speak ours, heaping tablespoons of words into their minds is one of the healthiest things parents can do for their brains. Speak to your children as often as you can. It is one of the most well-established findings in all of the developmental literature.

The linkage between words and smarts was discovered through some pretty invasive research. In one study, investigators descended upon a family's home every month for three years and jotted down every aspect of verbal communication between parents and their children. They measured size of vocabulary, diversity and growth rate of vocabulary, frequency of verbal interaction, and the emotional content of the speech. Just before the visits were finished, the researchers gave IQ tests. They did this with more than 40 families, then followed up years later. Through exhaustive analysis of this amazingly tough work, two very clear findings emerged:

- The variety and number of words matter.
- Talking increases IQ.

The more parents talk to their children, even in the earliest moments of life, the better their kids' linguistic abilities become and the faster that improvement is achieved. The gold standard is 2,100 words per hour. The variety of the words spoken (nouns, verbs, and adjectives used, along with the length and complexity of phrases and sentences) is nearly as important as the number of words spoken. So is the amount of positive feedback. You can reinforce language skills through interaction: looking at your infant; imitating his vocalizations, laughter, and facial expressions; rewarding her language attempts with heightened attention. Children whose parents talked positively, richly, and regularly to them knew twice as many words as those whose parents talked to them the least. When they entered the school system, their reading, spelling, and writing abilities soared above those of children in less verbal households. Even though babies don't respond like adults, they *are* listening, and it is good for them.

Talking to children early in life raises their IQs, too, even after controlling for important variables such as income. By age 3, kids who were talked to regularly by their parents (called the talkative group) had IQ scores 1½ times higher than those kids whose parents talked to them the least (called the taciturn group). This increase in IQ is thought to be responsible for the talkative group's uptick in grades.

Remember, it takes a real live person to benefit your baby's brain, so get ready to exercise your vocal cords. Not the portable DVD player's, not your television's surround-sound, but *your* vocal cords.

What to say and how to say it

Though 2,100 words per hour might sound like a lot, it actually represents a moderate rate of conversation. Outside of work, the typical person hears or sees about 100,000 words in a day. So there's no need to constantly babble to your baby in some 24-7 marathon. Overstimulation can be just as hazardous to brain development as understimulation (remember Goldilocks), and it's important to watch your baby for signs of fatigue. But no language exposure is too silly.

"Now we're going to change your diaper." "Look at the beautiful tree!" "What is that?" You can count steps out loud as you walk up a staircase. Just get in the habit of talking.

How you say those words matters, too. Picture this scene from an instructional DVD, developed at the Talaris Research Institute when I served as its director: A bunch of big tough men are watching a football game, passing a bowl of popcorn, eyes glued to the set. A baby is contentedly exploring in a playpen off to the side. At a critical juncture in the game, one of the couch potatoes growls to the quarterback: "Come on, you can do this. You can do this for me. I need this." There's a big play, and the guys all jump up and shout. The noise disturbs the baby, and you hear him start to cry. The biggest guy on the couch happens to be the dad. He runs to his little one, picks him up, and holds him in arms the size of tree trunks. "Hi, big guy," he soothes in a high-pitched voice. "Wanna join the party?" The guys on the couch look at each other, eyebrows raised. "Look at daddy's boy!" the father continues in his singsong voice. "How's d-a-a-a-ddy's boy? Are you h-u-u-u-ngry?" The dad seems to have forgotten all about the game. "Let's get some sp-a-a-g-heeeettti," he continues, marching to the kitchen. The guys on the couch stare at him in disbelief. The game resumes, dad in the background, feeding spaghetti to his happy son.

We have just witnessed the hypnotic effect babies can have on attentive fathers. But what's going on with the dad's voice? Turns out parents all over the world talk to their kids this way, a form of speech called "parentese." It is catnip to a baby's ear.

Parentese is characterized by a high-pitched tone and a singsongy voice with stretched-out vowels. Though parents don't always realize they do it, this kind of speech helps a baby's brain learn language. Why? A speaker who has slowed down is much easier to understand, for one. Parentese also makes the sound of each vowel more distinct; this exaggeration allows your baby to hear words as distinct entities and discriminate better between them. The melodic tone helps infants separate sounds into contrasting categories. And the high pitch may assist infants in imitating the characteristics of speech. After all, with a vocal tract one-quarter the size of yours, they can produce fewer sounds, at first only at higher pitches.

When should you start doing all this talking? The real answer is that nobody knows, but we have strong hints that the answer is going to be "as soon as the baby is born." As we saw with the newborn who stuck his tongue back out at Andy Meltzoff, babies are reliably capable of interacting with adults 42 minutes after birth. And pre-verbal infants are processing a lot of verbal information, even if they don't always seem to be taking it in. Even reading to a 3-month-old is probably good, especially if you hold the child close and allow her to interact with you.

Educational psychologist William Fowler trained a group of parents to talk to their children in a particular fashion, following some of the guidelines mentioned above. The children spoke their first words between 7 and 9 months of age, some even speaking sentences at 10 months. They had conquered most of the basic rules of grammar by age 2, while kids in the control group achieved a similar mastery around age 4. Longer-term studies showed that the kids did very well in school, including in math and science. By the time they entered high school, 62 percent of them were enrolled in gifted or accelerated programs. Critical parts of Fowler's training program need further study, but his work is terrific. It adds to the overwhelming evidence that a whole lot of talking is like fertilizer for neurons.

Clearly, speech is great soil for your baby's developing mind. As your child gets older, other elements become just as important. The next nutrient in our fertilizer is self-generated play, a delightful example of which I encountered when our boys were both younger than the age of 4.

3. Hurray for play!

It was Christmas morning. Wrapped under the tree was a racetrack toy for our two boys, and I was excited for them to open it. I knew they would immediately let out oohs and ahs as they discovered their gift. They tore open the box, and—puzzled silence. A minute passed. Then they tossed aside the racetrack and held the box over their heads. Their enthusiasm returned like inflation.

"I know!" one of them yelled. "It's an airplane!" "No," the other boy yelled, "It's a spaceship!" "Yeah, it's a *spaceship,*" the first quickly agreed, and they both seized some crayons lying on the floor. Soon they were drawing shapes all over the racetrack box, cryptic little circles, lines, and squares, completely neglecting the toy parts lying scattered around them. I was left wondering why I wasted the money.

The older child went upstairs looking for more crayons, then let out a war whoop. He had spotted an enormous, discarded cardboard box, which earlier that morning had carried a new chair my wife and I had purchased. "Yahoo!" he cried, struggling successfully to bring the box downstairs. "Our *cockpit!*" The next two hours became consumed with crayons and paints and tape and furious scribbling. They fastened the racetrack box to the big box. "Place to store aliens," one of them solemnly explained. They drew tiny dials. They fashioned laser cannons from wrapping paper tubes. They drew something that could cook French fries. For the rest of the day they flew their spacecraft, making up enemies with such diverse names as Evil Mountain Beaver and Kelp Queen. They were no longer in Seattle. They were in Alpha Quadrant, Captain Toddlerhood with Boy Pull-up in the World of Tomorrow. My wife and I laughed 'til we cried, watching them. Their creativity was a joy to behold for any parent.

But there was something much deeper, too: This kind of open-ended play was fertilizing their brains with the behavioral equivalent of Miracle-Gro. That sentence might seem strange. Open-ended *play*? Not "open-ended purchase of electronic educational toys"? Not French lessons, followed by hours of militant drilling? Actually, I do believe in a form of disciplined repetition as children begin formal schooling. But many parents are so preoccupied with their young child's future that they transform every step of the journey into a type of product development, recoiling at open-ended *anything*. From 1981 to 1997, the amount of free time parents gave their kids shrank by about a quarter. In the *Atlantic*, Esther Entin details more of that same study: Children "spent 18 percent more time at school, 145 percent more time doing school work, and 168 percent more time shopping with parents. The researchers found that, including computer play, children in 1997 spent only about eleven hours per week at play."

Children's free time hasn't improved since then. Researcher Peter Gray noted in 2011 that the number has been declining for more than half a century. The making-baby-smart product industry—fashioning toys that are the opposite of open-ended (what could be more claustrophobic than a DVD for *infants*?)—is a multibillion-dollar industry.

We now know that open-ended activities are as important to a child's neural growth as protein. Indeed, the box the flashcards come in is probably more beneficial to a toddler's brain than the flashcards themselves. Depending upon what you study and how you measure it, the benefits are stunning. Studies show that, compared with controls, kids allowed a specific type of open-ended playtime were:

- **More creative.** On tests of divergent thinking (which measure alternative uses for familiar objects), they came up with more than three times as many creative options as did controls.

- **Better at language.** The children's use of language was more facile. They displayed a richer store of vocabulary and a more varied use of words.

- **Better at problem solving.** This is fluid intelligence, one of the basic ingredients in the intelligence stew.

- **Less stressed.** Children regularly exposed to such activity had half the anxiety levels of controls. This may help explain the problem-solving benefit, as problem-solving skills are notoriously sensitive to anxiety.

- **Better at memory.** Play situations improved memory scores; for example, kids who pretended they were at the supermarket remembered twice as many words on a grocery list as controls.

- **More socially skilled.** The social-buffering benefits of play are reflected in the crime statistics of inner-city kids. If low-income kids were exposed to play-oriented preschools in their earliest years, fewer than 10 percent had been arrested for a felony by age 23. For children exposed to instruction-oriented preschools, that figure was more than 33 percent.

Chicken-or-egg questions are plentiful in these data, so we need to keep our grump factor high. Is play the method of learning something, for example, or is it merely practice or consolidation of skills that are already developing? Happily, such controversies triggered an event dear to the heart of any scientist: additional rounds of funding. In new studies, researchers asked: Were there specific behaviors embedded in open-ended play that produced the benefit? That answer, unequivocally, turned out to be yes.

Not just any type of open-ended play will give you the extraordinary findings. The secret sauce is not unstructured, do-anything-you-want play. Advocacy for this hands-off model hearkens back to a romantic notion that children are born with effervescent, perfectly formed imaginations and an unerring instinct to create make-believe worlds. The assumption is that if we just allow children to guide us, then all will be well. I subscribe to parts of this notion deeply. Kids are inventive and curious, and I've learned more about imagination from my children than from probably any other single source. But kids are also very inexperienced. They don't have all of the keys that can unlock their potential; that's why they need parents.

No, the type of play that gives all the cognitive benefits is a type that focuses on impulse control and self-regulation—those executive-function behaviors discussed in the previous chapter as ingredients of intelligence, revealed by the cookie experiment. The data are so clear, you could use them to design the family playroom.

Tools of the Mind: Mature dramatic play

The type of play is called mature dramatic play, or MDP. To get the benefits in those bullet points, MDP has to be engaged in many hours a day. This has been codified into a school program called Tools of the Mind, one of the few programs of its type that has been studied in randomized trials.

The ideas for Tools of the Mind come from Russian psychologist Lev Vygotsky, a handsome polymath who burned out quickly in the early years of the Soviet era. He was an inspiration for all budding geniuses who couldn't make up their minds about what they wanted to do when they grew up. He started out in literary analysis, writing a famous essay on Hamlet at the age of 18, then decided to go to Moscow University's medical school to become a doctor. He soon changed his mind, switching to law school, then immediately and simultaneously enrolled at a private university to study literature. Still not satisfied, he got a Ph.D. in psychology. A few years later, at the ripe old age of 38, he was dead. But the 10 years he actively pursued psychology were quite productive and, for the time, groundbreaking. Vygotsky was one of the few researchers of his era to study dramatic play in children. He predicted that the ability of the under-5 crowd to engage in imaginative activities was going to be a better gauge of academic success than any other activity—including quantitative and verbal competencies. The reason, Vygotsky believed, was that such engagement allowed children to learn how to regulate their social behaviors.

Hardly the carefree activity we think of in the United States, Vygotsky saw imaginative play as one of the most tightly restrictive behaviors children experience. If little Sasha was going to be a chef, he would have to follow the rules, expectations, and limitations of "chef-ness." If this imaginative exercise included friends, they would have to follow the rules, too. They might push and pull and argue with each other until they agreed on what those rules were and how they should be executed. That's how self-control developed, he posited. In a group setting, such a task is extremely intellectually demanding, even for adults. If this sounds like a prelude to the more modern notion of executive function, you are right on the money. Vygotksy's followers showed that children acting out imaginative scenes controlled their impulses much better than they did in non-MDP situations. While other parts of Vygotsky's work are starting to show some intellectual arthritis, his ideas on self-regulation have held up well.

The cascade of confirmatory research that followed these findings led directly to the Tools of the Mind program. It has a number of moving parts, but the three most relevant to our discussion involve planning play, direct instruction on pretending, and the type of environment in which the instruction takes place. Here's what happens in a Tools of the Mind classroom:

A play plan

Before the preschoolers take off into a day filled with imaginative play, they take colored markers and fill out a printed form called a play plan. This announces in explicit terms what the activity du jour will be: "I am going to have tea with my dollies at the zoo," or "I am going to make a Lego castle and pretend I'm the knight." The kids carry around a clipboard with the activities written on them.

Practice pretending

The children are then coached on dramatic play in a technique called "make-believe play practice." The kids receive direct, open-ended instruction about the mechanics of pretending! Here's a sentence from the training manual: "I'm pretending my baby is crying. Is yours? What should we say?"

The little ones are then let loose to their imaginations. At the end of each week, the children have a short "learning conference" with the instructor, listing what they experienced and learned during the period. They also have group meetings. Any discipline intervention usually becomes a group discussion centered around problem solving.

One big playroom

Most Tools of the Mind classrooms look like the equivalent of a late-Christmas-morning living room. Legos are scattered everywhere. Sandboxes are sprinkled around the room. There are jigsaw puzzles to figure out. Blocks with which to build entire new worlds. Clothes for dress-up. Places for crafts. Boxes! Lots of time—and space—for interaction with other kids. The combinations of situations in which individual imagination and creativity could be deployed are seemingly endless.

Many other activities occur in the course of a Tools of the Mind day, and we don't yet know which combinations work best. We also don't know about the long-term effects of the program. As of this writing, no fewer than four long-term, large-scale studies are under way to answer these questions. But we do know this about the program: It *works*. Kids in the program typically perform 30 percent to 100 percent better than controls on just about any executive function test you throw at them. That means better grades, too, as high executive function is one of the two greatest predictors of academic success that exist in the research literature. And it means the many benefits we described earlier, most of which come from studies of the Tools program.

These data radiate a light that can hurt unaccustomed eyes. They challenge the notion that rote-drilled learning atmospheres always equal better performance. These data flatly state that *emotional* regulation—reining in impulses—predicts better *cognitive* performance. That's a bombshell of an idea. It directly ties intellectual horsepower to emotional processing. I am not dismissing rote drills, as a memorized database is an extremely important part of human learning. But it is clear: Vygotsky was on to something.

4. Praise effort, not IQ

Though their lives are separated by many years, I imagine Vygotsky would have really liked Evelyn Elizabeth Ann Glennie. She is the world's foremost percussionist and possibly the most versatile. She loves imaginative play, too, though her friends range from entire symphony orchestras, like the New York Philharmonic, to rock groups like Genesis to the performance artist Björk. Glennie studied at Ellon Academy and at London's Royal Academy of Music, and she won a Grammy in 1989. As accomplished and powerful a musician as Glennie is, her musical talent is not her most remarkable feature.

Glennie is deaf. The effort she must put into her craft cannot be imagined. After her hearing collapsed at the age of 12, she would put her hands against the classroom wall to sense the vibrations when her music teachers played. Born with perfect pitch, she was able to translate what were now only rough sounds, felt in her body. She often plays barefoot onstage, saying it helps her feel the music. Glennie's genius is revealed through sheer determination, a resolve detectable in the response she once gave to a reporter who was annoyingly dwelling on her hearing loss. "If you want to know about deafness," she retorted, "you should interview an audiologist. My specialty is *music.*"

We know accomplishment like that comes from gritty effort, not necessarily from high IQ. As every experienced parent understands, a child with naturally high intelligence is not automatically guaranteed a starting spot on Harvard's freshman roster. It will not even guarantee her an A on a math test. Though it is a reliable predictor of high academic performance, IQ has a real love-hate relationship with an individual student's GPA, and it is ambiguously related even to other intellectually rich activities (chess is one surprising example).

What separates high performers from low performers is not some divine spark. It is, the most recent findings suggest, a much more boring—but ultimately more controllable—factor. All other things being equal, it is effort. Good old-fashioned neural elbow grease. Deliberate practice. From a psychological perspective, effort is in part the willingness to focus one's attention and then sustain that focus. Effort also involves impulse control and a persistent ability to delay gratification. Sounds like executive function, spiced with a few unique ingredients.

> **Kids praised for effort complete 50 percent more hard math problems than kids praised for intelligence.**

How can you get that kind of effort from your child? Surprisingly, it's how you *praise* him. What you praise defines what your child perceives success to be. Here is where parents make a common mistake—one that often creates the saddest sight a teacher can behold: a bright child who hates learning.

Ethan's parents constantly told him how brainy he was. "You're so smart! You can do anything, Ethan. We are so proud of you," they would say every time he sailed through a math test. Or a spelling test. Or any test. With the best of intentions, they consistently tethered Ethan's accomplishment to some innate characteristic of his intellectual prowess.

Researchers call this "appealing to fixed mindsets." The parents had no idea that this form of praise was toxic.

Little Ethan quickly learned that any academic achievement *that required no effort* was the behavior that defined his gift. When he hit junior high school, he ran into subjects that did require effort. He could no longer sail through, and, for the first time, he started making mistakes. But he did not see these errors as opportunities for improvement. After all, he was smart because he could mysteriously grasp things quickly. And if he could no longer grasp things quickly, what did that imply? That he was no longer smart. Since he didn't know the ingredients making him successful, he didn't know what to do when he failed. You don't have to hit that brick wall very often before you get discouraged, then depressed. Quite simply, Ethan quit trying. His grades collapsed.

What happens when you say, "You're so smart"

Research shows that Ethan's unfortunate story is typical of kids regularly praised for some fixed characteristic. If you praise your child this way, three things are statistically likely to happen:

First, your child begins to perceive mistakes as failures. Because you told her that success was due to some static ability over which she had no control, she starts to think of failure (such as a bad grade) as a static thing, too—now perceived as a lack of ability. Successes are thought of as gifts rather than the governable product of effort.

Second, perhaps as a reaction to the first, she becomes more concerned with looking smart than with actually learning something. (Though Ethan was intelligent, he was more preoccupied with breezing through and appearing smart to the people who mattered to him. He developed little regard for learning.)

Third, she becomes less willing to confront the reasons behind any deficiencies, less willing to make an effort. Such kids have a difficult time admitting errors. There is simply too much at stake for failure.

What to say instead: "You really worked hard"

What should Ethan's parents have done? Research reveals a simple solution. Rather than praising him for being smart, they should have praised him for working hard. On the successful completion of a test, they should not have said, "I'm so proud of you. You're such a bright kid." That appeals to a fixed, uncontrollable intellectual trait. It's called "fixed mindset" praise. His parents should have said, "I'm so proud of you. You must have studied *a lot.*" This appeals to controllable effort. It's called "growth mindset" praise.

More than 30 years of study show that children raised in growth-mindset homes consistently outscore their fixed-mindset peers in academic achievement. They do better in adult life, too. That's not surprising. Children with a growth mindset tend to have a refreshing attitude toward failure. Rather than seeing mistakes as failures over which to despair, they see mistakes simply as problems to be solved. In the lab as well as in school, they spend much more time banging away at harder tasks than fixed-mindset students. They solve those problems more often, too. Kids regularly praised for effort successfully complete 50 percent to 60 percent more hard math problems than kids praised for intelligence.

Carol Dweck, a noted researcher in the field, would check in on students taking her tests. She heard comments like "I should slow down and try to figure this out" and the delightful "I love a challenge!" Because they believe mistakes occur from a lack of effort, not from a lack of ability, the kids realize mistakes can be remedied simply by applying more cognitive elbow grease.

If you've already gone down the path of fixed-mindset praise, is it too late to switch? That specific question needs more study, but research has shown that even limited exposure to growth-mindset praise has positive effects.

Praise isn't the only factor, of course. We're starting to see that genes may play a role in effort, too. A group of researchers in London studied the self-perceived abilities (termed SPA) of nearly 4,000 twins. SPA measures a child's perceived ability to handle tough academic challenges. The twins' shared home environment, where growth-mindset behaviors would presumably be a factor, accounted for only 2 percent of the variance in SPA. The researchers concluded that there was a better-than-even chance that an SPA gene could be isolated. These observations require a great deal more research. If such a gene were characterized, it wouldn't let parents off the hook. It would simply change the strategies needed to raise certain kids. Some wouldn't need much instruction; others would need constant supervision, something we already know. Maybe effort simply allows children to better mobilize whatever intelligence they were born with. Either way, you want effort as the fourth nutrient in your fertilizer.

And then there are the things you want to limit.

The digital age: TV, video games, and the Internet

I had just finished a lecture to a group of educators and parents on visual processing and the high priority the brain gives it. As I paused for questions, a middle-aged mom blurted out, "So is TV good for the brain, then?" There was some grumbling in the room. An older gentleman joined in. "And what about all those newfangled video games? (Yes, he said "newfangled.") And that *Internet*?" A young man stood up, a bit defensive: "There's nothing wrong with gaming. And there is nothing wrong with the Internet." This exchange got increasingly heated: older folks on one side, younger on the other. Eventually, someone said loudly, "Let's ask the brain scientist." Turning to me, he said, "What do *you* think?"

"I like to quote my old 19th-century friend J. Watson," I began, hesitant to enter the fray. It's a quote I always pull out when controversies erupt. "He was a member of Congress, and he was something of a diplomat. Watson was once asked how he was going to vote on some controversial piece of legislation. His response was clever: 'I have friends on both sides of the issue, and I like to stand with my friends.'" Everybody laughed, and that seemed to defuse the tension in the room. It also ducked the question.

It's not a question that should be ignored, however. From smart TVs to even smarter cell phones, the digital age has affected virtually every student on the planet, and screen time is now a regular part of children's developmental experience. Should parents be concerned about TV? Video games? The Internet? I will tell you flatly: Except for some of the television work we'll discuss in a moment, I have never seen messier research literature in my life, particularly regarding brains, behaviors, and video games. Even a cursory review of the work that's out there reveals shoddy designs, biased agendas, lack of controls, non-randomized cohorts, too few sample sizes, too few experiments—and lots of loud, even angry, opinions. Promising studies are in the pipeline regarding video games and the Internet, but, as is typical for any new research effort, early findings show mixed results. Which means there's enough to make everyone, and no one, happy.

The toddler in the litter box

The main thing to consider when you think of exposing your kids to Screen World is the content of what your child will be consuming, for two reasons.

The first is that kids are really good at imitation. Remember the light box and the baby touching her forehead to it? This ability to reproduce a behavior, after witnessing it only once, is called deferred imitation. Deferred imitation is an astonishing skill that develops rapidly. A 13-month-old child can remember an event a week after a single exposure. By the time she is almost a year and a half, she can imitate an event *four months* after a single exposure. The skill never leaves children, something the advertising industry has known for decades. The implications are powerful. If toddlers can embed into memory a complex series of events after one exposure, imagine what they can consume in hours spent online and watching TV. (Not to mention what children are consuming as they view their parents' behaviors 24 hours a day, 365 days a year. Deferred imitation helps explain why we are still so prone to imitating our parents' behaviors years after we leave the nest, as I was doing with my wife and the car keys.)

With children, deferred imitation can reveal itself in unexpected ways, as this tale from a young mother reveals.

We had a great Christmas. At one point, I noticed that my three year old daughter had disappeared. I went looking for her and I found her in my master bathroom. I asked her why she used my bathroom instead of hers and she said she was "being a kitty." I look over at the litterbox and sure enough, she had gone poo in the litterbox! I was speechless …

This story reveals a lot about how children acquire information. The little girl had apprehended the general idea of "pooping places" and had created an expectation, and a plan, for her own resulting behavior. Gross topic. Delightful stuff.

The second reason content is so important is that our expectations and assumptions profoundly influence our perception of reality. This is because of the brain's eager willingness to insert its opinion directly into what you are currently experiencing—and then fool you into thinking this hybrid is the actual reality. It may disturb you to know this, but your perception of reality is not like a camcorder recording verbatim information to some cellular hard drive. Your perception of reality is a handshake agreement between what your senses bring to your brain and what your brain thinks ought to be there. And what you expect to be out there is directly tied to *what you allowed into your brain in the first place.* Experiences morph into expectations, which can, in turn, influence your behavior.

Yale psychologist John Bargh did an experiment illustrating this exquisite sensitivity. He told a bunch of healthy undergraduates that he was testing their language abilities. He presented them with a list of words and asked them to create a coherent sentence from it. You can try this right now. Make a sentence out of the following scramble:

DOWN SAT LONELY THE MAN WRINKLED BITTERLY THE WITH FACE OLD

Easy to do? You bet. "Bitterly, the lonely old man with the wrinkled face sat down" is one quick suggestion. But this was no linguistics test. Note how many words in the scramble are related to old age. Bargh was not interested in his subject's creative use of grammar. He was interested in how long it took the students to leave the lab and walk down the hall after they were exposed to the words. What he found was extraordinary. Those students who had been exposed to an "elderly" mix of words took almost 40 percent longer to walk down the hall than those who had been exposed to "random" words. Some students even stooped and shuffled as they left, as if they were 50 years older than they actually were. To cite Bargh's clinical observation, these words "activated the elderly stereotype in memory, and participants acted in ways consistent with that activated stereotype."

Bargh's result is just one in a long line of data demonstrating what a powerful force immediate, external influences can exert over internal behavior. What you allow into your child's brain influences his expectations about the world, which in turn influences not only what he is capable of perceiving but his very behavior. This is true whether you are looking at infants only a month old or undergrads 20 years later.

How do deferred imitation and expectations manifest themselves in the digital world? Television has the best research behind it.

No boob tube before age 2

The issue of kids' exposure to TV doesn't throw off as many sparks as it used to. There is general agreement that a child's exposure to television of any type should be limited. There is also general agreement that we are completely ignoring this advice.

I remember as a kid waiting every Sunday night for Walt Disney's *Wonderful World of Color* to come on, and loving it. I also remember my parents turning off the television when it was over. We don't do that anymore. Americans 2 years of age and older now spend an average of four hours and 49 minutes *per day* in front of the TV—20 percent more than 10 years ago. And we are getting this exposure at younger and younger ages, made all the more complex because of the wide variety of digital screen time now available. In 2003, 73 percent of kids under 6 watched television every day. And children younger than 2 got two hours and five minutes of "screen time" with TVs and computers per day. I mentioned earlier that the average American is exposed to about 100,000 words per day outside of work. Fully 45 percent of those words come from television.

The fact is, the amount of TV a child should watch before the age of 2 is zero.

TV can lead to hostility, trouble focusing

For decades we have known of the connection between hostile peer interactions and the amount of kids' exposure to television. The linkage used to be controversial (maybe aggressive people watch more TV than others?), but we now see that it's an issue of our deferred-imitation abilities coupled with a loss of impulse control. One personal example:

When I was in kindergarten, my best friend and I were watching *The Three Stooges*, a 1950s TV show. The program involved lots of physical comedy, including people sticking their fingers in other people's eyes. When the show was over, my friend fashioned his little fingers into a "V," then quickly poked me in both eyes. I couldn't see anything for the next hour and was soon whisked to the emergency room. Diagnosis: scratched corneas and a torn eye muscle.

Another example comes from a study that looked at bullying. For each hour of TV watched daily by children under age 4, the risk increased 9 percent that they would engage in bullying behavior by the time they started school. This is poor emotional regulation at work. Even taking into account chicken-or-egg uncertainties, the American Association of Pediatrics estimates that 10 percent to 20 percent of real-life violence can be attributed to exposure to media violence.

TV also poisons attention spans and the ability to focus, a classic hallmark of executive function. For each additional hour of TV watched by a child under the age of 3, the likelihood of an attentional problem by age 7 increased by about 10 percent. So a preschooler who watches three hours of TV per day is 30 percent more likely to have attentional problems than a child who watches no TV.

Just having the TV on while no one is watching—secondhand exposure—seemed to do damage, too, possibly because of distraction. In test laboratories, flashing images and a booming sound track continually diverted children from any activity in which they were otherwise engaged, including that marvelous brain-boosting imaginative play we discussed. The effects were so toxic for kids in diapers that the American Association of Pediatrics issued a recommendation that still stands today:

> Pediatricians should urge parents to avoid television viewing for children under the age of 2 years. Although certain television programs may be promoted to this age group, research on early brain development shows that babies and toddlers have a critical need for direct interactions with parents and other significant caregivers (e.g., child care providers) for healthy brain growth and the development of appropriate social, emotional, and cognitive skills.

Current research projects are addressing the potential effect of TV on grades, and preliminary work suggests that it affects both reading scores and language acquisition. But after age 2, the worst effects on kids' brains may come because television coaxes kids away from exercise, a subject we will examine when we get to video games.

TV aimed at babies not so brainy

What about all those store shelves lined with educational videos and DVDs? They certainly claim to boost cognitive performance in preschool populations. Such boasts inspired a group of researchers at the University of Washington to do their own studies. I remember reading a series of press releases about their work one sunny day—unusual for Seattle. At first I laughed out loud, then suddenly I turned sober. The president of our university had just received a phone call from no less than Robert Iger, head of the Disney Company. The mouse was not happy. The UW scientists had just published research testing a product Disney makes, *Baby Einstein* DVDs, and the results were damning.

This won't surprise you, given everything we have discussed so far. The products didn't work at all. They had no positive effect on the vocabularies of the target audience, infants 17 to 24 months. Some did actual harm. For every hour per day the children spent watching certain baby DVDs and videos, the infants understood an average of six to eight fewer words than infants who did not watch them.

Disney demanded a retraction, citing deficiencies in the studies. After consultations with the original researchers, the university held its ground and issued a press release saying so. After this initial flurry of activity, there was silence. Then, two years later, in October 2009, Disney announced what amounted to a product recall, offering refunds to anyone who had purchased *Baby Einstein* materials. Responsibly, the company has dropped the word "educational" from the packaging.

After age 5, the jury is out

Since the first studies on television, researchers have discovered that not everything about TV is negative. It depends upon the content of the TV show, the age of the child, and perhaps even the child's genetics. Before age 2, TV is best avoided completely. But after age 5, the jury is out on this harsh verdict—way out, in fact. Some television shows *improve* brain performance at this age. Not surprisingly, these shows tend to be the interactive types (*Dora the Explorer*, good; *Barney & Friends*, bad, according to certain studies). So although the case is overwhelming that television exposure should be limited, TV cannot be painted with a monolithic brush. Here are a few recommendations for TV viewing the data suggest:

1. Keep the TV off before the child turns 2. I know this is tough to hear for parents who need a break. If you can't turn it off—if you haven't created those social networks that can allow you a rest—at least limit your child's exposure to TV. We live in the real world, after all, and an irritated, overextended parent can be just as harmful to a child's development as an annoying purple dinosaur.

2. After age 2, help your children choose the shows (and other screen-based exposures) they will experience. Pay special attention to any media that allow intelligent interaction.

3. Watch the chosen TV show with your children, interacting with the media and helping your children to analyze and think critically about what they just experienced. And rethink putting a TV in the kids' room: Kids with their own TVs score an average of 8 points lower on math and language-arts tests than kids in households with TVs in the family room.

Video games: Don't just sit there

First, a disclaimer. I love *Myst*, an old computer-based video game. I was a graphics artist and professional animator before becoming a scientist, and *Myst* was love at first byte. Here was this beautifully rendered world, elegantly drawn with digital paint, dripping in what I could only describe as bit-mapped love. I spent hours in this world, exploring, problem solving, *reading* (there are books in this game!), examining star charts, and manipulating technologies that were visually inspired by equal parts Leonardo da Vinci, Jules Verne, and Gene Roddenberry. Even now, hearing real waves gently lapping against a shoreline sends me back to the dreamy digital world where I first learned the real power of computing. If I sound smitten, then I am communicating correctly. That's dangerous for a scientist, especially one about to comment on video games. Fortunately, cooler heads are out there; that's why it's called refereed literature, after all.

What does that literature say about video games and developing brains in babies? There's not much, and it paints a decidedly mixed picture. This is understandable. The subject is too new, and the technology undergirding it is changing too rapidly. So what parents of newborns and toddlers should know about gaming comes not from data about what video games do to the mind but from what video games do to the body.

As with television, most video games are consumed in a sedentary position: You sit there. Movement-oriented game consoles such as the Wii, which debuted in 2006, potentially provide an exception, but they seem to have made little dent: Kids' weight is still rising precipitously. So pronounced is this weight-gain trend that our children are starting to get diseases usually associated with middle and later life—including arthritis! Childhood obesity is three times more prevalent in gamers than in non-gamers.

The brain loves exercise

This rise in pediatric obesity is painful to hear in the brain science community, especially because we know so much about the relationship between physical activity and mental acuity. Exercise—especially aerobic exercise—is fantastic for the brain, increasing executive function scores anywhere from 50 percent to 100 percent. This is true across the life span, from young children to members of the golden-parachute crowd. Strengthening exercises, though there are many other reasons to do them, do not give you these numbers.

Parents who start their kids out on a vigorous exercise schedule are more likely to have children for whom exercise becomes a steady, even lifelong, habit—up to 1½ times more likely, depending upon the study. Fit kids score higher on executive function tests than sedentary controls, and those scores remain as long as the exercise does. The best results accrue, by the way, if you do the exercises *with* your children. Remember that deferred-imitation business? Encouraging an active lifestyle is one of the best gifts you can give your child. It may mean putting away *World of Warcraft*, getting off your butt, and providing a good example. This does not make *Myst* any less beautiful. It simply gives gaming a more nuanced perspective. I still love the genre, always will, but I am increasingly convinced that electronic games should come with a warning label.

Texting: A cautionary tale

How about the Internet and its associated digital communication vassals? Again, real data are few and far between. The little work that's out there suggests some reason for concern, as illustrated by this story:

A 9-year-old girl decided to invite five or six of her closest friends to her very first slumber party. The girl's mother, a sociologist by training, was delighted. Remembering her own childhood sleepovers, she anticipated nonstop talking, pillow fights, whispering secrets in the dark, and giggles at 2:00 a.m. None of that happened. As her daughter's friends gathered together, Mom immediately noticed things that set her sociologist's Spidey instincts tingling. The discourse between the girls seemed not like that of typical 9-year-olds, whose social exchanges can be surprisingly sophisticated, but more emotionally immature, like that of 4-year-olds. The culprit appeared to be the girls' consistent misreading and misinterpreting of each other's nonverbal cues. Mom also saw that within 30 minutes of the start of the party, five of the six girls had pulled out their cell phones. They were busily texting friends who weren't there, or taking pictures and sending them off. This continued throughout the day. Deep into the night, around 2:00 a.m., everything was absolutely still. Mom snuck upstairs to make sure everything was OK. Half of the girls had gone to sleep. The other half were still on their cell phones, little screens glowing underneath the sheets.

Could the text messaging be related to the social immaturity? It's not a trivial issue. The average youngster in 2008 sent and received 2,272 texts per month, about 80 per day. By 2009, 27 percent of the words they encountered came directly from a computer. Anything wrong with that? Nobody really knows yet. What we can say has to do with the inherent nature of the medium itself. The Internet and associated media encourage private consumption. This leads to the odd condition, as the slumber party illustrates, that even when we're together, we're often far apart. Unless all of their digital interactions involve a video camera, kids won't get much practice interpreting nonverbal cues. That's the world autistic kids live in, by the way.

Perfecting nonverbal communication skills takes years of practice, and, as we discussed in the previous chapter, it's critical that kids do it. Real-life experiences are much messier than life on the Internet and not at all anonymous. Flesh-and-blood people touch each other, get in each other's way, and constantly telegraph information to each other in a fashion not easily reformatted into emoticons and cute three-letter abbreviations. Recall that from marriages to workplaces, the largest source of conflict comes from the asymmetry between extrospective and introspective information. A great deal of asymmetry can be averted through the correct interpretation of nonverbal cues. The less practice humans get at it, the more immature their social interactions are likely to be, and the implications of that affect everything from future divorce rates to erosion of productivity in the workforce.

The sociologist mom's anecdotal observation may be a wake-up call. It is certainly fertile ground for research. Given what's at stake, a healthy skepticism toward a digital-only world is probably best. The best current advice may be keeping those machines mostly in the off position for as long as you can.

For better or for worse, we are social animals. It is probably wired into our DNA. You don't have to look much further than Theodore Roosevelt to see that human relationships are the number one ingredient for a child's future success. A culture marinated in technology might readily accuse researchers of being on the wrong side of history. The researchers, in turn, might accuse culture of being on the wrong side of humanity.

Hyper-parenting: "My baby is better than your baby"

I recently overheard this half of a cell-phone conversation while waiting for my plane to take off: "Is Stephanie walking yet? No? Brandon was walking by the time he was 9 months!" Then later: "Stephanie's still in diapers? Brandon was potty-trained before he was 2!" The conversation went on and on about various milestones Superbaby Brandon was accomplishing in the face of Pathetic Stephanie. I hear versions of this baby competition virtually everywhere I go. They're an element of hyper-parenting—another ingredient you want to limit in your smart-baby fertilizer. As the conversation ended, I imagined what Stephanie's mom might feel. Anger? Embarrassment? She may have gone out and bought every developmental toy out there to hasten her little girl's development. Or she may have just cried. And all for no good reason.

Creating comparisons like these is not only counterproductive (it puts pressure on a child that can be harmful to his or her brain) but also out of step with current neuroscientific understanding.

No two brains develop at the same rate

As you know by now, the brain follows a developmental timetable that is as individual as its owner's personality. Children do not go through the same developmental milestones in lock step, marching like little brain-soldiers on the path to their future. A child who is a math whiz at age 4 is not necessarily one at age 9. Einstein, arguably as bright as they come, is rumored not to have spoken in complete sentences until he was 3. (His family had christened him "the dopey one!") This individuality is partially genetic, but it also occurs because neurons are so responsive to the outer environment.

They easily form new connections and break off existing ones, a property known as neuroplasticity.

The brain appears to go through *some* commonly experienced developmental stages. But few in the brain science community completely agree on what they are. Developmental psychologist Jean Piaget (who worked for a time with Alfred Binet, the IQ guy) came up with four phases of cognitive development in kids, which he called sensorimotor, preoperational, concrete operational, and formal operational. Widely influential then, the concept of developmental stages is a contentious idea now. Researchers began to question the notion in the late 20th century when they showed that children acquire skills and concepts at much earlier stages than Piaget posited. Follow-up work revealed that, even within a given category, children go through developmental stages at their own pace. Many don't follow the order Piaget conceived; they sometimes skip a step or two or repeat the same stage several times in a row. Some go through no definable stages at all. There is nothing wrong with our children's brains. There is just something wrong with our theories.

Some parents, though, think brain development is like running an Olympic race. They want their child to win at every step, whatever the cost. You can still see the effect of this mindset when these parents' children get into college. Though I mostly teach graduate students, I occasionally instruct undergraduates who want to get into medical school, and they care about little else. Many describe being hot-housed by pushy parents who seem to see their kids more as merit badges than as people.

This is called hyper-parenting, and it has been studied. Developmental psychologist David Elkind, now professor emeritus of child development at Tufts University, has divided overachieving moms and dads into categories. Four of them are:

- *Gourmet parents.* These parents are high achievers who want their kids to succeed as they did.

- *College-degree parents.* Your classic "hot-housers," these parents are related to Gourmets but believe that the sooner academic training starts, the better.

- *Outward-bound parents.* Wanting to provide their kids with physical survival skills because the world is such a dangerous place, these parents are often involved in the military and law enforcement.

- *Prodigy parents.* Financially successful and deeply suspicious about the education system, these parents want to guard their kids against the negative effects of schooling.

Regardless of category, hyper-parents often pursue their child's intellectual success at the expense of their child's happiness. Though real numbers are hard to come by, a cautionary tale may exist with high-school students in South Korea, for whom parental pressure to perform well on standardized tests can be enormous. After traffic accidents, suicide is the leading cause of death for 15- to- 19-year-olds.

I understand where parents are coming from. In a competitive world whose winners increasingly are the smartest among us, it is reflexive for loving parents to be concerned about their child's intelligence. The dirty little secret, however, is that extreme intellectual pressure is usually counterproductive.

Hyper-parenting can actually hurt your child's intellectual development in several ways:

I. Extreme expectations stunt higher-level thinking

Children are extraordinarily reactive to parental expectations, aching to please and fulfill when little; aching to resist and rebel when older. If little kids sense a parent wants them to accomplish some intellectual feat for which their brains are not yet ready, they are inexorably forced into a corner. This coerces the brain to revert to "lower-level" thinking strategies, creating counterfeit habits that may have to be unlearned later. I saw this in action at a social gathering one evening. A proud parent announced to me that his 2-year-old understood multiplication. He had the little guy perform by reciting the times tables. It became obvious, with some gentle probing, that the boy had no understanding of multiplication and was merely parroting back a few memorized facts. Lower thinking skills had substituted for higher processing features. Elkind disparagingly calls these types of displays "pony tricks" and believes no child should be subjected to them. I agree.

2. Pressure can extinguish curiosity

Children are natural explorers. But if parents supply only rigid educational expectations, interest will be transformed into appeasement. Children will stop asking potent questions like "Am I curious about this?" and start asking, "What will satisfy the powers that be?" Exploratory behavior is not rewarded, so it is soon disregarded. Remember, the brain is a *survival* organ, and nothing is more important to a child than the safety (approval, in this case) parents can provide.

3. Continual anger or disappointment becomes toxic stress

There's another harm when parents press their children to perform tasks their little brains aren't yet capable of executing. Pushy parents often become disappointed, displeased, or angry when their kids don't perform—reactions children can detect at an astonishingly young age and want desperately to avoid.

This loss of control is toxic. It can create a psychological state called learned helplessness, which can physically damage a child's brain. The child learns he can't control the negative stimuli (the parent's anger or disappointment) coming at him or the situations that cause it. Think of a third-grade boy who comes home from school every night to a drunken dad, who then beats him up. The little guy has to have a home, but it is awful to have a home. He will get the message that there is no way out, and eventually he will not try to escape, even if a way later presents itself. That's why it is called *learned* helplessness. And you don't need a physically abusive situation to create it.

Learned helplessness is a gateway to depression, even in childhood. I knew the parents of a graduate student who killed himself; they were archetypically pushy, demanding, and, frankly, obnoxious. Though depression is a complex subject, the student's suicide note intimated that his drastic actions were partially a response to his perceived failure to live up to his parents' expectations. This is a powerful demonstration that the brain is not interested in learning; it is interested in surviving.

Write this across your heart before your child comes into the world: Parenting is a not a race. Kids are not proxies for adult success. Competition can be inspiring, but brands of it can wire your child's brain in a toxic way. Comparing your kids with your friends' kids will not get them, or you, where you want to go.

You can maximize your child's brain power in plenty of wonderful ways. After breast-feeding, focus on open-ended play, lots of verbal interaction, and praising effort—fertilizers statistically guaranteed to boost your child's intellect from almost any starting point. These things aren't fancy. After all, the brain's intellectual performance envelope was forged in a world that was not only pre-Internet but pre–Ice Age.

Key points

- The brain is more interested in surviving than in getting good grades in school.
- What helps early learning: breast-feeding, talking to your children—a lot, guided play every day, and praising effort rather than intelligence.
- What hurts early learning: overexposure to television (keep the TV off before age 2), a sedentary lifestyle, and limited face-to-face interaction.
- Pressuring children to learn a subject before their brains are ready is only harmful.

happy baby: seeds

brain rule

Make new friends but keep the old

happy baby: seeds

The only thing you did to this sweet, calm little baby girl is to put a new toy in her crib. But she reacts as if you had just taken her favorite one away. Her eyes dart up at you and her face begins to contort, stress building up in her heart like a looming squall. She lets loose a Category 4 wail, flailing her legs and arching her back in nearly catastrophic distress. But it isn't just you. This happens to the poor thing whenever a new experience comes her way: an unfamiliar voice, a strange smell, a loud noise. She is *so* sensitive. This infant simply falls apart whenever "normal" is disrupted.

A girl with long brown hair, about 15, is being asked about school and her extracurricular activities. As she starts to answer, you can tell something is wrong. She has the same troubled look on her face as the baby! She fidgets nonstop. She shakes her knee, twirls her hair, plays with her ear. Her answers come out in halting, constipated chunks. The girl doesn't have very many activities outside of school, she says, though she plays the violin and writes a little. When the researcher asks her what is on her list of worries, she hesitates and then lets out the storm. Holding back tears, she says, "I feel really uncomfortable, especially if other people around me know what they're doing. I'm always thinking, Should I go here? Should I go there? Am I in someone's way?" She pauses, then cries, "How am I going to deal with the world when I'm grown? Or if I'm going to do anything that really means anything?" The emotion subsides, and she shrinks, defeated. "I can't stop thinking about that," she finishes, her voice trailing to a troubled whisper. The temperament is unmistakable. She's that baby, 15 years later.

And she is clearly one unhappy child.

Researchers call her Baby 19, and she is famous in the world of developmental psychology. Through his work with her and others like her, psychologist Jerome Kagan discovered many of the things we know about temperament and the powerful role it plays in determining how happy a child ultimately becomes.

This chapter is all about why some kids, like Baby 19, are so unhappy—and other kids are not. (Indeed, most kids are just the opposite. Baby 19 is so named because babies 1 through 18 in Kagan's study were comparatively pretty jolly.) We will discuss the biological basis of happy children, your chances of getting an anxious baby, whether happiness could be genetic, and the secret to a happy life. In the next chapter, we'll talk about how you can create an environment conducive to your child's happiness.

What is happy?

Parents often tell me their highest goal is to raise a happy child. When I ask what they mean, exactly, I get varying responses. Some parents mean happiness as an emotion: They want their children to regularly experience a positive subjective state. Some parents mean it more like a steady state of being: They want their children to be content, emotionally stable. Others seem to mean security or morality, praying that their child will land a good job and marry well, or be "upstanding." Past a few quick examples, however, most parents find the notion hard to pin down.

Scientists do, too. One researcher who has spent many years trying to get at the answer is a delightful elf of a psychologist named Daniel Gilbert, at Harvard. Other definitions of happiness exist, of course, but Gilbert proposes these three:

- **Emotional happiness.** This is what most of the parents I ask probably mean. This type of happiness is, Gilbert wrote, "a *feeling*, an *experience*, a *subjective* state" untethered to something objective in the real world. Your child is delighted by the color blue, moved by a movie, thrilled by the Grand Canyon, satisfied by a glass of milk.

- **Moral happiness.** Intertwined with virtue, moral happiness is more akin to a philosophical suite of attitudes than to a spontaneous subjective feeling. If your child leads a good and proper life, filled with moral meaning, he or she might feel deeply satisfied and content. Gilbert uses the Greek word *eudaimonia* to describe the idea, a word Aristotle translated as "doing and living well." *Eudaimonia* literally means "having a good guardian spirit."

- **Judgmental happiness.** In this case, the word "happiness" is followed by words like "about" or "for" or "that." Your child might be happy *about* going to the park. She might be happy *for* a friend who just got a dog. This involves making a judgment about the world, not in terms of some transient subjective feeling but as a source of potentially pleasurable feelings, past, present, or future.

Where does this happiness, regardless of type, come from? The main source of happiness was discovered by the oldest ongoing experiment in the history of modern American science.

The secret of happiness

The psychologist presiding over this research project is named George Vaillant. And he deserves it. Since 1937, researchers for the Harvard Study of Adult Development have exhaustively collected intimate data on several hundred people. The project usually goes by the moniker the Grant Study, named for the department store magnate W. T. Grant, who funded the initial work. The question they are investigating: Is there a formula for "the good life"? What, in other words, makes people happy?

Vaillant has been the project's caretaker for more than four decades, the latest in a long line of scientific shepherds of the Grant Study. His interest is more than just professional. Vaillant himself is a self-described "disconnected" parent. Married multiple times, he has five children, one of whom is autistic and four of whom don't speak to him very often. His own father committed suicide when he was 10, leaving him with few happy examples to follow. So he's a good man to lead the search for happiness.

The project's scientific godfathers, all of whom are now dead, recruited 268 Harvard undergraduates to the study. They were all white males, seemingly well-adjusted, several with bright futures ahead of them—including longtime *Washington Post* editor Ben Bradlee and President John F. Kennedy. Their lives were to be stretched out like a rack for years so that teams of professionals, including psychologists, anthropologists, social workers, even physiologists, could keep track of everything that happened to them. And that's what they did.

With an initial thoroughness the Department of Homeland Security might envy, these men have endured exhaustive medical checkups every five years, patiently taken batteries of psychological tests, tolerated in-person interviews every 15 years, and returned questionnaires every other year, for nearly three-quarters of a century. Though supervised unevenly over the decades by what best might be called a tag team of researchers, the Grant Study is probably the most thorough research of its type ever attempted.

And what did they come up with after all these years? What in the end constitutes the good life? Consistently makes us happy? I'll let Vaillant, in an interview with the *Atlantic*, speak for the group:

> *"The only thing that really matters in life [is] your relationships to other people."*

After nearly 75 years, the only consistent finding comes right out of *It's a Wonderful Life*. Successful friendships, the messy bridges that connect friends and family, are what predict people's happiness as they hurtle through life. Friendships are a better predictor than any other single variable. By the time a person reaches middle age, they are the *only* predictor. Says Jonathan Haidt, a researcher who has extensively studied the link between socialization and happiness: "Human beings are in some ways like bees. We have evolved to live in intensely social groups, and we don't do as well when freed from hives."

The more intimate the relationship, the better. A colleague of Vaillant's showed that people don't gain access to the top 10 percent of the happiness pile unless they are involved in a romantic relationship of some kind. Marriage is a big factor. About 40 percent of married adults describe themselves as "very happy," whereas 23 percent of the never-marrieds do.

More research has since confirmed and extended these simple findings. In addition to satisfying relationships, other behaviors that predict happiness include:

- a steady dose of altruistic acts
- making lists of things for which you are grateful, which generates feelings of happiness in the short term
- cultivating a general "attitude of gratitude," which generates feelings of happiness in the long term

- sharing novel experiences with a loved one
- deploying a ready "forgiveness reflex" when loved ones slight you

If those things sound obvious—the usual suspects in self-help magazines—this one may be a surprise: Money doesn't make the cut. People who make more than $5 million a year are not appreciably happier than those who make $100,000 a year, the *Journal of Happiness Studies* found. Money increases happiness only when it lifts people out of poverty to about $50,000 a year in income. Past that, wealth and happiness part ways. This suggests something practical and relieving: Help your children get into a profession that can at least make around $50,000 a year. They don't have to be millionaires to be thrilled with the life you prepare them for. After their basic needs are met, they just need some close friends and relatives. And sometimes even siblings, as the following story attests.

My brother is JOSH!

My two sons, ages 3 and 5, were running around a playground one cloudy Seattle morning. Josh and Noah were happily playing on swings, rolling on the ground, and shouting with other boys, everyone acting like the lion cubs-in-training they were. Suddenly, Noah was pulled to the ground by a couple of local bullies, large 4-year- olds. Josh bolted to his younger brother's aid like a shot of Red Bull. Jumping between brother and bully, fists raised, Joshua growled through clenched teeth: "Nobody messes with my brother!" The shocked gang quickly scattered.

Noah was not only relieved but *ecstatic*. He hugged his older brother and ran around in circles, flooded with festive, excess energy. He inexplicably shot off lasers with make-believe sticks, shouting at the top of his lungs to anybody in earshot, "My brother is JOSH!" His good deed done, Joshua returned to his swing, grinning from ear to ear. It was an impressively joyous one-act show, applauded at length by our nanny, who was watching them. The essence of this story is the presence of happiness—generated by a close, intense relationship. Noah was clearly thrilled; Josh clearly satisfied. Sibling rivalry being what it is, such altruism is not the only behavior in which they regularly engage. But for the moment, these kids were well-adjusted and *happy*, observable in near-cinematic fashion.

Helping your child make friends

These findings about the importance of human relationships—in all their messy glory—greatly simplify our question about how to raise happy kids. You will need to teach your children how to socialize effectively—how to make friends, how to keep friends—if you want them to be happy.

As you might suspect, many ingredients go into creating socially smart children, too many to put into some behavioral Tupperware bowl. I've selected the two that have the strongest backing in the hard neurosciences. They are also two of the most predictive for social competency:

- emotional regulation
- our old friend, empathy

We'll start with the first.

Emotional regulation: How nice

After decades of research burning through millions of dollars, scientists have uncovered this shocker of a fact: We are most likely to maintain deep, long-term relationships with people who are nice. Mom was right. Individuals who are thoughtful, kind, sensitive, outward focused, accommodating, and forgiving have deeper, more lasting friendships—and lower divorce rates—than people who are moody, impulsive, rude, self-centered, inflexible, and vindictive. A negative balance on this spreadsheet can greatly affect a person's mental health, too, putting him at greater risk not only for fewer friends but for depression and anxiety disorders. Consistent with the Grant Study, those with emotional debits are some of the unhappiest people in the world.

Moody, rude, and impulsive sound an awful lot like faulty executive control, and that is part of the problem. But the deficit is even larger. These people are not regulating their emotions. To figure out what that means, we first need to answer a basic question:

What on earth is an emotion?

You can put this little vignette in the "Do as I say, not as I do" file:

Last night my son threw his pacifier. I was tired and frustrated and said, "We don't throw things!" And then I threw it at him.

Perhaps the son did not want to go to sleep and in defiance threw the pacifier. Mom already told us she was tired and frustrated; you can probably add angry. Lots of emotions on display in these three short sentences. What exactly were they experiencing? You might be surprised by my answer. Scientists don't actually know.

There is a great deal of argument in the research world about what exactly an emotion is. In part that's because emotions aren't at all distinct in the brain.

We often make a distinction between organized hard thinking, like doing a calculus problem, and disorganized, squishy emoting, like experiencing frustration or happiness. When you look at the wiring diagrams that make up the brain, however, the distinctions fade. There are regions that generate and process emotions, and there are regions that generate and process analytical cognitions, but they are incredibly interwoven. Dynamic, complex coalitions of networked neurons crackle off electrical signals to one another in highly integrated and astonishingly adaptive patterns. You can't tell the difference between emotions and analyses.

For our purposes, a better approach is to ignore what an emotion *is* and instead focus on what an emotion *does*. Understanding that will point us to strategies for regulating emotions—one of our two main players in maintaining healthy friendships.

Emotions tag our world the way RoboCop tags bad guys

One of my favorite science fiction movies, *RoboCop*, has a great definition of emotions. The 1987 film takes place in a futuristic, crime-infested Detroit, a city then as now deeply in need of a hero. That hero turns out to be the cyborg RoboCop, a hybrid human formed from a deceased police officer (played by Peter Weller). RoboCop is unleashed onto the criminal underworld of the unsuspecting city, and he goes to work cleaning up the place. The cool thing is, RoboCop can apprehend bad guys while reducing collateral damage to anyone else. In one scene, he scans a landscape filled with criminals and innocent bystanders. You're inside RoboCop's visor; you can see him digitally tagging only the bad guys for further processing, leaving everyone else alone. Aim, fire: He blows away only the bad guys.

This kind of filtering is exactly what emotions do in the brain. You're probably used to thinking of emotions as the same thing as feelings, but to the brain, they're not. In the textbook definition, emotions are simply the activation of neurological circuits that prioritize our perceptual world into two categories: things we should pay attention to and things we can safely ignore. Feelings are the subjective psychological experiences that emerge from this activation.

See the similarity to the software in RoboCop's visor? When we scan our world, we tag certain items for further processing and leave other items alone. Emotions are the tags. Another way to think of emotions is like Post-it notes that cause the brain to pay attention to something. Onto what do we place our little cognitive stickies?

Our brains tag those inputs most immediately concerned with our survival—threats, sex, and patterns (things we think we've seen before). Since most people don't put Post-it notes on everything, emotions help us prioritize our sensory inputs. We might see both the criminal pointing a gun at us and the lawn upon which the criminal stands. We don't have an emotional reaction to the lawn. We have an emotional reaction to the gun. Emotions provide an important perceptual filtering ability, in the service of survival. They play a role in affixing our attention to things and in helping us make decisions. As you'd expect, a child's ability to regulate emotions takes a while to develop.

Emotions are like Post-it notes, telling the brain to pay attention to something.

Why all the crying? It gets you to "tag" them

In the first few weeks after we brought our elder son home, all Josh seemed to do was cry, sleep, or emit disgusting things from his body. He'd wake up in the wee hours of the morning, crying. Sometimes I'd hold him, sometimes I'd lay him down; either one would only make him cry more. I had to wonder: Was this all he could do? Then I came home early from work one day. My wife had Josh in a stroller, and as I walked toward them both, Josh saw me and seemed to experience a sudden rush of recognition. He flashed me a megawatt smile that could have powered Las Vegas for an hour, then stared at me intently. I couldn't believe it! I yelped and stretched out my arms to give him a hug. The noise was too loud, however, and the move too sudden. He instantly reverted to crying. Then he pooped his diapers. So much for variety.

My inability to decode Josh in his earliest weeks did not mean he—or any other baby—had a one-track emotion. A great deal of neurological activity occurs in both the cortex and limbic structures in all babies' early weeks. We'll take a look at these two brain structures in a few pages. By 6 months of age, a baby typically can experience surprise, disgust, happiness, sadness, anger, and fear. What babies don't have are a lot of filters. Crying for many months remains the shortest, most efficient means of getting a parent to put a Post-it note on *them*. Parental attention is deep in the survival interests of the otherwise helpless infant, so babies cry when they are frightened, hungry, startled, overstimulated, lonely, or none of the above. That makes for a lot of crying.

Big feelings are confusing for little kids

Babies also can't talk. Yet. They will—it is one of their first long-term, uniquely human goals—but their nonverbal communication systems won't be connected to their verbal communication systems for quite some time. The ability to verbally label an emotion, which is a very important strategy for emotional regulation, isn't there yet.

Until they acquire language, what's in store for young children as their tiny, emotion-heavy brains stitch themselves together is lots of confusion. This struggle is especially poignant in the early toddler years. Young children may not be aware of the emotions they are experiencing. They may not yet understand the socially correct way to communicate them. The result is that your little one may act out in anger when he is actually sad, or she may just become grumpy for no apparent reason. Sometimes a single event will induce a mixture of emotions. These emotions and their attendant feelings can feel so big and so out of control that the kids become frightened on top of it, which only amplifies the effect.

Because kids often express their emotions indirectly, you need to consider the environmental context before you attempt to decode your child's behavior. If you are concluding that parents need to pay a lot of attention to the *emotional* landscapes of their kids to understand their behavior—all to get them properly socialized—you are 100 percent correct.

Things eventually settle down. The brain structures responsible for processing and regulating emotions will wire themselves together, chatting like teenagers on their cell phones. The problem is that it doesn't happen all at once. The job really isn't finished until you and your child start applying for student loans. Though it takes a long time, establishing this communication flow is extremely important.

Once it matures, here's what emotional regulation looks like: Suppose you are at a play with some friends, watching a moving scene from the musical *Les Misérables*. It's the strangely powerful (some say sappy) song "Bring Him Home." You know two things: (a) when you cry, you really sob, and (b) this scene can really skewer you. To save yourself from social humiliation, you reappraise the situation and attempt to suppress your tears. You succeed, barely. This overruling is emotional regulation. There is nothing wrong with crying, or any other number of expressions, but you realize that there are social contexts where certain behavior is appropriate and social contexts where it is not. People who do this well generally have lots of friends. If you want your kids to be happy, you will spend lots of time teaching them how and when this filtering should occur.

Where emotions happen in the brain

"It glows!" a little girl squealed in a mixture of delight and horror. "Ooh, I can see its claws!" said a little boy, just behind her. "And there's its stinger!" said another girl, to which the boy replied, "Ooh. It looks just like your sister's nose!" This was followed by some pushing. I laughed. We were on a field trip at a museum, and I was completely surrounded by a group of bubbling, lively third graders in awe of the way scorpions glow under a black light.

One of the most beautiful parts of this exhibit was also its focal point, a display just out of reach above their shoulders. Here was a large, lonely scorpion, motionless on a rock, sitting inside in a larger, lonelier fishbowl. Ultraviolet light shining from above, the animal looked just like a glow-in-the-dark Lord of the Arachnids. Or, if you are a brain scientist, one of the most complex structures in the brain—the ones that generate and process our emotions.

Picture, if you will, that same scorpion suspended in the middle of your brain. The brain has two lobes, or hemispheres, which can be likened to two fishbowls that have been partially fused together. I'll describe the fishbowls first, the scorpion second.

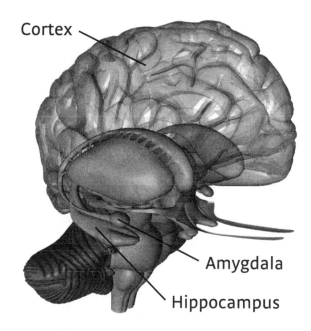

The cortex: Senses and thinking

The partially fused fishbowls are the brain's main hemispheres, logically called the left and right hemispheres. Each hemisphere is covered with a thick surface, made not of glass but a mixed layer of neurons and molecules. This cellular rind of tissue is the cortex. The cortex is only a few cells thick, and it is unlike the cortex of any other animal in the world. It is the tissue that makes us human. Among many other functions, ours is involved in abstract thinking (like doing algebra). It is also involved in processing external sensory information (like spotting a saber-toothed tiger). But we don't feel threatened by either algebra or tigers because of the cortex. That's the job of the scorpion.

The amygdala: Emotions and memories

This cerebral arachnid is part of a set of structures called the limbic system, which means "border" system. The scorpion's claws, one for each hemisphere, are called amygdala, which for good reason means "almond" (that's what they look like). The amygdala helps to generate emotions and then store memories of the emotions it generates. In the real world of the brain, you would not see the scorpion shape. The limbic regions are obscured by other structures, including an impenetrable thicket of cellular connections dangling down from every millimeter of the fishbowl's surface. But the amygdala is not connected just to your cortex. It is connected to regions that regulate your heartbeat, your lungs, and areas that control your ability to move. Emotions really are distributed among assemblies of cells scattered throughout the brain.

Still with me? Things are about to get more complex.

What a gossip!

The central region of the amygdala possesses big, fat connections to an area of the brain called the insula, a smallish region near the middle of the organ. That's an important finding. The insula, with assistance from its amygdalar buddy, helps create subjective, emotionally relevant contexts for the sensory information arising throughout the body from our eyes, ears, nose, fingertips, and more. How does that occur? We haven't the foggiest idea. We know the insula collates perceptions of temperature, muscle tension, itch, tickle, sensual touch, pain, stomach pH, intestinal tension, and hunger from the rest of the body. And then it chats about what it finds with the amygdala. Some researchers believe this communication is one of the reasons gathering information south of the head is so important to the creation and perception of emotional states. It may be involved in certain mental illnesses, like anorexia nervosa.

You get the impression this scorpion does a lot of talking. These connections are the phone lines allowing this part of the brain—and indirectly just about everywhere else in the body—to hear what the rest of the brain says. This is a big hint that emotion functions are distributed all over the brain, or at least announced all over the brain.

How the amygdala learns to brew up emotions and why it needs so many other neural regions to assist it are to some degree a mystery. We know the brain takes its own sweet time getting these connections wired up to one another—years, in some cases. Ever watched a selfish little boy blossom into a thoughtful young man? All it takes is a little time, sometimes.

Empathy: The glue of relationships

Along with the ability to regulate emotions, the ability to perceive the needs of another person and respond with empathy plays a huge role in your child's social competence. Empathy makes good friends. To have empathy, your child must cultivate the ability to peer inside the psychological interiors of someone else, accurately comprehend that person's behavioral reward and punishment systems, and then respond with kindness and understanding. The outward push of empathy helps cement people to each other, providing a long-term stability to their interactions. See what happens between mother and daughter in this story:

> I have GOT to learn not to be so crude when I get home. I was bitching to Shellie on the phone after work [about] how much of a pain in the butt my boss is. A few minutes later I smelled diaper rash cream, then felt some one trying to lift up my skirt. My dear two-year-old daughter had opened a tube of Desitin and was

trying to smear it on my backside! I said "What in the world are you doing?" She said, "Nothing Mommy. It's for the pain in your butt." I love this girl so much. I could have squeezed her til she burst!

Notice what the daughter's creative empathy did for her mom's attitude toward their relationship. *It seemed to bind them together.* These empathetic interactions have names. When one person is truly happy for another, or sad for another, we say they are engaging in active-constructive behaviors. These behaviors are so powerful, they can keep not only parents and children together but husbands and wives together. We talked in the Relationship chapter about the role of empathy in the transition to parenthood. If your marriage has a three-to-one ratio of active-constructive versus toxic-conflict interactions, your relationship is nearly divorce-proof. The best marriages have a ratio of five to one.

Mirror neurons: I feel you

There is a neurobiology behind empathy, and I was reminded of it the first time my younger son got a shot. As the doctor filled the syringe, my wary eyes followed his movements. Little Noah, sensing something was wrong, began wriggling in my arms. He was getting ready to receive his first set of vaccinations, and he already didn't like it. I knew the next few minutes were going to be excruciating. My wife sat this one out in the waiting room, having endured the process with our elder child and being no friend of the needle herself (when she was a little girl, her pediatrician's nurse actually had Parkinson's). It was up to me to hold Noah firmly in my arms to keep him still while the doctor did the dirty work. That shouldn't have been a big deal. I have a familiar research relationship with needles. In my career I have injected mice with pathogens, neural tissues with glass electrodes, and plastic test tubes with dyes, sometimes missing the tube but not my finger. But this time was different. Noah's eyes locked onto mine as the needle pushed into his little arm like a metallic mosquito from hell. Nothing prepared me for the look of betrayal on my youngest son's face. His forehead wrinkled like cellophane. He howled. I did too, silently. For no rational reason, I felt like a failure. My arm even ached.

Blame it on my brain. As I witnessed the pain in Noah's arm, some researchers believe, neurons that mediate the ability to experience the pain in *my* arm were suddenly springing to life. I was not getting the shot, but that didn't matter to my brain. I was mirroring the event, literally experiencing the pain of someone about whom I care a great deal. No wonder my arm ached.

These so-called mirror neurons are scattered across the brain like tiny cellular asteroids. We recruit them, in concert with memory systems and emotional processing regions, when we encounter another person's experiences. Neurons with mirrorlike properties come in many forms, researchers think. In my case, I was experiencing the mirrors most closely associated with extremity pain. I was also activating motor neurons that governed my arm's desire to withdraw from a painful situation.

Many other mammals appear to have mirror neurons, too. In fact, mirror neurons initially were discovered by Italian researchers trying to figure out how monkeys picked up raisins. The researchers noticed that certain brain regions became activated not only when monkeys picked up raisins but also when they simply watched others pick up raisins. The animals' brains "mirrored" the behavior. In humans, the same neural regions are activated not only when you tear a piece of paper and when you see Aunt Martha tearing a piece of paper—but also if you hear the words "Aunt Martha is tearing a piece of paper."

It's like having a direct internal link to another person's psychological experience. Mirror neurons permit you to understand an observed action by experiencing it firsthand, even though you're not. Sounds a lot like empathy. Mirror neurons may also be profoundly involved in both the ability to interpret nonverbal cues, particularly facial expressions, and the ability to understand someone else's intentions. This second talent falls under an umbrella of skills called Theory of Mind, which we'll describe in detail in the Moral chapter. Some researchers think Theory of Mind skills are the engines behind empathy.

Not all scientists agree about the role mirror neurons play in mediating complex human behaviors like empathy and Theory of Mind. It is definitely a matter of contention. The preponderance of evidence suggests a role for them, but I also think a great deal more research needs to be done. With more research, we may find that empathy is not a touchy-feely phenomenon but, rather, has deep neurophysiological roots. That would be an astonishing thing to say.

An uneven talent

Because this type of neural activity easily can be measured, it is possible to ask if every child has an equal talent for empathy. The unsurprising answer is no. Autistic children, for example, have no ability to detect changes in people's emotional states. They simply can't decode another person's psychological interiors by looking at his or her face. They cannot divine people's motivations or predict their intentions. Some researchers think they lack mirror-neuron activity.

Even outside of this extreme, empathy is uneven. You probably know people who are naturally highly empathetic and others with the emotional understanding of dirt. Are they born that way? Though separating social and cultural influences is tough, the equally tough answer is: probably.

This neural hardwiring suggests that there are aspects of a kid's social skill set a parent just can't control. It's a big thing to say, but there may be a genetic component to the level of happiness your offspring can achieve. This somewhat scary idea deserves a more detailed explanation.

Could happiness or sadness be genetic?

My mother says I was born laughing. Even though I entered the world prior to video cameras—or dads—in the delivery room, I do have a way to independently verify this observation. The pediatrician supervising my birth left a note, which my mother kept and I still have. The note says: "Baby appears to be laughing."

That's funny, for I love to laugh. I'm also an optimist. I tend to believe things will work out just fine, even when no shred of evidence warrants the attitude. My glass will always be half-full, even if the glass is leaking. This predisposition has probably saved my emotional bacon more than once, given the number of years I have dealt with the often-depressing genetics of psychiatric disorders. If I was born laughing, was I also born happy? No, of course not. Most babies are born crying, and it doesn't mean they are born depressed.

But is a tendency toward happiness or sadness genetic? Researcher Marty Seligman, one of the most well-regarded psychologists of the 20th century, thinks so. Seligman was among the first to directly link stress with clinical depression. His previous research involved shocking dogs to the point of learned helplessness; perhaps in reaction to that, many years ago he switched gears. His new topic? Learned optimism.

The happiness thermostat

After years of researching optimism, Seligman concluded that everyone comes into this world with a happiness "set point," something akin to a behavioral thermostat that allows us to experience happiness within a certain behavioral range. This notion is based on the ideas of the late David Lykken, a behavioral geneticist at the University of Minnesota. Some children's set points are programmed to high; they are naturally happy regardless of the circumstances life throws at them. Some children's set points are programmed to low. They are by nature depressive, regardless of the circumstances life throws at them. Everybody else is in the middle.

This might sound a bit deterministic, and it is—sort of. Seligman is quick to caution us that what happiness you consistently experience also has nurture components. He even has a formula, the Happiness Equation, to measure how happy people are. It is the sum of that set point, plus certain circumstances in your life, plus factors under your voluntary control.

Not everybody agrees with Seligman; the Happiness Equation has elicited special criticism. A preponderance of evidence suggests there is something to this set-point idea, but it needs work. To date, no neurological regions have been found devoted exclusively to the thermostat. Or to being happy in general. At the molecular level, researchers have yet to isolate a "happiness" gene or its thermostatic regulators, though researchers are working on both. We'll take a closer look at these genes at the end of the chapter.

All of this work—starting with Baby 19, the distressed girl at the beginning of this chapter—suggests that genetic influences play an active role in our ability to experience sustained happiness.

Born with a temperament

Parents have known for centuries that babies come to this world with an inborn temperament. Scientist Jerome Kagan, who studied Baby 19, was the first to prove it. Human temperament is a complex, multidimensional concept—a child's characteristic way of responding emotionally and behaviorally to external events. These responses are fairly fixed and innate; you can observe them in your baby soon after he or she is born. Parents often confuse temperament with personality, but from a research perspective they aren't the same thing. Experimental psychologists often describe personality in much more mutable terms, as behavior shaped primarily by parental and cultural factors. Personality is influenced by temperament the same way a house is influenced by its foundation. Many researchers think temperament provides the emotional and behavioral building blocks upon which personalities are constructed.

High reactives vs. low reactives

Kagan was interested in one layer of temperament: how babies reacted when exposed to new things. He noticed that most babies took new things in stride, gazing calmly at new toys, curious and attentive to new inputs. But some babies were much edgier, more irritable. Kagan wanted to find a few of these more sensitive souls and follow them as they grew up. Babies 1 through 18 fit the first model just fine. These calm babies are said to have low-reactive temperaments. Baby 19 was completely different. She, and babies like her, have high-reactive temperaments.

The behavior remains remarkably stable over time, as Kagan found in his most well-known experiment. The study is still ongoing, having survived even the old sage's retirement (a colleague has taken it over). The experiment enrolled 500 kids, starting at 4 months of age, who were coded for low reactivity or high reactivity. He retested these same kids at ages 4, 7, 11 and 15; some beyond that. Kagan found that babies coded as highly reactive were four times more likely than controls to be behaviorally inhibited by age 4, exhibiting classic Baby 19 behavior. By age 7, half of these kids had developed some form of anxiety, compared with 10 percent of the controls. There is almost no crossover. In another study of 400 kids, only 3 percent switched behaviors after five years. Kagan calls this the long shadow of temperament.

Will you get an anxious baby?

A researcher friend of mine has two little girls, ages 6 and 9 as of this writing, and their temperaments could not be more Kaganesque. The 6-year-old is little Miss Sunshine, socially fearless, prone to taking risks, ebullient, confident. She will charge into a playroom full of strangers, initiate two conversations at once, quickly survey all of the toys in the room, and then lock down on the dolls, playing for hours. Her big sister is the opposite. She seems fearful and tentative, cautiously tiptoeing into the same playroom after only reluctantly leaving her mother's side. She then finds some safe corner and sits there. She shows no interest in exploring, hardly speaks at all, and appears scared if somebody tries to talk to her. My friends have their own Baby 19.

Will you have one, too? You stand a one-in-five chance. High reactives composed about 20 percent of the population in Kagan's studies. But how a highly reactive baby turns out depends on many things. Every brain is wired differently, so not every brain state sparks the same behavior. That's an important point. On top of that, high vs. low reactivity is only one dimension of temperament. Researchers look at everything from types of distress to attention span to sociability to activity level to the regularity of bodily functions. Studies like Kagan's make conclusions about tendencies, not destinies. The data do not forecast what these children will become so much as they predict what they will NOT become. Highly reactive infants will not grow up to be exuberant, outgoing, bubbly, or bold. The older daughter will never become the younger daughter.

And if your infant is highly reactive? She might seem hard to parent, but there's a silver lining. As these highly reactive children navigated through school, Kagan noticed, most were academically successful, even if they were a bucket of nerves. They made lots of friends. They were less likely to experiment with drugs, get pregnant, or drive recklessly. We think that's because of an anxiety-driven need to acquire compensatory mechanisms. Kagan regularly employed high reactives during his research career. "I always look for high reactives," he told the *New York Times*. "They're compulsive, and they don't make errors; they're careful when they're coding data."

Why are fussy babies later the most likely to comply with parental wishes, be better socialized, and get the best grades? Because they are the most sensitive to their environments, even if they snarl about being guided all the way. As long as you play an active, loving role in shaping behavior, even the most emotionally finicky among us will grow up well.

No one gene for temperament

So you can see temperament at birth, and it remains stable over time. Does that mean temperament is completely controlled by genes? Hardly. As we saw with the ice-storm children in the Pregnancy chapter, it is possible to create a stressed baby simply by increasing the mother's stress hormones—not a double helix in sight. The involvement of genes is a scientific question, not a scientific fact. Happily, it is being researched.

Studies of twins so far show that there is no one gene responsible for temperament. (Gene work almost always begins with twins, the gold standard being twins separated at birth and raised in different households.) When you look at the temperaments of identical twins, the degree of resemblance, the correlation, is about 0.4. This means there is probably some genetic contribution, but it is not a slam dunk. For fraternal twins and non-twin siblings, the correlation is between 0.15 and 0.18, even less of a slam dunk.

Studies suggest that fussy babies are later more likely to comply with your wishes, be better socialized, and get better grades.

But a few genes have been isolated that might help explain one of the most baffling phenomena in all of developmental psychology: the resilient kid.

How can a kid go through all that and turn out OK?

The civil war that gave rise to South Sudan, the world's newest nation, also generated the so-called Lost Boys of Sudan. Their story is familiar.

Families experienced unbelievable suffering during the war, resulting in the untethering of 20,000 young boys from their homes. Sometimes the untethering was deliberate: families encouraged sons to leave home, fearful they would be conscripted into soldiery.

Sometimes their parents were killed. These kids wandered around a war zone with no visible means of support, sometimes for years. Many died—from disease, wild animals, crime. The last thing you'd think is that one of these boys would graduate from Michigan State University with a master's degree in public health, and then return to Sudan to open up a health clinic.

Yet that is exactly what happened to Jacob Atem. Atem made it to Ethiopia and then a refugee camp in Kenya. At age 15, he was among a group of Lost Boys resettled in the United States. Atem later returned to Sudan to build a clinic that treats 100 patients a day. How could someone be so resilient after living through such violence? What not only kept Jacob from wilting but drove him to then become a force for good? Joan Hecht, who created the Alliance for the Lost Boys of Sudan, has an idea. The *New York Times* quoted Hecht in a story about Atem: "[S]o many of them had 'an inner strength and inner faith and inner drive to succeed,' motivated 'to bring pride and dignity to their family's name.' That same impulse, [Hecht] said, pushed many of them to leave the safety and comfort of the United States and return to their homeland to try to help."

How do we explain people like Jacob? The short answer is that we can't. Many kids are severely traumatized by abusive experiences. But not all. Kids like Jacob have an almost supernatural ability to rise above their circumstances. Researchers have spent entire careers trying to uncover the secrets of this resiliency. Geneticists recently have joined in, and their surprising results represent the cutting edge of behavioral research today.

Three resiliency genes

Human behavior is almost always governed by the concerted team-work of hundreds of genes. Nonetheless, as with any team sport, there are dominant players and minor ones. Though this work is at best preliminary, here are three genetic franchise players worth keeping an eye on. They may have a role in shaping the temperament and personality of our children.

Slow MAOA: Lessoning the pain of a trauma

Children who are sexually abused are at a much higher risk for becoming alcoholics—a fact researchers have known for years. They also are at greater risk for developing a debilitating mental-health issue called antisocial personality disorder. But this is decidedly *not* true if the child has a variant of a gene called MAOA, which stands for monoamine oxidase A. There are two versions of this gene, one we'll call "slow" and the other "fast." If the child has the slow version, she is surprisingly immune to the debilitating effects of her childhood. If she has the fast version, she falls into the stereotype. The fast version of this gene assists in hyper-stimulating the hippocampus and parts of the amygdala when a traumatic memory is remembered. The pain is too great; Jack Daniels is often turned to for relief. The slow version of this gene calms these systems remarkably. The traumas are there, but they lose their sting.

DRD4-7: A guard against insecurity

Children who grow up without parental support, or children who have cold and distant parents, often feel deeply insecure and act out in an effort to gain attention. The behavior is both understandable and obnoxious. But not all kids who have such mothers have this insecurity, and a group of researchers in the Netherlands think they know why. A gene called DRD4, which stands for dopamine receptor D4, is deeply involved. It is one of a family of molecules capable of binding to the neurotransmitter dopamine and exerting specific physiological effects. If children have a variation of this gene called DRD4-7, this insecurity never develops. It's as if the gene product coats the brain in Teflon. Kids without this variant have no such protection from the effects of insensitive parents; for kids who do, the increase is *sixfold*.

Long 5-HTT: Stress resistance

Researchers have known for years that some adults react to stressful, traumatic situations by taking them in stride. They may be debilitated for a while, but they eventually show solid signs of recovery. Other adults in the same situations experience deep depression and anxiety disorders, showing no signs of recovery after a few months. Some even commit suicide. These twin reactions are like grown-up versions of Kagan's low-reactive and high-reactive infants.

The gene 5-HTT, a serotonin transporter gene, may partially explain the difference. As the name suggests, the protein encoded by this gene acts like a semitruck, transporting the neurotransmitter serotonin to various regions of the brain. It comes in two forms, which I'll term "long" and "short" variants.

If you have the long form of this gene, you are in good shape. Your stress reactions, depending upon the severity and duration of the trauma, are in the "typical" range. Your risk for suicide is low and your chance at recovery high. If you have the short form of this gene, your risk for negative reactions, such as depression and longer recovery times, in the face of trauma is high. Interestingly, patients with this short variation also have difficulty regulating their emotions and don't socialize very well. Though the link has not been established, this sounds like Baby 19.

There really do appear to be children who are born stress-sensitive and children who are born stress-resistant. That we can in part tie this to a DNA sequence means that we can responsibly say it has a genetic basis. Which means that you could no more change this influence on your child's behavior than you could change her eye color.

Tendencies, not destinies

Take this genetic discussion with a boulder of salt. Some of these DNA-based findings require much more research to tie up important loose ends before we can label them as true. Some need to be replicated a few more times to be convincing. All show associations, not causations. Remember: Tendency is NOT destiny. Nurturing environments cast a large shadow over all of these chromosomes, a subject we will take up in the next chapter. Yet DNA deserves a place at the behavioral table, even if it's not always at the head, because the implications for moms and dads are staggering.

In the brave new world of medicine, genetic screens for these behaviors probably will become available to parents. Would it be valuable to know if your new baby is high or low reactive? A child who is vulnerable to stress would obviously need to be parented differently from one who is not. One day your pediatrician may be able to give you this information based on something as simple as a blood test. Such a test is far off in the future. For now, understanding your child's seeds of happiness will have to come from getting to know your child.

Key points

- The single best predictor of happiness? Having friends.
- Children who learn to regulate their emotions have deeper friendships than those who don't.
- No single area of the brain processes all emotions. Widely distributed neural networks play critical roles.
- Emotions are incredibly important to the brain. They act like Post-it notes, helping the brain identify, filter, and prioritize.
- There may be a genetic component to how happy your child can become.

reminder: references at www.brainrules.net/references

happy baby: soil

brain rule

Labeling emotions calms big feelings

happy baby: soil

 "Not CARROT!" shrieked 2-year-old Tyler as his mother, Rachel, tried to provide a sensible alternative to his growing interests in sweets. "COOKIE! Tyler wants COOKIE!" Tyler collapsed into a screaming heap, fists pounding the floor. "COOKIE! COOKIE! COOKIE!" he raged. When Tyler found out about chocolate-chip cookies, his sole goal in life became to stuff as many as he could into his mouth.

Rachel, a hyper-organized marketing executive turned stay-at-home mom, had been someone who rarely lost her temper. Or her to-do list. But these battalion-strength temper tantrums were too much. And they were inescapable. If Rachel left the room, Tyler became a cruise missile. He would stop crying while he sought her out and then, maternal target acquired, would throw himself back on the floor and resume his explosive grand mals. Most days, Rachel would become furious, then hide, sometimes locking herself in the bathroom and putting her fingers in her ears. She told herself that any feeling—joy, fear, anger—was good to express, whether hers or her son's. Tyler would eventually work things out by himself, she hoped, if she left him to his own devices. Instead, Tyler's behavior steadily worsened. So did Rachel's. Familial clouds regularly gathered in the morning for a day's worth of behavioral storms. Rachel became increasingly anxious and uncomposed as the day progressed, rather like her son. Nothing in her life—professional or personal—had prepared her for anything like this. She wanted to take parenting one day at a time, but when Tyler acted like this, she felt as if several days assaulted her simultaneously.

Rachel, along with every other parent, can do some concrete things to increase the probability of raising a happy child—regardless of the temperamental dictates we discussed in the previous chapter. I start with Tyler's tantrum because of a startling fact: How Rachel responds to Tyler's intense emotions *profoundly* matters to his future happiness. In fact, her response is one of the greatest predictors of how he will turn out as a young man. It affects his ability to empathize with people and thus maintain friendships—big factors in human happiness. It will even affect his grade-point average. Starting with the process of bonding with baby, parents who pay close attention to the emotional lives of their children, in a very particular manner, have the best shot at making them happy. The point of this chapter is to explain what "very particular manner" means.

Attentive, patient ping-pong

One excellent person to start off our discussion is a researcher who has studied the emotional lives of children—and how parents interact with them—for decades. He sports a name right out of a 1950s science-fiction movie, Ed Tronick.

Tronick has a ready smile, deep-blue eyes, and a shock of white hair. He likes to attend Boston Red Sox games, though he can practically watch them from his research office, which overlooks the players' entrance on Yawkey Way. He was an antiwar activist in the

1960s and one of the first "parenting" researchers to live in other cultures, spending quality time with moms and dads in Peru, in the Democratic Republic of the Congo, and in plenty of other places. But he's most known for something you can see in a game of peekaboo. It's the power of two-way communication in cementing relationships between a parent and child. Here's an example, taken from Tronick's research files:

> The infant abruptly turns away from his mother as the game reaches its peak of intensity and begins to suck on his thumb and stare into space with a dull facial expression. The mother stops playing and sits back, watching.... After a few seconds, the infant turns back to her with an inviting expression. The mother moves closer, smiles, and says in a high-pitched, exaggerated voice, "Oh, now you're back!" He smiles in response and vocalizes. As they finish crowing together, the infant reinserts his thumb and looks away. The mother again waits ... the infant turns ... to her, and they greet each other with big smiles.

Notice two things: (1) the 3-month-old has a rich emotional life, and (2) the mother paid close attention to it. She knew when to interact and when to withdraw. I have seen dozens of delightful research videos showing this choreography between thoughtful parents and their babies, and every one of them looks like a wonderful, messy ping-pong game. The communication is uneven, doled out in fits and starts, mostly led by baby, and always two-way. Tronick calls it "interaction synchrony." Attentive, patient interactivity actually helps your baby's neural architecture develop in a positive way, tilting her toward emotional stability. The brain of a baby who doesn't experience synchronous interaction can develop very differently.

In that game of peekaboo, it is obvious that the baby and his mother have already formed a reciprocating relationship. In the late 1960s, researchers coined a term to describe it: attachment.

Attachment theory springs from the finding that babies come into this world preloaded with lots of emotional and relational abilities. At birth, babies appear to express disgust, distress, interest, and contentment. Within six months, they experience anger, fear, sadness, surprise, and joy. Give them another year and they will feel embarrassment, jealousy, guilt, and maybe even pride. These emotions are like RoboCop's tags (or Post-it notes, if you prefer) telling the brain, "Pay attention to this!" Different kids tag different things. It's as random as a newborn's fascination with Dad's beard, an infant's distress at wearing socks, or a toddler's fear or love of dogs. Knowing what your kids tag—what things they have an emotional reaction to—and then responding to that knowledge in specific ways is not only part of the attachment process, but one of the big secrets to raising happy kids.

Babies are born with the ability to relate for the evolutionary reasons we discussed in the Relationship chapter: It's an especially handy skill for a helpless infant who needs to quickly establish secure relationships with those who can feed him. Given that most adults are oddly moved by the presence of a baby, the relationship soon becomes an exercise in mutual tagging. As this two-way communication solidifies, the baby is said to become "attached." Attachment is understood as a reciprocal emotional relationship between an older baby and an adult.

The attachment bond is made stronger and more intimate through a variety of experiences, many involving how attentive a parent is to the baby in the early years (though genetic factors appear to play a strong role, too). If the bonding process runs into turbulence, the baby is said to be insecurely attached. These kids don't grow up to be as happy. Their scores on social responsiveness tests are almost two-thirds lower than those of securely attached children. As they grow up, they exhibit more than twice the emotional conflict in their interpersonal lives as do securely attached infants. They show less empathy and tend to be more irritable. They also get the poorest grades.

Attachment takes years

Attachment theory has been wildly misinterpreted in the media, at one point couched as if babies were born with a quick-drying relational paste. Immediately after birth, all kinds of things had to be done in hurry—setting the baby on mom's belly was popular—before the paste dried and the critical attachment period passed. These notions are still out there.

One colleague told me he had just finished a lecture on attachment when a woman named Susan came up to him at the lectern. "I am not sure what to do," she began. Susan had had her first baby a month prior, and after an extraordinarily difficult labor, she had fallen into an exhausted stupor. "I slept through my attachment!" Susan said, tears welling in her eyes. "Will my baby still like me?" Susan was in a panic that her relationship had been permanently damaged. She had heard from a friend that one maternity ward had put up a sign saying, "Please do not remove babies from mothers until after bonding has taken place." Good grief.

My colleague tried to reassure her that nothing was wrong, that no developmental insult had irreversibly exerted itself, and that she could look forward to many mutually fulfilling hours with her newborn.

Attachment is more like slow-drying cement than quick-setting superglue. Infants start to develop flexible working models of how people relate to each other almost as soon as they are born. They then use this information to figure out how to survive, with parents being the natural first target. The relationships that form from this activity slowly develop over time, perhaps two years or longer. Parents who consistently apply attention—especially in these early years—statistically raise the happiest kids.

Parenting is not for sissies

Is synchronously playing with your baby on a sustained basis all you need to do? Hardly. It may be necessary (and delightful) to interact with your 3-month-old, but that is not enough to turn him into a happy citizen. Kids have to grow up sometime, a process that naturally changes their behavior and complicates their relationships with just about everybody. As a parent, you will have to adapt to their changes. Parenting is wonderful. But it is not for sissies. How radical can these behavioral changes appear? Listen in on these parents:

> How the hell did my sweetie pie daughter turn into the devil overnight upon turning 3? Today she told me that she doesn't like me and is going to stab me. She tried to step on the fingers of a 14 month old and exclaimed, "Goddammit" out of the blue.

> Ugh. I just screamed at my 5 yr old. I asked him to stop running around several times because I have things out that he and his sister keep tripping over. (I'm cleaning). He looked at me with a snide grin and kept running. Like a test. I LOST it. I'd tried giving him stuff to help me with to keep him occupied, but he wanted to run around instead. I felt bad about losing it, but geez, what do you do when nice doesn't work?

You can feel the transitions occurring in the hearts of these poor mothers. But even though potty-mouthed 3-year-olds and strong-willed preschoolers almost certainly exist in your future, there is also this:

> I fixed my 3 year old daughter's hair today, and she looked in the mirror, gave me a thumbs up and said "Rock on, girlfriend!" LOL!!!

This strange sinner/saint combination of behaviors is often described as the terrible twos (though it is actually threes, fours, and beyond, as these forum posts attest). By the second year of baby-world, moms and dads are evolving, too. They have begun switching from cooing caregivers and glorified playmates to rule-breathing, hair-pulling, count-to-10-before-you-yell *parents*. The transition is natural. So is the frustration. Most people learn a lot from kids at these stages, including how little patience they possess. Soldiering on is a must, of course, but the way you do it matters if your goal is to raise a happy kid.

A terrific kid

What kind of kid are we talking about? I think of my friend Doug, who attended my high school in the early 1970s. Doug was as sharp as a whip—really good at math, but he could just as easily have joined the debate team. He held his own in just about every subject to which he applied himself. Doug would eventually become valedictorian, a fact he seemed to take as a given even as a freshman. Doug was also athletic (wide receiver on varsity), comfortably self-confident (with an easy smile), and graced with an almost pharmaceutical-grade optimism. To top it off, Doug was as disarmingly humble as he was socially confident. This made him extremely popular. By all appearances Doug seemed intelligent, gifted, motivated, well socialized, *happy*. Was it all an act, or was it something in Doug's physiology?

A fair amount of data suggests that kids like Doug are, in fact, measurably different. Their unconscious ability to regulate their autonomic nervous systems—something we call vagal tone—shows off-the-charts stability. Doug is emblematic of a small but very important cadre of terrific kids who exist all over the world. These children:

- have better emotional regulation, calming themselves more quickly.

- have the highest academic achievement.
- show greater empathetic responses.
- show greater loyalty to parents and have a higher compliance rate with parental wishes, the obedience coming from feelings of connection rather than from fear.
- have fewer incidences of pediatric depression and anxiety disorders.
- have the fewest infectious diseases.
- are less prone to acts of violence.
- have deeper, richer friendships, and lots more of them.

That last fact gives them their best shot at being happy. These findings have prompted more than one parent to ask:

"Where do you go to get kids like this?"

Doug's parents weren't psychologists. They were owners of a moderately successful grocery store, married for 20 years, apparently happy and well-adjusted. And clearly they were doing something right.

Researchers, too, wanted to know how to get kids like Doug. It's about as important an issue to the success of a culture that exists. In the absence of rigorous, randomized, longitudinal studies, some terrific investigators did the next best thing. They studied families who consistently produced terrific kids, then analyzed what their parents did that was so darned nourishing. They wondered if perhaps these parents had a few things in common. In other words: Did certain parenting skills correlate so strongly with the hoped-for outcomes that they could predict how *any* kid turned out?

Yes, it turns out. Though the data are associative, they are sophisticated. Regardless of race or income, parents who end up with great kids do similar kinds of things over and over again. We can certainly argue about what a happy kid really looks like and the fundamentals of parenting practice. But if those bullet points look compelling to you, we know how to get you there. The research is statistically complex, but I will recruit a recipe from one of America's favorite chefs to help us describe those common traits. His name is Bobby Flay, and his recipe is for barbecued chicken.

Bobby Flay has red hair and a New York accent, owns a line of successful restaurants, and has been celebrity chef in chief of the United States for years. He is known for creating Southwestern recipes for people who enjoy taking regular trips to the top of the food pyramid, where all the fats and meats dwell. Fortunately for health-conscious consumers, Flay has also created tasty dishes that don't add girth simply by inhaling their aromas. One of them is a dry rub for baked chicken. Dry rubs are spices mixed together, then massaged into the meat to season it before cooking.

For our purposes, the chicken is your child's emotional life. The spices, six of them, are your parenting behaviors. When parents properly spice this chicken on a regular basis, they increase their probability of raising a happy kid.

Emotions must be central

Parents face many issues on a daily basis in the raising of kids, but not all of them affect how their children turn out. There is one that does. How you deal with the *emotional* lives of your children—your ability to detect, react to, promote, and provide instruction about emotional regulation—has the greatest predictive power over your baby's future happiness.

Fifty years of research, from Diana Baumrind and Haim Ginott to Lynn Katz and John Gottman, have come to this conclusion. That's why your child's emotional life takes the central role, the chicken, in our metaphor. You won't get any of the other benefits of the recipe unless you have placed the meat of the matter squarely in the center of your parenting behavior. The critical issue is your behavior when your children's emotions become intense (Gottman would say "hot") enough to push you out of your comfort zone.

Here are the six spices that go into this parental dry rub:

- a demanding but warm parenting style
- comfort with your own emotions
- tracking your child's emotions
- verbalizing emotions
- running toward emotions
- two tons of empathy

1. A demanding but warm parenting style

We know a great deal about what works thanks, in part, to developmental psychologist Diana Baumrind. She was born in New York City in 1927 to lower-middle-class Jewish immigrants. She is spicy as cayenne and known for taking a fellow researcher to task over an ethics violation (Yale psychologist Stanley Milgram, who duped a group of undergraduates into thinking they were shocking people to death). Baumrind had a second career as a human-rights activist and was investigated for un-American activities by Joe McCarthy in the 1950s. She does her science at—where else?—the University of California–Berkeley. In the mid-1960s, Baumrind published her ideas on parenting, a framework so robust that researchers still use it today. You can think of her ideas as the four styles of child rearing. Baumrind described two dimensions in parenting, each on a continuum:

- **Responsiveness.** This is the degree to which parents respond to their kids with support, warmth, and acceptance. Warm parents mostly communicate their affection for their kids. Hostile parents mostly communicate their rejection of their kids.

- **Demandingness.** This is the degree to which a parent attempts to exert behavioral control. Restrictive parents tend to make and enforce rules mercilessly. Permissive parents don't make *any* rules.

Putting these dimensions in the form of a two-by-two grid creates four parenting styles that have been studied. Only one style produces happy children.

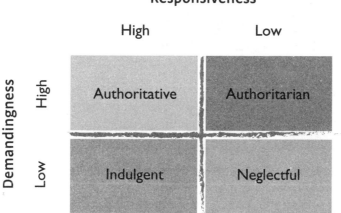

Responsiveness

Authoritarian: Too hard

Unresponsive plus demanding. Exerting power over their kids is very important to these parents, and their kids are often afraid of them. They do not try to explain their rules and do not project any warmth.

Indulgent: Too soft

Responsive plus undemanding. These parents truly love their kids but have little ability to make and enforce rules. They subsequently avoid confrontation and seldom demand compliance with family rules. These parents are often bewildered by the task of raising kids.

Neglectful: Too aloof

Unresponsive plus undemanding. Probably the worst of the lot. These parents care little about their children and are uninvolved in their day-to-day interactions, providing only the most basic care.

Authoritative: Just right

Responsive plus demanding. The best of the lot. These parents are demanding, but they care a great deal about their kids. They explain their rules and encourage their children to state their reactions to them. They encourage high levels of independence, yet see that children comply with family values. These parents tend to have terrific communication skills with their children.

Neglecting parents tended to produce the worst-behaved, most emotionally challenged kids on the block; they got the worst grades, too. Authoritative parents produced Doug.

Baumrind's insights were confirmed in a massive 1994 study involving thousands of students as they entered adolescence in California and Wisconsin. Based solely on parenting behavior, researchers successfully predicted how the kids would turn out, regardless of ethnicity. Further work has supported and extended Baumrind's initial ideas. This later generation of researchers asked a simple question: How did the parents come to fall into one of those four parenting styles? The answer is in our next spice.

2. Comfort with your own emotions

Imagine your best friend is over for a chat, and her 4-year-old fraternal twins, Brandon and Madison, are playing in the basement. Suddenly, you're interrupted by shouting. The twins have gotten into an argument: One wants to play "army men" with some figurines; the other wants to play house with them. "Gimme those!" you hear Brandon shout, trying to corral the figurines for himself. "No fair!" shouts Madison, grabbing some from Brandon's stash. "I want some, too!" Your friend wants you to think she has little angels, not devils, and she marches downstairs. "You brats!" she bellows. "Why can't you play nice? Can't you see you're embarrassing me?" Brandon begins to cry, and Madison sulks, glaring at the floor. "I am raising a bunch of wimps," she mutters, marching back upstairs.

What would you do in that situation, if you were the twins' parent? Believe it or not, psychologists can, with some certainty, predict what you will do. John Gottman calls it your meta-emotion philosophy. A meta-emotion is how you feel about feelings ("meta" literally means ascending, or looking from above).

Some people welcome emotional experiences, considering them an important and enriching part of life's journey. Others think that emotions make people weak and embarrassed and that emotions should be suppressed. Some people think a few emotions are OK, like joy and happiness, but some should stay on a behavioral no-fly list; anger, sadness, and fear are popular choices. Still others don't know what to do with their emotions and try to run from them. That's Rachel at the beginning of this chapter. Whatever you feel about feelings—your own or other people's—is your meta-emotion philosophy. Can you discern Baumrind's four parenting styles in these attitudes?

Your meta-emotion philosophy turns out to be very important to your children's future. It predicts how you will react to their emotional lives, which in turn predicts how (or if) they learn to regulate their own emotions. Because these skills are directly related to a child's social competency, how you feel about feelings can profoundly influence your child's future happiness. You have to be comfortable with *your* emotions in order to make your kids comfortable with *theirs*.

3. Tracking emotions

You can get a snapshot of family life by the way people talk about it. Sometimes an entire relationship spills out of a few sentences. Gwyneth Paltrow, star of stage and screen, grew up in the business, her mom an actress, her dad a director. Her parents stayed together their entire lives, which, given the gravitational pull of the profession, is something of a miracle. In *Parade* magazine in 1998, Paltrow related the following story about her dad.

When I was 10, we went to England. My mother was shooting a miniseries there.... My dad took me to Paris for the weekend. We had the most amazing time. On the plane back to London, he asked me, "Do you know why I took you to Paris, only you and me?" And I said, "Why?" And he said, "Because I wanted you to see Paris for the first time with a man who would always love you."

When Paltrow won an Oscar in 1999, she gave a famously gushing and tearful acceptance speech, saying she was full of gratitude that, because of her family, she could know what love is. Bruce Paltrow died four years later. But his loving comment remains an excellent example of what I'll call "balanced emotional surveillance."

Earlier I mentioned parents paying close attention to the emotional lives of their children *in a particular manner.* You could see it with the mom and baby playing peekaboo in Tronick's laboratory:

The mother stops playing and sits back, watching.... After a few seconds, the infant turns back to her with an inviting expression. The mother moves closer, smiles, and says in a high-pitched, exaggerated voice, "Oh, now you're back!" He smiles in response and vocalizes.

The mom was extraordinarily attuned to her child's emotional cues. She knew that her baby's turning away probably meant he needed a break from the sensory flood he was receiving. Mom withdrew, waited patiently, and did not resume until baby signaled he was no longer flooding. He could then be delighted when mom returned, smiling, rather than staying overstimulated by her persistence and probably crying. The total elapsed time was less than five seconds, but, stretched over years, this emotional sensitivity can make all the difference between a productive kid and a juvenile delinquent.

Parents with the happiest kids started this habit early in their parenting careers and then continued it over the years. They kept track of their children's emotions the way some people keep track of their stock portfolios or favorite baseball team. They did not pay attention in a controlling, insecure style but in a loving, unobtrusive way, like a caring family physician. They knew when their kids were happy, sad, fearful, or joyful, often without asking. They could read and interpret with astonishing accuracy their child's verbal and nonverbal cues.

The power of prediction

Why does this work? We know only a couple parts of the story. The first is that parents who possess *emotional* information gain the great power of behavioral prediction. Moms and dads become so acquainted with their children's psychological interiors, they become pros at forecasting probable reactions to almost any situation. This results in an instinctive feel about what is most likely to be helpful, hurtful, or neutral to their child, and in a wide variety of circumstances. That's about as valuable a parenting skill as you can have.

The second is that parents who continue paying attention over the years are not caught off guard by their children's ever changing emotional development. That's important, given the tectonic shifts that occur in the brain's development during childhood. As kids' brains change, their behavior changes, which results in more brain changes. These parents experience fewer surprises as their children grow up.

Emotional surveillance comes with a caveat, however, for it is possible to give too much of a good thing. In the late 1980s, researchers were somewhat startled to find that when parents paid too much attention to their kids' cues—responding to every gurgle, burp, and cough—the kids became *less* securely attached. Children (like anybody) didn't take too well to being smothered. The stifling seemed to interfere with emotional self-regulation, messing with a natural need for space and independence.

In that game of peekaboo, note how many times the mother backed off in response to the baby's cues. Most parents initially have a tough time understanding when their children are feeling loved and when they are feeling crowded. Some never get it. One probable reason is that the ratio is different from one kid to the next—and maybe from one day to the next. Nonetheless, you need a balance (go ahead and insert our entire Goldilocks discussion right here). Parents who resisted giving in to their inner helicopter helped create the most secure attachments.

4. Verbalizing emotions

"I don't like it," the 3-year-old muttered to herself as the guests left. Miserable throughout her older sister's birthday party, she was now growing angry. "I want *Ally's* doll, not *this* one!" Her parents had bought her a consolation present, but the strategy went down like a lead balloon. The girl threw her doll to the floor. "Ally's doll! Ally's doll!" She began to cry. You can imagine a parent making any of several choices in the face of this bubbling brew.

"You seem sad. Are you sad?" is what the girl's dad said. The little girl nodded, still angry, too. The dad continued. "I think I know why. You're sad because Ally's gotten all the presents. You only got one!" The little girl nodded again. "You want the same number and you can't have it, and that's unfair and that makes you sad." The dad seemed to be pouring it on. "Whenever somebody gets something I want and I don't, I get sad, too." Silence.

Then the dad said the line most characteristic of a verbalizing parent. "We have a word for that feeling, honey," he said. "Do you want to know what that word is?" She whimpered, "OK." He held her in his arms. "We call it being jealous. You wanted Ally's presents, and you couldn't have them. You were jealous." She cried softly but was beginning to calm down. "Jealous," she whispered. "Yep," Dad replied, "and it's an icky feeling." "I been jealous all day," she replied, nestling into her daddy's big strong arms.

This big-hearted father is good at (a) labeling his feelings and (b) teaching his daughter to label hers. He knows what sadness in his own heart feels like and announces it easily. He knows what sadness in his child's heart looks like, and he is teaching her to announce it, too. He is also good at teaching joy, anger, disgust, concern, fear—the entire spectrum of his little girl's experience.

Research shows that this labeling habit is a dominant behavior for all parents who raise happy children. Kids who are exposed to this parenting behavior on a regular basis become better at self-soothing, are more able to focus on tasks, and have more successful peer relationships. Sometimes knowing what to do is tougher than knowing what to say. But sometimes saying is all that's needed.

Labeling emotions is neurologically calming

Notice in the story that as the dad addressed his daughter's feelings directly, the little girl began to calm down. This is a common finding; you can measure it in the laboratory. Verbalizing has a soothing effect on the nervous systems of children. (Adults, too.) Thus, the Brain Rule: Labeling emotions calms big feelings.

Here's what we think is going on in the brain. Verbal and nonverbal communication are like two interlocking neurological systems. Infants' brains haven't yet connected these systems very well. Their bodies can feel fear, disgust, and joy way before their brains can talk about them. This means that *children will experience the physiological characteristics of emotional responses before they know what those responses are.* That's why large feelings are often scary for little people; tantrums often self-feed because of this fear. That's not a sustainable gap. Kids will need to find out what's going on with their big feelings, however scary they seem at first. They need to connect these two neurological systems. Researchers believe that learning to label emotions provides the linkage. The earlier this bridge gets constructed, the more likely you are to see self-soothing behaviors, along with a large raft of other benefits. Researcher Carroll Izard has shown that in households that do not provide such instruction, these nonverbal and verbal systems remain somewhat disconnected or integrate in unhealthy ways. Without labels to describe the feelings they have, children can remain confused by a cacophony of physiological experiences.

I've seen the power of labeling firsthand. One of my sons could easily conjure up Richter-scale tantrums. I knew from the research literature that occasional tantrums are normal for kids in the first couple of years, mostly because their sense of independence plays a game of chicken with their emotional maturity. But my heart would sometimes break for him. He seemed so unhappy and sometimes quite scared. I would always move as close as I physically could to him when this occurred, just to reassure him that someone who will always love him was nearby (everyone can learn from Bruce Paltrow).

One day, as he was subsiding from a particularly fierce temblor, I looked at him squarely and said, "You know, son. We have a word for this feeling. I would like to tell you that word. Is that OK?" He nodded, still crying. "It is called being 'frustrated.' You are feeling frustrated. Can you say 'frustrated'?" He suddenly looked at me as if he had been hit by a train. "Frustrated! I am FRUSTRATED!!" Still sobbing, he grabbed my leg, holding on for dear life. "Frustrated! Frustrated! Frustrated!" he kept repeating, as if the words were some kind of harness tossed to him from a first responder. He quickly calmed down.

There they were, just as the research literature said: the powerful calming neurological effects of learning to verbalize one's feelings. Now it was my turn to become misty-eyed.

What if you're not used to examining emotions?

You may need to practice labeling your *own* emotions out loud. When you experience happiness, disgust, anger, joy, just say so. To your spouse, to the air, to God and His host of angels. This can be tougher than you think, especially if you are not used to delving into your psychological interiors and declaring what you find. But do it for your kids. Remember, adult behaviors influence child behaviors in two ways: by example and through direct intervention. Establish a habit of labeling emotions now. Then, by the time your little bundle of joy goes verbal, she will have a heaping dose of examples to follow while you raise her. The benefit will last the rest of her life.

Just one note: The point of this training is to increase your awareness. You can be aware of your emotions without being highly emotive. You are not obligated to perform an emotional striptease to just anybody simply because you are aware of what you are feeling. What's key is that:

- you know when you are experiencing an emotion.
- you can identify the emotion quickly and can verbalize it on demand.
- you can recognize that same emotion in other people just as quickly.

10 years of music lessons

There's another powerful way to fine-tune a child's hearing for the emotional aspects of speech: musical training. Researchers in the Chicago area showed that musically experienced kids—those who studied any instrument for at least 10 years, starting before age 7—responded with greased-lightning speed to subtle variations in emotion-laden cues, such as a baby's cry. The scientists tracked changes in the timing, pitch, and timbre of the baby's cry, all the while eavesdropping on the musician's brain stem (the most ancient part of the brain) to see what happened.

Kids without rigorous musical training didn't show as much discrimination. Their brains didn't pick up on the fine-grained information embedded in the signal and were, so to speak, more emotionally tone deaf. Dana Strait, first author of the study, wrote: "That their brains respond more quickly and accurately than the brains of nonmusicians is something we'd expect to translate into the perception of emotion in other settings."

This finding is remarkably clear, beautifully practical, and a bit unexpected. It suggests that if you want happy kids later in life, get them started on a musical journey early in life. Then make sure they stick with it until they are old enough to start filling out their applications to Harvard, probably humming all the way.

5. Running toward emotions

It's every parent's worst nightmare: your child caught in a life-threatening situation, clinging for dear life by the slimmest of margins, you impotent to help. In February 1996, 15-year-old Marglyn Paseka and a friend were playing in Mantanzas Creek when they were suddenly swept up in a central California flash flood. Her companion managed to scramble up the bank, running to safety. Not Marglyn. She was left clinging to a branch, water racing around her like rush-hour traffic, for 45 minutes. By the time the first responders arrived, she did not have much strength left. Onlookers, including her mom, were screaming.

Fireman Don Lopez did not scream. Without hesitation, he lowered himself into the raging, frigid waters and began trying to attach a safety harness to the young girl. He failed, once, twice … several times. The girl's strength was nearly exhausted when Lopez, at the last second, finally got her attached. Photojournalist Annie Wells was on the scene working for the Santa Rosa *Press Democrat*, and she captured that moment (along with a Pulitzer Prize). It is an incredible photo to see, the weakened teenager nearly letting go of the branch, the muscular fireman saving her life. Like first responders everywhere, when everyone else was either screaming, sitting on the sidelines, or running away, Lopez ran toward trouble.

Parents who raise kids like my friend Doug, the valedictorian, have this type of courage in spades. They are fearless in the face of raging floods of emotions from their child. They don't try to shoot down emotions, ignore them, or let them have free reign over the welfare of the family. Instead, these parents get involved in their kids' strong feelings. They have four attitudes toward emotions (yes, their meta-emotions):

- They do not judge emotions.
- They acknowledge the reflexive nature of emotions.
- They know that behavior is a choice, even though an emotion is not.
- They see a crisis as a teachable moment.

They do not judge emotions

Many families actively discourage the expression of tough emotions like fear and anger. Happiness and tranquility, meanwhile, make it to the top of the list of "approved" emotions. To parents of Dougs all over the world, there is no such thing as a bad emotion. There is no such thing as a good emotion. An emotion is either there—or it is not. These parents seem to know that emotions don't make people weak and they don't make people strong. They only make people human. The result is a savvy let the children be-who-they-are attitude.

They acknowledge that emotional reactions are reflexive

Some families deal with hot emotions by actively ignoring them, hoping their kids will "snap out of it" as adults do. But denying the existence of emotions can make them worse. (People who deny their feelings often make bad choices, which is what usually gets them into trouble.) Parents in the studies who raised the happiest children understood that no technique known to humankind can make a feeling go away, even if nobody wants the feeling around. Initial emotional reactions are as automatic as blinking. They don't disappear simply because someone thinks they should.

How might the attitudes of discouraging or ignoring emotions play out in real life? Imagine that the family goldfish, the only pet your 3-year-old son Kyle has ever known, suddenly dies. Visibly upset, Kyle mopes around the house all day, saying things like "I want fishy back!" and "Bring him back!" You've tried to ignore him, but his moodiness eventually grates on you. What do you do?

One response might be: "Kyle, I'm sorry your fish is dead, but it's really no big deal. He's just a fish. Death is part of life, and you need to learn that. You wipe those tears away, son, and go outside and play." Another might be: "That's OK, honey. You know, the fish was already old when you were born. We'll go to the store tomorrow and get you another one. Now put on that happy face, and go outside and play."

Both responses completely ignore how Kyle is feeling at the moment. One seems to actively disapprove of Kyle's grief; the other is trying to anesthetize it. Neither *deals* with his intense emotions. They give him no tools that might help him navigate through his grief. Know what Kyle might be thinking? "If this is not supposed to matter, why do I still have this big feeling? What I am supposed to do with it? There must be something really wrong with me."

They know that behavior is a choice, even though an emotion is not

Day to day, parents of happy kids do not allow bad behavior simply because they understand where it came from. A little girl might slap her baby brother because she feels threatened. That does not make slapping OK. These parents understand that kids have a choice in how they express emotions, reflexive though emotions can be. They have a list filled not with *emotions* that are approved and disapproved but *actions* that are. And the parents put teeth into it, consistently teaching their kids which choices are appropriate and which are not. Parents of kids like Doug speak softly but carry an obvious rule book.

Some families don't make a rule book. Some parents let their kids freely express whatever emotions they have, then allow whatever behavior the kid engages in to spew forth all over the world. They believe there is little you can do about a stream of negative emotions, except perhaps to scramble up the bank and let the flood pass by. Parents with these attitudes are descending into an abdication of their parenting responsibilities. Statistically, they will raise the most troubled children of any parenting style ever tested.

It's a myth that releasing emotions makes everything better (that blowing your top will defuse your anger, for example). "Better out than in," the saying goes. Almost half a century's worth of research shows that "blowing off steam" usually *increases* aggression. The only time expressing anger in that style helps is when it is accompanied immediately by constructive problem solving. As C. S. Lewis observed in *The Silver Chair*, one book in the Chronicles of Narnia series: "Crying is all right in its own way while it lasts. But you have to stop sooner or later, and then you still have to decide what to do."

They see a crisis as a teachable moment

Parents who raise the happiest kids constantly rummage through their offspring's intense feelings looking for stray teachable moments. They seem to have an intuitive sense that people produce lasting change only in response to a crisis. And they often welcome these intense moments of possibility.

"You never want a serious crisis to go to waste" is an attitude as common in these households as it is in certain political circles. The problem the child is having may seem ridiculously small to the parents, not something that should take up precious time. But these parents realize they don't need to like the problem to solve it. They regularly replace the words "potential catastrophe" with "potential lesson," which puts a very different spin on what a catastrophe is.

This has two long-term consequences. First, it makes parents remarkably relaxed in the face of the emotional meltdowns. That pays dividends, for it gives children a powerful example to emulate when their own crises come into their adult lives. Second, there are fewer emotional disasters. That's because timing is important: The best way to limit the damage of a house fire is to put it out quickly. If you run toward the fire rather than ignore it, your repair bills are likely to be smaller. How do you put out the fire? That's our sixth spice.

6. Two tons of empathy

Let's say you are waiting in a long line at the post office with your rest-less 2-year-old, Emily. She announces, "I want a glass of water." You calmly respond, "Honey, I can't get you water right now. The drinking fountain is broken." Emily starts to whine. "I want some water!" Her voice cracks. You anticipate what's coming, and your blood pressure begins to rise. "We'll have to wait until we get home. There's no water here," you say. She retorts, "I want water NOW!" The exchange escalates in intensity, in danger of erupting into a very public fight.

What now? Here are three tactics you might take:

- You choose to disregard the child's feelings and say brusquely, "I said, wait until we get home. There's no water here. Now be quiet."

- Anxious about a potential embarrassing meltdown, you condemn your child's reactions and hiss, "Will you *please* be quiet? Do *not* embarrass me in public."

- Not knowing what to do, you shrug your shoulders and smile limply as your child takes over. Her emotions reach critical mass, then explode all over your parenting skills.

Haim Ginott, one of the most influential child psychologists of his generation, would say none of those are good choices. He proposed a series of parental "to-dos" in the late 1960s that have since proved, after years of testing in John Gottman's labs and others', to be quite prescient.

Here's what you are supposed to do instead: You acknowledge the child's feelings and empathize. "You're thirsty, aren't you? Getting a big gulp of cold water would feel so good. I wish that drinking foun-tain was working so I could lift you up and let you drink as much as you wanted."

Sound odd? Many parents would expect this response to make things worse, like trying to extinguish a flame by dousing it with lighter fluid. But the data are remarkably clear. Empathy reflexes and the coaching strategies that surround them are the only behaviors known consistently to defuse intense emotional situations over the short term—and reduce their frequency over the long term. Note how you're running toward your child's reactions in that fourth response rather than away from them. Note how you verbalize her feelings, validating them, signaling understanding. This is empathy. Lynn Katz at the University of Washington calls it the "coaching of emotions." So does Gottman. The idea springs directly from Ginott's insights about how to raise happy children. So what should Rachel have said to Tyler, the kid who wanted cookies instead of carrots at the beginning of this chapter? She should have started with stating the obvious: "You want a cookie, don't you, dear?"

We think there are several physiological reasons empathy works, thanks to seemingly unrelated research efforts: an attempt to understand crowd behavior and an attempt to characterize the optimal doctor-patient relationship.

Emotions are contagious

A person tends to experience feelings generated by the emotions of surrounding crowds. If people around you are fearful, angry, or violent, you often "catch" the same feelings, as if they were a virus. Investigators interested in how mobs influence individual behavior discovered this emotional contagion. It applies to a broad swath of emotional experiences, including humor. You have been exposed to this for years. In an attempt to get you to "catch" feelings of humor, TV-based sitcoms often include laugh tracks.

Empathy calms the nerves

The second set of studies looked at how to optimize doctor-patient relationships. It was puzzling: Therapists whose heart rates and skin temperatures were synchronized to their patients' during clinical interviews found that their patients got better faster, and more completely, than therapists whose physiologies didn't synchronize. The term is called, appropriately enough, physiological synchrony. Patients of these "empathetic" doctors routinely recovered from colds faster, bounced back from surgery more quickly and with fewer complications, and were less likely to sue for malpractice. The presence of empathy is actually a health-cost issue.

This biological finding led directly to the discovery that empathy calms people down. When the brain perceives empathy, the vagus nerve relaxes the body. This nerve connects the brain stem to other areas of the body, including the abdomen, chest, and neck. When it is overstimulated, it causes pain and nausea.

This may take practice

It's understandable if you find it hard to project empathy on a sustained basis. You may discover when you first have children how profoundly your former world was about you, you, you. Now it is all about them, them, them. This is one of the hardest parts of that social contract. But your ability to move from *you* to *them*, which is what empathy forces anyone to do, makes all the difference to your child's brain.

Even though empathy seems to spring from innate sources, children must experience it on a regular basis to become good at expressing it. "Empathy comes from being empathized with," says Stanley Greenspan, clinical professor of psychiatry and pediatrics at the George Washington University School of Medicine, in his book *Great Kids*. In order for you to grow empathetic kids, practice empathy on a regular basis, with your friends, with your spouse, with your coworkers. As in tennis, novices learn to play the game best when they can practice regularly with pros. The more empathy your child sees, the more socially competent he'll become, and the happier he'll be. He in turn will produce more empathetic grandkids—nice to have in old age, especially in a rickety economy!

Fortunately, to give your child the gift of emotional regulation, you don't have to juggle all six spices 24 hours a day. If 30 percent of your interactions with your child are empathetic, Gottman contends, you'll raise a happy kid. Does this mean 70 percent of the time you can cut yourself some slack? Perhaps. Really, the statistic points to the great power of paying attention to feelings. A lot of parents don't raise kids like my friend Doug. But there is no reason why *you* can't.

Key points

- Your infant needs you to watch, listen, and respond.
- How you deal with your toddlers' intense emotions is a huge factor in how happy your child will be as an adult.
- Acknowledge, name, and empathize with emotions. Save judgment for any unacceptable behavior arising from emotions.
- One parenting style is most likely to produce terrific kids: demanding and warm.

moral baby

brain rule

Firm discipline with a warm heart

moral baby

 Daniel has wealthy parents, but they are nearly bankrupt when it comes to controlling their children. Daniel, the eldest, is Exhibit A. Daniel's mother took him and his sister on a weekend trip to the family's opulent vacation home. As they hurtled down the freeway, 5-year-old Daniel suddenly unbuckled his seat belt. He grabbed his mom's cell phone and started playing with it. "Please put that down," his mom said. Daniel completely ignored the request. "Please put that *down*," his mom repeated, to which Daniel replied, "No." Mom paused. "OK, you can use it to call your dad. Now please buckle your seat belt." Daniel ignored both directives and proceeded to play video games on the phone.

When they stopped for gas a few hours later, Daniel crept out the window and climbed over the roof of the car. Horrified, his mother commanded, "Stop that!" Daniel replied, "You stop it!" and crawled down the windshield. With Daniel back in the car, the family drove on. Daniel found the cell phone again; this time he threw it on the floor and broke it. As this little Napoleon grew older, Daniel saw just how easily he could ignore his family's social boundaries, then any social boundaries. He got used to demanding his way everywhere. He started hitting kids at school who did not pay attention to him. He developed a sulfurous relationship with authority. He stole things from classmates. Eventually, his moral clutch slipped completely, and he stabbed a little girl in the cheek with a pencil. He was expelled from school. As of this writing, the family is embroiled in a lawsuit, as is the school.

Daniel was a behavioral—one is tempted to say *moral*—wreck. Though it is easy to be a backseat parent, each year there seems to be a bumper crop of out-of-control kids and helpless parents. No loving parent wants to raise a Daniel. In this chapter, we'll talk about how to avoid doing so. You *can* create moral maturity in most children. And, perhaps surprisingly, there is neuroscience behind it.

Are babies born moral?

What exactly does "moral" mean? Are any moral absolutes embedded into our brains, or is moral awareness only culturally understood? These questions have occupied philosophers for centuries. The word "moral," in both its Greek and Latin incarnations, has a strong social underpinning. It originally outlined a code of conduct, a consensus of manners and customs possessing equal parts "heartily recommend it" and "don't you dare." That's the definition we'll use: a set of value-laden behaviors embraced by a cultural group whose main function is to guide social behavior.

Why would we need such rules in the first place? It may have to do with that strong evolutionary requirement for social cooperation. Some researchers believe our moral sense—really a specific suite of socializing behaviors—developed to aid that cooperation. Regular massacres, after all, are not exactly in the best interests of a species whose effective founding population was less than 18,500 individuals (some say less than 2,000). In this Darwinian view, our brains come preloaded at birth with certain limited moral sensibilities, which then develop in a semi-variable fashion, depending upon how we are raised. "[W]e are born with a universal moral grammar," says cognitive scientist Steven Pinker, "that forces us to analyze human action in terms of its moral structure ..."

Popular candidates for which moral sensibilities we possess include distinctions between right and wrong, proscriptions against social violence such as rape and murder, and empathy. Yale psychologist Paul Bloom lists a sense of justice, emotional responses to thoughtfulness and altruism, and a willingness to judge another person's behavior. Psychologist Jon Haidt sees five categories: harm, fairness, loyalty, respect for authority, and something intriguingly called spiritual purity.

If such moral sensibilities are an innate part of our brain's function, we might be able to see shards of them in some of our evolutionary neighbors. And we can, looking no further than a zoo in England. Kuni, a female chimpanzee, lived in a pen that was part glass and part open air, mostly surrounded by a moat. One day a starling collided with the glass and fell into the cage, and the chimp captured it. Though dazed and limp, the bird was not beyond recovery. Kuni reacted with what can only be described as a humanitarian gesture. She picked up the limp bird and put it on its feet, but the bird didn't fly. She tossed it a short distance. That didn't work. Kuni then picked up the starling with one hand and climbed to the top of a tree in the pen, looking like King Kong with an avian Fay Wray. Using her legs as support, she gently pried open the wings of the bird and threw it toward the moat. That didn't work, either. The bird landed just inside the bank, where a curious juvenile ape came over to investigate. Kuni scrambled down and just stood over her tiny charge, apparently guarding it. She stayed at her post until the bird could fly away on its own.

This is an extraordinary example of ... something. Though we cannot get into the mind of a chimp, it is one of a host of observations that suggest animals have an active emotional life, including, perhaps, notional altruism. Humans tend to have that altruistic quality in spades, and in much more sophisticated forms than our genetic neighbors. If moral awareness is universal, we might also expect to see general agreement across cultures. Harvard researchers developed the Moral Sense Test, which hundreds of thousands of people from more than 120 countries have taken. You can take it, too, at *http://moral.wjh.harvard.edu*. The data they've compiled appear to confirm a universal moral sense.

A third hint that moral awareness is innate, which we'll get to in a few pages, has to do with the fact that damage to a specific part of the brain can affect the ability to make certain types of moral decisions.

Why don't kids just do the right thing?

If children are born with an innate sense of right and wrong, why don't they just *do* the right thing—especially as they get older (puberty comes to mind)?

Turns out it's surprisingly difficult to explain proactive moral behavior, like voluntarily helping someone cross the street. Even enlightened self-interest does not fully explain certain types of human altruism. The road between moral reasoning and moral behavior is quite rocky. In fact, the concept of "conscience" was developed in a partial attempt to pave over this difficulty. A conscience is something that makes you feel good when you do good things and makes you feel bad when you don't. The late Harvard psychologist Lawrence Kohlberg believed that a healthy conscience was the top rung in the ladder of all moral reasoning. But not all scientists think conscience is innate. Some think it's a social construct. For them, internalization is the most important measure of moral awareness.

A child who can resist the temptation to defy some moral norm, *even when the possibility of detection and punishment is zero,* has internalized the rule. These children not only know what is proper, an awareness that might have been preloaded into their brains, but they now agree with it and attempt to align their behaviors accordingly. This is also sometimes called inhibitory control, which sounds suspiciously like well-developed executive function. They may be the same thing. Either way, a willingness to make the right choices—and to withstand pressure to make the wrong ones, even in the absence of a credible threat or in the presence of a reward—is the goal of moral development. Which means your parenting objective is to get your child to pay attention to and align himself with his innate sense of right and wrong.

This takes time. A lot of time.

One lie every two hours

One reason we know this is by the way kids lie, which changes with their age. I once heard a psychology professor discuss what happens when a child first becomes capable of lying, and he livened up his talk with an old Bill Cosby routine. With apologies to both the professor and Cosby, here is my recollection of his story.

Bill and his brother Russell were jumping on the bed in the middle of the night—in violation of their parents' strictest orders. They broke the bed frame, and the snap and crash awakened a furious father. Dad stormed into the room, pointed to the broken furniture, and bellowed, "Did you do this?" The older boy stammered, "No, Dad! I didn't do it!" Then the boy paused, a light jumping into his eyes. "But I know who did. A teenager came into our room from the bedroom window. He jumped up and down on the bed 10 times and broke it, then he leaped out the window and ran down the street!" The dad's brow wrinkled. "Son, there is no window in this room." The boy didn't miss a beat. "I know, Dad! He took it with him!"

Yes, children are bad at lying, at least at first. In the magical fairy dust of the childhood mind, kids initially have a hard time distinguishing reality from fancy, which you can see in their eagerness to engage in imaginative play. They also perceive their parents to be essentially omniscient, a belief that won't be completely destroyed until the 20-kiloton blast of puberty. The fuse gets lit early, though, around 3 years of age, when kids begin to realize that parents can't always read their minds. To their delight (or horror), children discover they can give their parents false information without it being detected. Or, as the Cosby story relates, they *think* they can. The child's realization that you can't always read his or her mind coincides with the flowering of something we call Theory of Mind skills.

Theory of Mind develops over time

What is Theory of Mind? A literary example may help explain it. Ernest Hemingway was once challenged to write an entire novel in only six words, and what he wrote is a perfect illustration of Theory of Mind. That's because when you read it, it will activate yours.

For sale: Baby shoes. Never used.

Do these six words make you sad? Make you wonder what happened to the person who wrote the advertisement? Can you infer that person's mental state?

Most humans can, and we use Theory of Mind skills to do it. The basis of these skills is the understanding that another's behavior is motivated by a range of mental states—beliefs, intentions, desires, perceptions, emotions. Theory of Mind, first coined by noted primatologist David Premack, has two general components. The first is the ability to discern someone else's psychological state. The second is the realization that although these states may be different from your own, they are still valid for the person with whom you are interacting. You develop a theory of how the other person's mind works, even if it differs from your own.

Those six words could have been written by a couple whose baby died shortly after birth, and you feel the pangs of their sadness. You may never have experienced the grief of having lost a child; you may not even have children. Nonetheless, using your advanced Theory of Mind skills, you can experience their reality and empathize. The shortest novel in the world can reveal a universe of feeling because of it. Hemingway considered it his best work.

Even though Theory of Mind is a hallmark of human behavior, we don't think it is fully developed at birth. It is extremely difficult to measure in very young children. The skill appears instead to unfold progressively, influenced by social experiences. You can see this timeline in the way kids lie. Pulling the wool over someone's eyes requires Theory of Mind— the ability to peer into someone else's mind and predict what they will think if you tell them one thing. The talent improves over time.

By age 4, a child will lie about once every two hours; by age 6, it's once every 90 minutes.

After age 3, kids begin to lie in earnest, though they usually do so imperfectly. The nasty habit picks up astonishing speed. By age 4, a child will tell a lie about once every two hours; by age 6, she will do it every 90 minutes. As a child grows in vocabulary and social experience, the lies become more sophisticated, more prevalent, and harder to spot.

This timeline suggests to researchers that children have an age-dependent relationship with certain types of moral reasoning, too. Kids might be born with certain moral instincts, but it takes a while to coax them into their mature form.

How moral reasoning develops

Kohlberg, the Harvard psychologist, believed that moral reasoning depended upon general cognitive maturity—another way of saying that these things take time. If, indeed, decisions have strong emotional roots, as we will explore, I would also argue that moral reasoning depends upon emotional maturity. Though Kohlberg has his critics, his ideas remain influential, as do those of his intellectual mentor, Jean Piaget. The ideas of both men have been applied in schools, juvenile detention facilities, even prisons. Kohlberg outlined a progressive process for moral development:

1. *Avoiding punishment.* Moral reasoning starts out at a fairly primitive level, focused mostly on avoiding punishment. Kohlberg calls this stage pre-conventional moral reasoning.

2. *Considering consequences.* As a child's mind develops, she begins to consider the social consequences of her behaviors and starts to modify them accordingly. Kohlberg terms this conventional moral reasoning.

3. *Acting on principle.* Eventually, the child begins to base her behavioral choices on well-thought-out, objective moral principles, not just on avoidance of punishment or peer acceptance. Kohlberg calls this coveted stage post-conventional moral reasoning. One could argue that the goal of any parent is to land here.

Kids don't necessarily arrive at this third stage all by themselves. Along with time and experience, it can take a wise parent to get a child to consistently behave in a manner congruent with his or her inborn moral grammar. Part of the reason it's tough is that when children observe bad behavior, they have *learned* it. Even if the bad behavior is punished, it remains easily accessible in the child's brain. Psychologist Albert Bandura was able to show this, with help from a clown.

Lessons from Bobo the clown

In the 1960s, Bandura showed preschoolers a film involving a Bobo doll, one of those inflatable plastic clowns weighted on the bottom. In the film, an adult named Susan kicks and punches the doll, then repeatedly clobbers it with a hammer—buckets o' violence. After the film, the preschoolers are taken into another room filled with toys, including (surprise) a Bobo doll and a toy hammer. What do the children do? It depends.

If they saw a version of the film where Susan was praised for her violent actions, they hit the doll with great frequency. If they saw a version where Susan got punished, they hit Bobo with less frequency. But if Bandura then strides into the room and says, "I will give you a reward if you can repeat what you saw Susan do," the children will pick up a hammer and start swinging at Bobo. Whether they saw the violence as rewarded or punished, they learned the behavior.

Bandura calls this "observational learning." He was able to show that kids (and adults) learn a lot by observing the behaviors of others. It can be positive, too. A Mexican soap opera in which the characters celebrate books, and then ask viewers to sign up for reading classes, increased literacy rates across the country. Bandura's finding is an extraordinary weapon of mass instruction.

Observational learning plays a powerful role in moral development. It is one of many skills hired in the brain's ethical construction project. Let's take a peek inside.

Would you kill one to save five?

Imagine what you'd do in these two hypothetical situations:

1. Suppose you are on a terrifying ride in a trolley that has lost its brakes. You're the driver, and you're able to steer. Rushing at breakneck speed, you suddenly see a fork in the track—and something else ahead. It's a construction site! Horrified, you notice that there are five construction workers on the tracks of the left fork—and one on the right. You realize you are going to kill people. Which fork do you choose?

2. Suppose you are on a bridge overlooking the tracks of a trolley careening out of control. This time, you are standing next to a really big guy. This time there's no fork in the track. The dysfunctional trolley will soon come roaring underneath the bridge, killing five construction workers in its path. You realize that if you push the big guy over the bridge before the trolley gets to the site, the trolley will be blocked. The five construction workers will be saved. Again, what do you do?

Each case presents the same ratio, five deaths to one. The vast majority of people find the first scenario easy to answer. The needs of the many outweigh the needs of the few. They'd steer the trolley to the right. But the second situation involves a different moral choice: deciding whether to murder someone. The vast majority of people choose not to murder the man.

But not if they are brain-damaged. There's a region above the eyes and behind the forehead called the ventromedial prefrontal cortex. If this area of the brain suffers damage, moral judgment is affected. For these people, the fact of murder is not particularly relevant to their choice. Convinced that the needs of the many still outweigh the needs of the one, they push the large man over the bridge—saving five people and killing one.

What does this mean? If morality is an innate part of our brain's neural circuitry, then damage to those areas should change our ability to make moral decisions. Some researchers think these results show just that. Some researchers don't think trolley experiments demonstrate anything at all. They argue that no one can relate hypothetical decisions to real-life, in-the-moment experiences. Any way out of this controversy? There might be, though it involves the ideas of philosophers who have been dead for more than 200 years. Philosophy titans such as David Hume thought that base passions powered moral decisions. Modern neuroscience is betting that Hume was right.

Some researchers believe that we have two sets of moral reasoning circuits, and that moral conflicts arise because the two systems get into arguments so frequently. The first system is responsible for making rational moral choices, the kind that decides that saving five lives makes more sense than saving one. The second system is more personal, even emotive. These neurons let you visualize the large man plunging to his death, imagine how the poor fellow and his family would feel, and realize that his untimely death would be your responsibility. This Hume-like view causes most people's brains to pause, then issue a veto order over this choice. The brain's ventromedial prefrontal cortex is involved in mediating this philosophical struggle. When it is damaged, Hume takes a hike.

If you lose emotions, you lose decision making

What does this mean for parents wanting to raise a moral child? As we saw in the previous chapter, emotions are the foundation of a child's happiness. It appears that they are also the basis of moral decision making. A bombshell of a finding comes from a man named Elliot, under the observant eyes of neuroscientist Antonio Damasio. Damasio relates the story of a man he calls Elliot. It is a clinical case similar to the famous example of Phineas Gage, a 19th-century railroad worker who suffered a horrendous accident (a tamping iron shot through his frontal lobes) and lived to tell the tale, though his personality was changed forever. Elliot suffered not from an accident but from a tumor. When the surgeons removed the tumor from his frontal lobes, Elliot, like Gage, had become a different man. Four unusual changes were worth noting:

Formerly a responsible, upstanding member of his community, Elliot became impulsive, undisciplined, and socially odious enough that he lost his wife, his job, and his standing in the community. He went bankrupt. A very similar thing had happened to Gage more than a century before. Fascinated, Damasio put Elliot through a series of cognitive tests. Elliot scored in the superior range on IQ tests and other assays of memory. He scored typically on certain per-sonality tests. What was missing? The clue comes from the second change Elliot displayed after surgery: Elliot failed to show emotion. Show him images that typically arouse people (gory images, sexually suggestive pictures, and the like), and Elliot flatlined physiologically. Windswept. Nothing at all.

The third change turned out to be Elliot's core deficit. It was extraordinary, mostly because it sounds so benign. Elliot lost his ability to make up his mind. About almost anything. He couldn't decide, for example, which restaurant to go to, or what to order once he got there. He couldn't decide which radio station to listen to, which pen to write with, or what order tasks should be done in. His life became one long equivocation.

This led Damasio to the fourth trait. *Elliot had trouble making moral judgments.* He couldn't have cared less that his indecisive behav-iors led to a divorce or to bankruptcy or to any loss of social standing. Abstract tests showed that he knew right from wrong, yet he behaved and felt as if he didn't. He could remember that he used to experi-ence such feelings, but they were now lost in a distant moral fog. As scholar Patrick Grim has observed, what Elliot *did* was clearly unteth-ered from what Elliot *knew*.

This is an incredible finding. Because Elliot could no longer inte-grate emotional responses into his practical judgments, he completely lost his ability to make up his mind. His entire decision-making machinery collapsed, including his moral judgment.

Other studies confirm that a loss of emotion equals a loss of decision making. We now know that children who have suffered damage to the ventromedial and frontopolar prefrontal cortices before their second birthday have symptoms quite similar to Elliot's.

How the brain bridges facts and emotions

If you eavesdrop on the human brain while it is busy wres-tling with ethical choices, you see a bewildering number of regions becoming as active as an *Iron Chef* episode. The lateral orbitofrontal cortex; the dorsolateral prefrontal cortex, right lateralized; the ventral striatum; the ventromedial hypothalamus; the amygdala—all get involved. Emotions and logic, as we discussed in the previous chapter, are freely and messily intertwined in the brain. We are only in the beginning stages of understanding how the two function in moral decisions. We know there is a regional division of labor: The surface regions are preoccupied with assessing facts. The deeper regions are preoccupied with processing emotions. They are connected by the ventromedial prefrontal cortex. This is oversimplified, but think of the ventromedial prefrontal cortex as the Golden Gate Bridge, connecting San Francisco (emotions) to its northern neighbor, Marin County (just the facts, ma'am). Here's how some scientists think the traffic flows:

1. *An emotional reaction occurs.* When a child's brain is confronted with a moral dilemma, San Francisco is alerted first. The child's deep, mostly unconscious circuitry generates an emotional reaction—a Post-it note.

2. *The signal is carried across the bridge.* That message is spirited across the VMPFC, the cellular Golden Gate connecting lower and higher centers of the brain.

3. *Fact centers analyze it and decide what to do.* The signal arrives at the neuroanatomical equivalent of Marin County. The child's brain reads the note and makes up its mind about what to do. It judges right from wrong, critical from trivial, necessary from elective, and ultimately lands on some behavioral course of action. The decision is executed.

This all occurs in the space of a few milliseconds, a speed requiring that the emotion-generating areas of the brain work in such close concert with the rational areas that it is impossible to tell where one starts and the other leaves off. The integration is so tight, we can actually say that without the irrational, you can't achieve the rational.

This biology tells us that emotional regulation is an important component of raising a moral child. So is executive function. The healthy integration of both processes will go a long way toward keeping a child in touch with her inner Mother Teresa.

Raising a moral child: Rules and discipline

So the question now becomes: If kids are born with an innate number of moral construction materials, how do we help our children build moral houses worth inhabiting? How do we get them to that coveted stage of moral internalization?

Families who raise moral kids follow very predictable patterns when it comes to rules and discipline. The patterns are not a behavioral insurance policy, but they are as close as research gets us right now. Many interlocking components make up these patterns; an illustration from my wife's kitchen may simplify things. We used to keep a three-legged stool near the refrigerator to help our boys reach the shelves. Think of the flat seat of that stool as representing the development of a moral awareness, or conscience. Each leg represents what researchers know about how to support it. You need all three legs for the stool to provide children with the sturdiest seat—the most finely attuned moral reflexes.

The three legs are:

- Clear, consistent rules and rewards
- Swift punishment
- Rules that are explained

I'll borrow scenes from a TV show to illustrate each.

I. Clear, consistent rules and rewards

A little boy at the dinner table punches his brother, demanding, "I want your ice, *now!*" Mom and Dad look horrified. A plump, elegant stranger with a British accent also sits at the table. She doesn't seem horrified at all. She is, however, taking notes, something like a product tester. "What are you going to do?" she asks the parents calmly. The boy punches his brother again. "I will take away your dessert if you do that again," Mom says sternly to the child. He does it again. Mom looks down at her plate. Dad looks away, angry. The parents, it seems, have no idea how to answer the British woman's question.

Welcome to the invasive world of the TV nanny. You've probably seen these reality shows, all of which follow a familiar formula: Families clearly out of control allow a camera crew access to their lives, all in the company of a professional nanny. Invariably blessed with an authoritative accent from the British Isles, she proceeds to act like a Nottingham sheriff come to clean house. The nanny has a week to perform her domestic miracle, transforming the harried parents into loving disciplinarians and their little helllions into angels. Among the scenes:

Toddler Aiden refuses to go to bed, wailing at the top of his lungs. He knows that when his parents say, "Lights out—I mean it," they don't really mean it at all. If there is a curfew, it is unannounced or unenforced, and its absence makes Nanny's brow wrinkle. It takes Aiden hours to go to bed.

A little boy named Mike accidentally trips on the stairs, dropping a bunch of books he was carrying. The little guy cringes and tries to hide, expecting a yelling from his moody father. He gets one, gale force. Nanny intervenes: She goes over to the boy, helps him pick up the books, and says with a sad kindness, "You look really afraid, Mike. Did your dad frighten you?" Little Mike nods, then bolts up the stairs. Later that night, like a British bulldog, Nanny gives the dad a biting lecture about the child's need to feel safe.

Amanda makes an effort to go to bed on time all by herself, which she previously had resisted. This effort goes unnoticed, however, because the parents are busy chasing her younger twin brothers, trying to get them to brush their teeth. Once finished, the parents flop down in front of the television. Nanny tucks Amanda into bed and says, "Good job. You did that all by yourself, and no fuss! Wow!"

The TV nannies' solutions are sometimes irritating, sometimes spot-on. But in these cases they follow the behavioral science of our first leg of discipline: consistent rules that are rewarded on a regular basis. Watch what they do, paying attention to four characteristics.

Your rules are reasonable and clear

In the example of Aiden above, the toddler either does not have a set bedtime or ignores the one that's supposed to be in place. His only guidance is his parents' behavior, which is waffling and ambiguous. Aiden has no direction and, at the end of a busy, tiring day, very little social reserve. No wonder he shrieks.

Nanny's solution? Next day, she brings in a physical chart with rules and expectations written right on it—including a reasonably formulated time for bed—then mounts it where the entire family can see. The chart produces an objective authority where the rule is (a) realistic, (b) clearly stated, and (c) visible to all.

You are warm and accepting when administering rules

Mike, the boy who wants to hide because of dropped books, clearly has been yelled at before. Cringing with fear is an obvious sign that the kid does not feel safe at that moment and may not feel safe generally. Getting yelled at for something as innocent as accidently dropping books is consistent with the latter. This is a warning flag for Nanny. She tries to communicate safety to the little guy—note her immediate empathy—and she later upbraids Mike's dad, telling him he needs to choose a calmer, more measured response if he wants Mike's behavior to change. Remarkably, the dad listens.

You know by now that the brain's chief interest is safety. When rules are not administered in safety, the brain jettisons any behavioral notion except one: escaping the threat. When rules are administered by warm, accepting parents, moral seeds are more likely to take root.

So you have crystal-clear rules, and you administer them in a certain manner. The next two steps involve what you do when the rules are followed.

Every time your child follows the rules, you offer praise

Scientists (and good parents) discovered long ago that you can increase the frequency of a desired behavior if you reinforce the behavior. Children respond to punishment, certainly, but they also respond to praise—and in a way that risks less damage and usually produces better results. Behaviorists call this positive reinforcement. You can even use it to encourage behavior that hasn't happened yet.

Suppose you want your increasingly sedentary 3-year-old, who happily still craves your attention, to get some exercise outside and play on the swings in the backyard more often. Problem is, he rarely even goes outside. What are you going to do? Instead of waiting for your 3-year-old to get on the swings, you can reinforce his behavior every time he gets near the door. After a while, he will spend more time at the door. Then you reinforce his behavior only when he opens the door. Then only when he goes outside. Then when he spends time near the swing set. Eventually, he'll get on the swings and you two can play together. This process, called shaping, can take much patience, but it usually doesn't take much time. Famed behaviorist B. F. Skinner, using a shaping protocol, got a chicken to turn the pages of a book as if it were reading in less than 20 minutes. Humans are much easier to shape than chickens.

You also praise the absence of bad behavior

Remember Amanda, the little girl who put herself to bed while her parents watched TV? The parents did not praise her obvious lack of fussy behavior, but the nanny did. Praising the *absence* of a bad behavior is just as important as praising the *presence* of a good one.

Researchers have measured the effects of these four parenting strategies on moral behavior. When warm, accepting parents set clear and reasonable standards for their kids, then offer them praise for behaving well, children present strong evidence of an internalized moral construct, usually by age 4 or 5. These are hallmark behaviors of Baumrind's gold-medal authoritative parenting style. They're not everything you need in your moral tool kit, but from a statistical point of view, you won't get a good kid without them.

Seeing yourself

Do you do these things, or do you think you do? One of the obstacles to getting parents to change their behavior is making them understand how they are actually coming across to their kids. Nanny helps parents see what she sees by videotaping the families, looking for each person's cues, and pointing them out. Researchers use the technique, too.

Marian Bakermans-Kranenburg at Leiden University, for one, carried a video camera into the homes of 120 families with kids ages 1 to 3. Bakermans-Kranenburg was examining some of the hardest kids on earth to treat: pathologically resistant children who displayed a toxic brew of aggression, uncooperativeness, whining, and screaming. She and her crew edited the video for teachable moments and created a lesson plan for the parents. The researchers taught the parents to spot cues they'd previously missed or had misinterpreted. They were shown behaviors that proved counterproductive, ones to which the children had responded poorly. Afterward, even in this tough group, the children's hellion acts dropped by more than 16 percent! That's huge for this field. Most moms in the group were able to resume reading to their children on a regular basis. In an interview, Bakermans-Kranenburg said the parents found a "peaceful time that they had dismissed as impossible." That's powerful stuff.

2. Swift punishment

Though I don't want to, I sometimes think of Ted Bundy. The serial killer did a great deal of his mayhem at the University of Washington around the same time I was attending as an undergraduate. A panicky parenting feeling sets in when I remember the time: How do I keep my kids from being exposed to the Ted Bundys of this world? How do I know my kids won't grow up to *be* like Ted Bundy?

Ted Bundy's favorite method of murder was a crowbar to the head, and he often raped his victims after they died. He may have killed as many as 100 women. Most of us cannot conceive of such horror and depravity. Bundy's case was made all the worse because he seemed perfectly normal. Smart, handsome, and witty, Bundy was on the fast track in the legal profession, at one point even mentioned as a future politician. He navigated "proper" society with the ease of a diplomat. There is a haunting photo of him with his girlfriend opening a bottle of wine, a smiling and caring young man, obviously in love. Yet by the time that picture was taken, he had already killed 24 women.

Researchers over the years have tried to make sense of the behavior of people like Bundy. They have no good answers. There are the usual suspects: broken home; violent, abusive parents, and Bundy had these. But other people do, too, and most don't become serial killers. Most so-called psychopaths—people with an inability to connect emotionally to their actions, among other traits—aren't even violent. Bundy was clearly emotionally competent. He could not only fake pro-social behaviors, but he also had an abundance of genuine emotions concerning himself. Narcissistic until the end, he had to be dragged to Florida's electric chair on the morning of his execution, doubled over in terror, sobbing inconsolably with tears he probably spent years storing up for himself. To this day there are no good explanations for Bundy's complete moral collapse.

Ted Bundy knew the rules, but he sure didn't follow them. How do we make sure our kids do? How do we correct any behavior we don't like—and get the child to internalize the change? Discipline.

Addition by subtraction: Negative reinforcement

Researchers distinguish between two discipline strategies: negative reinforcement and punishment. Both deal with aversive situations, but negative reinforcement tends to strengthen behaviors, whereas punishment tends to weaken them.

As a child you probably discovered that when you burn your finger, cold water provides immediate pain relief, removing the obnoxious experience. When a response pays off, it tends to get repeated. The next time you got a burn—an aversive stimulus—the probability multiplied of you running to the nearest sink. This is negative reinforcement, because your response was strengthened by the removal (or avoidance) of an aversive stimulus. It's different from positive reinforcement, which is when an action leads to such a wonderful experience, you want to repeat the action. Negative reinforcement can be as powerful, but it is also trickier to apply.

I knew a preschool girl who craved her mom's attention. She started off her terrible twos by throwing her toys down the stairs on a regular basis, disrupting the entire family. The little girl seemed to enjoy misbehaving and was soon throwing lots of things down the stairs. Mom's books were a favorite target, which, this being Seattle, proved to be the last straw. Mom tried talking to her, reasoning with her, and, when these failed, yelling at her. She eventually brought out the heavy artillery—spanking—but nothing changed.

Why were Mom's strategies failing? Because her punishments were actually providing the little girl what she desired most: Mom's undivided attention. As difficult as this might seem, Mom's best shot at breaking this cycle was to ignore her daughter when she misbehaved (after first locking away some of the books), destroying this unholy alliance between the stairs and attention. Instead, Mom would reinforce her daughter's desirable behaviors by paying rich, undivided attention only when she acted in accordance with the laws of the family. Mom tried it, consistently lavishing praise and attention when the daughter opened one of the remaining books rather than tossing it. The throwing stopped within a few days.

Sometimes the situation requires more direct interventions. For this there is the concept of punishment, which is closely related to negative reinforcement. The research world recognizes two types.

Letting them make mistakes: Punishment by application

The first type is sometimes called punishment by application. It has a reflexive quality to it. You touch your hand to a stove, your hand gets burned immediately, you learn not to touch the stove. This automaticity is very powerful. Research shows that children internalize behaviors best when they are allowed to make their own mistakes and feel the consequences. Here's one example:

> *The other day my son had a tantrum in the phone store and took his shoes and socks off. Instead of arguing with him to put them back on, I let him walk outside a few feet in the snow. It took about 2 seconds for him to say, "Mommy, want shoes on."*

This is the most effective punishment strategy known.

Taking away the toys: Punishment by removal

In the second type of punishment, the parent is subtracting something. Appropriately, this is called punishment by removal. For example, your son hits his younger sister, and you do not allow him to go to a birthday party. Or you give him a time-out. (Jail time for crimes is the adult form of this category.) Here's how it worked for one mom:

> *My 22 month old son threw another fit at dinner tonight because he didn't like what was served. I put his little self in time out and let him sit there until he finished screaming (took about 2 min). Brought him back to the table and for the first time after one of*

his fits, HE ATE THE FOOD! He ate the mashed potatoes and the hamburger from the shepherd's pie!! Mommy—1, son—0. WOO HOO!!

Either type of punishment, under proper conditions, can produce powerful, enduring changes in behavior. But you have to follow certain guidelines to get them to work properly. These guidelines are necessary because punishment has several limitations:

- It suppresses the behavior but not the child's knowledge of how to misbehave.

- It provides very little guidance on its own. If it's not accompanied by some kind of teaching moment, the child won't know what the replacement behavior should be.

- Punishment always arouses negative emotions—fear and anger are natural responses—and these can produce such resentment that the relationship may become the issue rather than the obnoxious behavior. You risk counterproductivity, or even real damage to your connection with your child, if you punish incorrectly.

Punishment that's actually effective

How *not* to punish kids? Try the 1979 movie *Kramer vs. Kramer.* The film is about a divorcing couple and the impact of the experience on their young son. Dustin Hoffman plays the workaholic, unengaged dad whose parenting instincts have the subtlety of dog food.

The scene opens with the little boy refusing to eat dinner, instead demanding chocolate-chip ice cream. "You're not going to have any of it until you eat all your dinner," the dad warns. The son ignores him, gets a chair, and reaches up for the freezer. "Better not do that!" dad admonishes. The kid opens the freezer anyway. "You'd better stop right there, fella. I'm warning you." The son brings the ice cream to the table, acting as if his dad were invisible. "Hey! Did you hear me? I'm warning you, you take one bite out of that, and you're in big trouble!" The boy dips the spoon in the ice cream, staring intently at his father. "Don't you dare! You put that ice cream in your mouth, and you are in very, very, very big trouble." The kid opens his mouth wide. "Don't you dare go anywhere beyond that." When the boy does, his dad snatches him up out of his chair and throws him in his bedroom. "I hate you!" the kid yells. The dad shouts, "And I hate you back, you little shit!" He slams the door.

The coolest heads, obviously, were not prevailing. The following four guidelines show the way to punishment that's actually effective.

- **It must be punishment.** The punishment should be firm. This does NOT mean child abuse. But it also doesn't mean a watered-down version of the consequences. The aversive stimulus must, in fact, be aversive to be effective.

- **It must be consistent.** The punishment must be administered consistently—every time the rule is broken. That is one of the reasons why hot stoves alter behavior so quickly: *Every* time you put your hand on it, you get burned. The same is true with punishment. The more exceptions you allow, the harder it will be to extinguish the behavior. To borrow a familiar phrase: Let your yes be yes and your no be no. Consistency must be there not only from one day to the next but from one caregiver to the next. Mom and Dad and Nanny and stepparents and grandparents and in-laws all need to be on the same page regarding both the household rules and the consequences for disobeying them. Punishments are obnoxious by definition—everyone wants to escape them—and kids are unbelievably talented at discovering loopholes. You can't give them the opportunity to play one caregiver against another if you want them to have a moral backbone. All they'll form is cartilage.

- **It must be swift.** If you are trying to teach a pigeon to peck on a bar but delay the reinforcement by 10 seconds, you can do it all day and the pigeon won't get it. Shrink that delay to 1 second, and the bird learns to peck the bar in 15 minutes. We don't have the same brains as birds, but whether we are being punished or rewarded, we have remarkably similar reactions to delay. Researchers have measured this in real-world settings. The closer the punishment is to the point of infraction, the faster the learning becomes.

- **It must be emotionally safe.** The punishment must be administered in the warm atmosphere of emotional safety. When kids feel secure even in the raw presence of parental correction, punishment has the most robust effect. This evolutionary need for safety is so powerful, the presence of rules themselves often communicates safety to children. "Oh, they actually care about me" is how the child (at almost any age in childhood) views it, even if he or she seems less than appreciative. If the kids don't feel safe, the previous three ingredients are useless. They may even be harmful.

No toy for you

How do we know about these four guidelines? Mostly from a series of experiments whose name and design would be right at home in a Tim Burton retrospective. They are called the Forbidden Toy paradigms. If your preschooler were enrolled in an experiment in Ross Parke's laboratory, she would experience something like this:

Your daughter is in a room with one researcher and two toys. One toy is very attractive, begging to be touched. The other is unattractive, one she'd never play with. As she reaches out to touch the attractive toy, she hears a loud, obnoxious buzzer. She touches it again and gets the same unpleasant noise. In some experiments, after the buzzer sounds, the researcher issues a stern admonishment not to touch the toy. The buzzer never goes off when your child touches the unattractive toy, however. And the researcher remains silent. Your daughter quickly learns the game: The attractive toy is *forbidden*.

The researcher now leaves the room, but not the experiment, for your child is being recorded. What will she do when flying solo? Whether she chooses to obey depends on many variables, Parke discovered. Experimenters manipulated the timing between the touch and the buzzer, the script of the authority figure, the level of perceived aversion, the attractiveness of the toy. From literally hundreds of such manipulations using this paradigm, researchers discovered the effects of severity, consistency, timing, and safety—the very guidelines that we just covered.

3. Rules that are explained

Want a simple way to make any form of punishment more effective, long-lasting, and internalized—everything a parent could ask for? It's the third leg supporting our stool of moral awareness. It just takes one magic sentence, Parke found, added to any explicit command.

Without rationale
"Don't touch the dog, or you'll get a time-out."

With rationale
"Don't touch the dog, or you'll get a time-out. The dog has a bad temper, and I don't want you to get bitten."

To which sentence would *you* be more likely to positively respond? If you're like the rest of the world, it is the second sentence. Parke was able to show that compliance rates soar when some kind of cognitive rationale is given to a child. The rationale consists of explaining why the rule—and its consequences—exist. (Works well with adults, too.) You can use this after a rule has been broken, too. Say your child yells in a quiet theater. The punishment would include an explanation of how his yelling affected other people and how he might offer amends, such as apologizing.

Parenting researchers call this inductive discipline, and it is incredibly powerful. The parents of kids with a mature moral attitude practice it. Psychologists even think they know why it works. Let's say little Aaron has been punished for a moral infraction—stealing a pencil from classmate Jimmy—just before a test. The punishment was subtractive in nature: Aaron would have no dessert that night. But Aaron was not just punished and left alone. He was also given the magic follow-up sentence, involving explanations ranging from "How could Jimmy possibly complete his test without his pencil?" to "Our family doesn't steal." Aaron also was instructed to write a note of apology.

Here's what happens to Aaron's behavior when explanations are supplied consistently over the years:

1. When Aaron thinks about committing that same forbidden act in the future, he will remember the punishment. He becomes more physiologically aroused, generating uncomfortable feelings.

2. Aaron will make an internal attribution for this uneasiness. Examples might include: "I'd feel awful if Jimmy failed his test," "I wouldn't like it if he did that to me," "I am better than that," and so on. Your child's internal attribution originates from whatever rationale you supplied during the correction.

3. Now, knowing why he is uneasy—and wanting to avoid the feeling—Aaron is free to generalize the lesson to other situations. "I probably shouldn't steal erasers from Jimmy, either." "Maybe I shouldn't steal things, period."

Cue the applause of a million juvenile correction and law-enforcement professionals. Inductive parenting provides a fully adaptable, internalizable moral sensibility—congruent with inborn instincts.

Kids who are punished without explanation do not go through these steps. Parke found that such children only externalize their perceptions, saying, "I will get spanked if I do this again." They are constantly on the lookout for an authority figure; it is the presence of an *external* credible threat that guides their behavior, not a reasoned response to an internal moral compass. Children who aren't guided to step 2 can't get to step 3, and they are one step closer to Daniel, the boy who stabbed a classmate in the cheek with a pencil.

The bottom line: Parents who provide clear, consistent boundaries *whose reasons are always explained* generally produce moral kids.

No such thing as one-size-fits-all

Note that I said "generally." Inductive discipline, powerful as it is, is not a one-size-fits-all strategy. The temperament of the child turns out to be a major factor. For toddlers possessed of a fearless and impulsive outlook on life, inductive discipline can be too weak. Kids with a more fearful temperament may react catastrophically to the sharp correctives their fearless siblings shrug off. They need to be handled much more gently. All kids need rules, but every brain is wired differently, so you need to know your kid's emotional landscapes inside and out—and adapt your discipline strategies accordingly.

Should you spank?

Few issues are more incendiary than deciding whether spanking will be in your parenting tool kit. Many countries ban the practice. Ours doesn't. More than two-thirds of Americans approve of the practice; 94 percent of Americans have spanked by their kid's fourth birthday. Generally, spanking is in the punishment-by-removal category.

Over the years, many studies have been devoted to assessing the usefulness of this method, often coming to confusing—even opposing—conclusions. One of the latest lightning rods is a five-year review of the research literature by a committee of child development specialists sponsored by the American Psychological Association. The committee came out against corporeal punishment, finding evidence that spanking causes more behavioral problems than other types of punishment, producing more aggressive, more depressed, more anxious children with lower IQs. A spring 2010 study, led by Tulane University School of Public Health researcher Catherine Taylor, confirms the findings. It found that 3-year-olds who were spanked more than twice in the month prior to the study were 50 percent more likely to be aggressive by age 5, even when controlling for differing levels of aggression among kids and for maternal depression, alcohol or drug use, or spousal abuse.

> **3-year-olds spanked more than twice in a month were 50 percent more likely to be aggressive by age 5.**

Hear that furious typing sound? That is the clatter of a thousand blogs springing to life, violently disagreeing with these findings. "It's associative data only!" says one (true). "Not all experts agree!" says another (also true). "Context-dependent studies are missing!"—i.e., do we know that spanking done in a loving, inductive household is different from spanking done in a harsh, noninductive atmosphere? (We don't.) What about parental intention? The list of objections goes on and on. Many come from a growing concern that today's children are being parented less and less, that contemporary moms and dads are increasingly afraid to discipline their kids. I am in deep sympathy with this concern. The numbers aren't, however. In the brain, the fight appears to be between deferred-imitation instincts and moral-internalization proclivities. Spanking is just violent enough to trigger the former more often than the latter.

Sociologist Murray Straus has been investigating spanking for a long time. As he noted in an interview with *Scientific American Mind*, the linkage between spanking and behavioral unpleasantness is more solid than the linkage between exposure to lead and lowered IQ. More solid, too, than the association between secondhand smoke and cancer. Few people argue about these associations; indeed, people win lawsuits with associative numbers in those health-related cases. So why is there so much controversy about whether to spank, when there should be none? Good question.

I do know that inductive parenting takes effort. Hitting a kid does not. In my opinion, hitting is a lazy form of parenting. If you're wondering, my wife and I don't do it.

The discipline kids prefer

A number of years ago, several groups of researchers decided to get kids' opinions of parenting styles. Using sophisticated surveys, they asked kids between the ages of preschool and high school what they thought worked and what they thought failed. The questions were cleverly couched: The kids listened to stories about misbehaving kids, and then were asked, "What should the parent do? What would you do?" They were given a list of methods of discipline. The results were instructive. By a large margin, inductive parenting got the biggest statistical high five. The next most-favored behavior was actual punishment. What came in dead last? The withdrawal of parental affection or laissez-faire permissiveness.

Taken together, the style of correction kids liked the best was an inductive style spiced with a periodic sprinkling of a display of power. The results to some extent depended upon the age of the responder. The 4- to 9-year-old crowd hated permissiveness more than any other behavior, even love-withdrawal styles. That was not true of the 18-year-olds.

Overall, a clear picture emerges about how to raise well-adjusted, moral children. Parents whose rules issue from warm acceptance and whose rationales are consistently explained end up being perceived as reasonable and fair, rather than as capricious and dictatorial. They are most likely to evince from their kids committed compliance rather than committed defiance. Remind you of Diana Baumrind's authoritative parenting style—restrictive but warm? This was the one style statistically most likely to produce the smartest and happiest children.

It turns out these smart and happy children will be the most moral, too.

Key points

- Your child has an innate sense of right and wrong.
- In the brain, regions that process emotions and regions that guide decision making work together to mediate moral awareness. Lose emotions and you lose decision making.
- Moral behavior develops over time and requires a particular kind of guidance.
- How parents handle rules is key: realistic, clear expectations; consistent, swift consequences for rule violations; and praise for good behavior.
- Children are most likely to internalize moral behavior if parents explain why a rule and its consequences exist.

sleepy baby

brain rule

Test before you invest

sleepy baby

 The video clip should have come with a disclaimer: "Warning: The video you are about to enjoy will intrude on your normally scheduled dose of decency."

Samuel L. Jackson—denizen of such violent fare as *Pulp Fiction* and *Django Unchained*—is shown reading from a script in a sound studio. This isn't the dangerous Jackson you know and love, as the video soon reveals. His normally stern face is instead graced with a gentle smile, scholarly glasses perched atop his nose. He intones with the surprising tenderness of a loving father: *"The windows are dark in the town, child. The whales huddle down in the deep."*

The script seems more in common with the children's book *I'll See You in the Morning* than the Jackson movie *Snakes on a Plane*—except that lulling a child to sleep is the text's furthest goal. The next words hit you like a time-delayed ordnance, resonating with almost every newly minted parent I have ever met, and preserving Mr. Jackson's foul-mouthed reputation. *"I'll read you one very last book if you swear / You'll go the fuck to sleep!"*

Jackson is reading from *Go the F**k to Sleep*, written by author Adam Mansbach. The book was wildly popular several years ago, topping Amazon's charts 30 days before it was published.

The popularity of Mansbach's salty text underscores just how challenging infant nighttime sleeping can be for rookie parents. After the fourth sleep-deprived night in a row, you may begin to crave sleep like an exhausted swimmer craves oxygen. You may become desperate for an answer to your child's sleep issue. Any answer. You may even regret having signed on the biological dotted line, making baby your own. You will almost certainly mutter your own string of profanity. No wonder Mansbach's first book has received so much attention.

Sleep consolidation, the formal term for a child's process of sleeping through the night, is the subject of this chapter. Focusing mostly on the first year of life, we will explore some of the basic neuroscience of sleep, discuss insights from "sleep gurus," and end with a few practical suggestions.

The science of infant sleep

So how do you get your child to sleep through the night? I can almost guarantee you won't like my response: I can't give you an answer for your baby.

The variables predicting successful sleep consolidation in pediatric populations are so numerous, we haven't even finished cataloging them. We are even further from understanding how to shape the known factors into a slumber-inducing protocol providing every sleepless parent their well-deserved answer. We don't even know the basics, like how many hours of sleep per day babies actually need. We can track how much sleep babies get, but that's a different question from how much they need. We know sleep requirements vary by age; newborns undoubtedly need more sleep than 6-month-olds. Sleep varies by nation, too. Six-month-olds in Switzerland get about 14 hours a day. Six-month-olds in Japan get about 11. Infants in the United

States get about 13. Undoubtedly both environment and genetics play a role, though we have no idea about the relative influences of each. We simply have the observations of an unpredictable system.

That's why there are so many books on the subject: everybody is currently guessing. The situation isn't hopeless, of course, but the disclaimer is necessary. I know, if you are a sleep-deprived parent, this is the last thing you want to hear. You are not alone in wanting an answer. Between 25 percent and 40 percent of babies born in the United States experience sleep problems in the first six months of life. And it's not just an American problem. Depending on the country, between 10 percent and 75 percent of new parents all over the world report having problems getting their child to sleep through the night. Parents in Western cultures have three chief complaints: baby has difficulty falling asleep at bedtime; baby wakes up too many arousal times during the night; and baby awakens too early the next day.

What's so difficult about going to sleep? Factors published by the scientific literature reveal the complexities in both baby and parent. Infant issues include biological temperament, the individual brain-wiring of their various "sleep centers," the developmental changes that affect those centers over time, and even environmental factors (such as reactions to food, light, or being held). Adult factors include beliefs and expectations about sleep, the social context shaping those beliefs, individual adult temperaments, and memories of how the adults themselves were raised.

Getting a child to sleep through the night can be likened to a dance between two people who don't know each other very well, and end up regularly stepping on each other's toes. Both cry. A lot. Just how different are these dance partners? One of my son's favorite rides at Disney World can help explain.

Tower of Terror

My sons have always loved elevators—their dad does, too—enjoying the feeling of near free fall you can sometimes get in the otherwise predictable experience of being in an office building. So you can probably imagine how we felt the day we climbed aboard the Twilight Zone Tower of Terror on a visit to Disney's Hollywood Studios in central Florida.

The ride starts with a slow ascent to the top, similar to your standard office-building elevator. Suddenly you are pulled downward (as opposed to just letting gravity do its thing), creating the terrifying sensation of an uncontrolled free fall. The ride continues with a series of seemingly random drops and lifts, stops and starts, even sideways lurches. At least one fall traverses the entire vertical length of the tower. It's a nauseating, exhilarating series of experiences.

These two elevator rides, the calm office building and the Tower of Terror, describe quite well what we know about adult vs. infant sleep.

Adult sleep

Mature adult sleep might best be likened to your boring, standard-issue workplace elevator. You start at the top floor, fully awake. Then you get drowsy, signaling that your normal sleep cycle has commenced. You begin slowly descending through various sleep stages, losing consciousness, and arriving at the bottom floor where "real sleep" occurs. This happens about 90 to 100 minutes after the elevator began its journey. It is very hard to wake someone in this stage. We call this slow-wave sleep, or non-rapid eye movement sleep stage 4 (NREM4).

You don't stay at the bottom long. In our evolutionary history, if we remained unconscious for a full eight hours, we'd probably wind up in some predator's stomach. So after about 30 minutes in NREM4, the elevator begins to ascend again. Your eyes, still closed, start moving back and forth in a truly creepy, increasingly vigorous fashion, a stage called REM sleep (short for rapid eye movement, as you might suspect). At the top of this stage, you are restless and can be easily awakened.

If all is well, however, you may not fully awaken. After a period of time, you start the cycle again, your elevator executing another descent. It will move in the same deliberate, stately manner as before, returning eventually to the bottom. After another 30-minute sojourn in the land of NREM4, the elevator again rises, your eyes move back and forth, and you reenter an REM state. You will travel up and down in this smooth, calm manner on average five times a night.

There's a bit of a surprise here. Even in the normal state, no one sleeps through the night in one continuous, uninterrupted chunk. Regretfully, that includes children.

Infant sleep

The central fact of newborn sleep is that it is *nothing* like adult sleep. Instead of gradual cycles of descent and ascent, newborns have only two speeds, christened by sleep researcher Richard Ferber as "active sleep" and "quiet sleep." Both speeds are established in the womb, detectable by the middle of the third trimester.

The presence of just two tempos means infants are only beginning to learn how to sleep. They won't exhibit a predictable sleep cycle for several months—or adult-like sleep behaviors for years. Sleep for them seems spasmodic, and parents get jerked along for the ride. On a good night, adults ride a smoothly moving elevator. On a good night, babies ride the Tower of Terror.

Why? Here's what researchers know so far:

When babies are safely tucked inside their mother's womb, they may respond to—even follow—mom's natural biochemical rhythms. This is because they are plugged into the maternal central computer via the placenta and umbilical cord. It's not just humans. All mammals get warmth, food, water, and hormones (including sleep-regulating melatonin) from mom on a regular basis. At birth, the comforting supply of warmth, food, water, and sleep cues become immediately and violently disconnected. (I literally cut the umbilical cord off both my sons with a pair of sharp scissors.)

In this one act, babies become completely out of sync with the cycles of adult existence. The newborn must solve these problems immediately after birth, the most important problem being food. Some researchers think the altered waking/sleeping patterns initially concentrate on getting a consistent food supply. Newborns' task is Herculean. They need to eat about every two to three hours, some much more often. Consistent with this notion, infant sleep patterns have been shown initially to closely follow feeding patterns: the amount of time it takes babies to consume food, digest food, metabolize food, and then become hungry again. Baby may sleep, but only after the tank has been topped off.

Notice that I said "may." Some babies are energized by food, in which case they are not ready to sleep after a midnight snack; they are ready to play, cry, or otherwise demand attention. So feeding doesn't always ensure a round of sleep.

Active and quiet sleep

Babies' two sleep tempos do have a rough equivalent to adult sleep. Active sleep is somewhat similar to adult REM sleep, which means baby is restless and more easily awakened in this stage. Breathing is shallower, more irregular. Babies move their eyeballs. Eyelids tremble. They might flex their little arms and legs. They may even vocalize. When babies first start nodding off, unlike adults, they immediately enter into active sleep. For most newborns, this active state lasts 20 or 30 minutes.

Then the quiet sleep mode, similar to adult NREM sleep, kicks in. Baby's breathing becomes deeper and more rhythmic. Baby's eyes stop moving. Limbs go limp. They are not very easily aroused. This means you can probably put them in the crib without fear of waking them. I have spent many hours gazing at both my little boys in this tranquil newborn state of theirs. How long does this heaven last? Usually an hour or less, which means I was too quickly jolted out of my reverie.

Quiet sleep represents the end of junior's sleep cycle. The baby then does one of two things: either reenters active sleep for another go-round, or wakes up. I am convinced that some infants sleep through the night fairly early in life because they are born capable of reentering their active/quiet sleep cycle without much need to consult Mom and Dad. Some have problems for months because they can't. At this point, we only have vague ideas about how to increase the probability of the former.

Do not disturb

I can offer one piece of advice for helping baby stay in active sleep in the first place. The instant an infant shows signs of sleepiness, exhausted parents often want to immediately put their kid in a crib. Frustratingly, the baby senses the disruption, begins to fuss, to wiggle, to arouse. That's the opposite of what you want! Why did this occur? Remember, baby is still in active sleep mode, and easily aroused. Once you detect signs of sleep, don't disrupt the process. If you are holding baby, continue to hold baby. Pay attention to how long it takes her to reach quiet sleep. Give it an extra 10 minutes as an insurance policy, and then place baby in the crib.

This way, you can perhaps avoid identifying with the person who tacked up a poster I saw in an office. It depicted a famous scene from *Raiders of the Lost Ark*. Harrison Ford is kneeling in front of that small but iconic golden idol, which is sitting on a pedestal in the middle of a heavily booby-trapped room. Harrison wants to steal the statue without triggering the booby traps. He has in hand a bag of sand, similar in weight to the idol, with which he hopes to quickly replace the statue. The poster shows Harrison poised at the tensest moment just before the exchange occurs.

The caption above Harrison's head reads HOW I FEEL ... and the caption below reads ... TRYING TO LEAVE MY SLEEPING BABY SO HE STAYS SLEEPING.

I laughed so hard only because it rang true.

If you do the math, a change in the drowse/arouse cycle seems to occur every 90 minutes or so. This has been noticed by researchers, most notably famed sleep researcher Nathan Kleitman. He termed the 90-minute time frame the BRAC, short for Basic Rest Activity Cycle.

Adults' drowse/arouse cycles are about the same length. But, of course, there is great variation in both babies and adults, and no one fast rule each child must obey. (Like I said, the variables are complex.) I suggest that parents time their baby's active/quiet sleep cycles to find their child's schedule.

When will this ride end?

How long will baby ride the Tower of Terror? With most newborns, you don't see strong evidence of something approaching a socially acceptable circadian rhythm (as measured by melatonin production) for almost three months, and nothing approaching sanity—defined as getting five straight hours of sleep—for almost six months. Some kids take longer to learn to sleep through the night. My son Joshua did not successfully sleep five hours straight until he was 7 months old.

It's not that babies don't want to cooperate, however difficult this may be to believe. German researchers showed that just 48 hours after birth, babies were struggling to stay awake longer in the daytime than in the night. Japanese scientists demonstrated this effort had begun to pay off by the second week of life: infants had fewer arousals during nighttime sleep than during the day. The finding remained consistent even when babies were fed several times at night.

Infants' efforts result in the eventual establishment of a sleep cycle. Authentic NREM sleep as part of a normal awake/asleep cycle has been detected in babies as young as 6 months old. But it does take a while to sync up. It is not unusual for an infant to wake up three times a night for the first six months of his life. He may still wake up once or twice a night before his first birthday, and may wake up once a night until his second. It takes a lot of time for a little one to leave the Tower of Terror and instead firmly plant themselves on the boring office elevator of the adults.

Bedtime routines

Sleep experts agree that one thing helps babies make this transition: having a consistent bedtime routine. This starts with choosing a time for bedtime, sometime around 6 months old. Around the world, bedtime depends upon baby and culture. Whatever time you choose, the advice is to make it consistent.

Next, create a series of predictable bedtime rituals. These rituals can be almost anything, from singing favorite lullabies to turning all the lights in the house down low. Part of the ritual may involve giving your infant a warm bath, followed by a nursing session to "top off" the child before slumber. If the child is a tough sleeper, your routine may involve a slow ride over a bumpy road. The Medina family found this to be the most successful method when sleep was a problem. Whatever the activities, they should be consistently applied: same content, same order, same environment. Babies quickly learn to associate these behaviors, especially when dependably applied, with the fact that sleep time is coming.

There is no guarantee they will always welcome it, however. Or that you will, as Samuel L. Jackson can clearly testify.

(Not) sleeping through the night

So let's say it's been six months since the birth of your child, your child isn't sleeping through the night, and you're dropping f-bombs like Jackson (or would like to). Many books out there are willing to give you advice, purporting to know the secret formula for getting baby to sleep. Many of them contradict each other, which is the most frustrating thing about reading multiple books about the subject.

Ava Neyer, a mom from Fort Bragg, North Carolina, got so frustrated with the plethora of incongruous suggestions out there that she wrote a post about it, republished on the *Huffington Post* with the title "I Read All The Baby Sleep Books." Here's an excerpt:

> *Put the baby in a nursery, bed in your room, in your bed. Co-sleeping is the best way to get sleep, except that it can kill your baby, so never, ever do it. If your baby doesn't die, you will need to bed-share until college.*

> *Don't let your baby sleep too long, except when they've been napping too much, then you should wake them. Never wake a sleeping baby. Any baby problem can be solved by putting them to bed earlier, even if they are waking up too early. If your baby wakes up too early, put them to bed later or cut out a nap. Don't let them nap after 5 p.m. Sleep begets sleep, so try to get your child to sleep as much as possible. Put the baby to bed awake but drowsy. Don't wake the baby if it fell asleep while nursing.*

Funny—unless you're the new parent who's wondering what to do. These contradictory opinions are like a boxing match between two heavyweight philosophical ideas, fighting for the title of "Best way to get your baby to sleep through the night."

NAP vs. CIO

In one corner, we have the Nighttime Attachment Parenting (NAP) styles of pediatric sleep consolidation. In the other corner, we have what people call Cry-It-Out (CIO) styles of pediatric sleep consolidation. The contenders have very different ideas about how nighttime sleeping issues should be addressed in the first year of life. Their fans regularly get into the ring, too, some of whom throw some pretty nasty punches.

NAP advocates' underlying philosophy, as described by pediatrician William Sears, is this: "During the first year, an infant's wants and needs are usually one and the same." CIO advocates believe the two are not necessarily always the same. When an infant cries at night, NAP says the parental response should be instantaneous, to show your baby you're there when he wants you. CIO says you should wait a bit, because your baby needs to learn how to fall asleep on his own.

Which side wins? At this point in sleep research, neither. NAP styles are not well studied (tough to do because parents implement them in such variable ways), and they are undergirded by attachment theory, a concept that's in flux. CIO styles have been shown to get kids to sleep through the night more quickly, but science hasn't weighed in on whether that's best for baby or just more convenient for our modern culture. In the end, it's up to you to decide what feels right, based on *your* baby.

We'll detail how each method works and look at the science, inconclusive as it is.

Fighting for NAP: William Sears

Nighttime Attachment Parenting is an extremely infant-driven style. Advocates encourage feeding on demand rather than keeping to a schedule, both day and night; wearing your newborn in a sling during the day; and sleeping with your baby at night (whether in the same bed or in the same room), or at least making "comfort visits" to baby's crib when baby cries. The idea is to have as much contact with your child as possible. Baby will be calmer and feel secure during the day, NAP advocates argue, and thus baby will be calmer and more likely to sleep at night.

Like Athena leaping from the forehead of an elderly Zeus, Nighttime Attachment Parenting styles spring from attachment theories first developed in the late '60s (discussed in more detail in "Attentive, patient ping-pong," on page 190). Needs not fulfilled when junior is a baby, the theory goes, create problems for junior as an adult. Ignoring your baby at night is a way of ignoring those needs, say NAP advocates; paying attention is a way of gratifying them.

NAP's champion is the aforementioned William Sears. He is an experienced, handsome pediatrician, the epitome of a California doctor. To say he likes kids is an understatement. He and his wife, a nurse and parenting health advocate, have raised eight children. Three of them grew up to become practicing doctors, one with his own television show. Dr. Bill (as the elder Sears likes to be called) and his wife, Martha, have authored more than 30 parenting books. The most well-known of these is probably *The Baby Book*, which they wrote with two of their sons, Robert and James. More than a million sold, the book is chock-full of practical advice from the NAP corner of the sleep consolidation ring.

The Sears family doesn't pull punches when it comes to defending their ideas. Here's how one edition of *The Baby Book* describes the concept of sleeping in the same bed with your baby, called bed sharing:

> *Which do you think your baby prefers: to drift off to sleep peacefully at his mother's breast or in his father's arms, or to soothe himself to sleep with a tasteless, emotionless, rubber pacifier?*

At another point, the Sears book goes on:

> *Is it all right to let your baby sleep in your bed? Yes! We are astonished how many baby books flatly put thumbs down on this most time-tested universal sleeping arrangement. Are they also against motherhood and apple pie? How dare self-proclaimed baby experts discourage what science is proving and veteran parents have long known*—most babies and mothers sleep better together.

You can see why I opened this section with a prize-fighting metaphor.

To be fair, the Sears family is more nuanced about exactly how to practice sleeping with your child, describing several variants that range from sleeping in the same bed (bed sharing) to sleeping in the same room with your child (room sharing). The Sears family readily discusses alternatives to seven nights a week of co-sleeping. They also address important fears many parents raise about the practice, including:

- Will I create an unhealthy emotional dependency? (No.)
- Will my baby ever learn to sleep on her own? (Yes.)
- What will happen to our sex life? (You will learn to be creative.)
- How long should you co-sleep with your child? (Depends on how long you can tolerate it.)

We are now ready to march over to the other side of the sleep-consolidation boxing ring, where overtired parents really love their kids, but also need to get up in the morning and go to work.

Fighting for CIO: Richard Ferber

It is not often a scientist becomes so engrained in popular culture that his name becomes a verb. But that is exactly what happened to pediatric sleep researcher Dr. Richard Ferber, a prominent advocate of the Cry-It-Out method. Dr. Ferber, founder of Boston's Center for Pediatric Sleep Disorders, didn't make up CIO. Core CIO ideas can be found as far back as the 19th century. But his name is so closely associated with the practice that parents who embraced his protocol were accused—yes, accused—of "Ferberizing" their children.

How does CIO work? Researchers call CIO methods "extinction styles." In psychology, "extinction" is a general term for weakening a behavior by restricting its reward structure. The reward structure is attacked because it is the reinforcing agent keeping a behavior alive, a behavior whose extinction is desired.

With infant sleep, a reinforcing agent looks like this: (a) baby is crying at 3:00 a.m. for attention; (b) parent comes into the room, picks him up, and comforts him, providing the attention; (c) baby stops crying, thus reinforcing the behavior. The baby learns that crying is a good way to get attention, day or night. He cries in anticipation of parental response, creating an internal attitude called a "reinforcement expectation." The parent learns that the most successful method to calm the infant at night is to go in and hold him, which rewards the crying.

The way to "break" this cycle is to not provide attention every time baby wants it. He must instead be taught to fall back asleep independently, CIO advocates say. Baby then learns to sleep on his own, and the nighttime crying is extinguished. This process is not usually greeted with enthusiasm on the part of the child. That's why it's called "crying it out."

CIO can properly be described as a continuum between "unmodified extinction," in which the parent refuses to respond regardless of how long the crying continues (researchers don't recommend this), and "camping out" or "fading," in which the parent is close but spends less and less time by the child's crib providing assurance. In the middle of the continuum, we find "graduated extinction." The parent does respond to the child's nighttime cries, but on a strict schedule. The amount of time a child is allowed to cry gradually lengthens. The delays are deliberately timed and incremental, hence the term "graduated." The schedule, taken from Ferber's book *Solve Your Child's Sleep Problems*, goes like this:

First day

Put the baby into his crib as usual, or perhaps even a little later than usual, letting him fall asleep. Then leave the room.

1. The first time you hear baby cry, break out the stopwatch and wait three minutes before reentering the room to provide comfort. Ferber calls this the "first wait." Don't spend more than one or two minutes reassuring your baby. Now leave the room again, even though he has not stopped crying.

2. Wait five minutes (the "second wait") before reentering, leaving again after one to two minutes.

3. Wait a third time, for 10 excruciating minutes. For the rest of the night, the magic wait time will be 10 minutes. Continue this routine until the child awakens in the morning, generally between 5:00 a.m. and 6:00 a.m.

Second day

Continue this schedule, but make the first wait five minutes, the second wait 10, the third and subsequent waits 12 minutes.

Third day

Increase the first wait to 10 minutes, the second to 12 minutes, and the third to 15.

Fourth day and beyond

I think you get the picture. By the seventh day, the first wait has expanded to 20 minutes; the ceiling is 30 minutes. Babies don't like it at first. Outbursts of crying may increase for a period of time (the "post-extinction burst") just before the behavior subsides. Even so, by the third or fourth night, things should be substantially better.

Dr. Ferber emphasizes that these numbers are advisory only, and that a wide variety of schedules will work. (Some parents can stand only a minute at first.) But he is also very clear that, whatever schedule you design, the waiting intervals need to be consistently and progressively longer. That is the core idea driving the CIO models, the reason the crying behavior is eventually extinguished. Ferber calls this the Progressive Waiting approach. Other researchers call it controlled comforting/controlled crying. Critics call it "Ferberizing."

Whatever you call it, you can see how different the NAP and CIO approaches are.

What the research says

Let's compare graduated extinction, the most popular CIO method, to Nighttime Attachment Parenting in terms of a few issues of importance to parents: how each approach supports sleep consolidation (baby's ability to sleep through the night); whether the parties involved get better sleep; the level of stress they cause baby; and how easy each is to implement.

Will baby sleep through the night?

CIO says: Wait to comfort baby

Graduated extinction has undergone the most scientific scrutiny of all the styles. Overwhelmingly, the evidence shows that it works—if you define "works" as getting the child to quit crying during the night so that everyone can sleep through the night. And it works surprisingly quickly, typically within a week. This is true whether you use the harsh unmodified extinction protocols, gentler graduated extinction methods, or room-sharing approaches.

There is an important caveat to these data, however. It comes from a secret Las Vegas slot-machine designers know well.

One of the hardest behaviors to quench in anyone is a habit that is only occasionally rewarded. Want to keep a gambler at a slot machine longer? Make sure the payout schedule is random. Studies show that people who experience random rewards in response to a behavior cling to that behavior much more solidly than those who don't.

This is true for adults, but it is also true for the diaper-an-hour crowd. That's why consistency is considered non-optional if you go down the CIO road. The fastest way to keep your child clinging to his cries at night is to make sure your attentive rewarding behavior is unpredictable. Go in sometimes. Don't go in at other times. Like someone welded to the slots, the poor little baby will actually cry longer, harder, more frequently. He becomes increasingly disorganized if he can't detect a regular pattern. The sleep goal is unmet, for both parent and baby, and everyone is miserable. So CIO works, but only if applied consistently.

NAP says: Make "comfort visits"

One hallmark of the NAP style is persistent parental nocturnal visitations to the crib, providing verbal/physical contact in response to the nighttime demands of the infant. A team of researchers from the United Kingdom specifically focused on whether this approach helps infants establish sleep consolidation.

The results were not reassuring. The more a parent "rescued" their infant at night, the more sleep problems the infant displayed over time. The infants displayed a marked reduction in the capacity to return independently to sleep after arousal, for example. "Comfort visits" also had consequences for childhood sleep far past the first year, other researchers discovered.

Actively "rescued" children at 18 months old still had problems getting a solid night's rest (now defined as six uninterrupted hours). Things were not substantially better when the children reached their second year of life. Excessive interference at night appeared to be a gift that kept on giving, but it was not the gift the parent wanted.

Will our family sleep better?

Co-sleeping, and the ease of breast-feeding that comes with it, are often pitched by the NAP crowd as a way for both parents and babies to get more rest at night.

A number of laboratories studying this have uncovered a surprising finding: nocturnal breast-feeding is negatively associated with a stable sleep cycle. As you know, I am a real fan of breast-feeding. If a mom is at all capable, she should do it. Nonetheless, the on-demand style of nocturnal breast-feeding was correlated with a greater frequency of nighttime arousals, even when the rates were compared to infants fed on formula, and infants were fed at roughly comparable rates.

This mom's post at *TruuConfessions.com* illustrates what a problem that can be:

> *I am such a mess. My 13 mo still does not sleep through the night and is addicted to the boob like a crack fiend at night. She wants to nap with my boob in her mouth too. I'm exhausted and sleep deprived and my patience is running real short with her now. I feel like a horrible mom because out of frustration I have ignored her crying and have not been the happiest person to be around. She favors my husband over me and I think it's because of this ... Today I cried for hours in front of her while she watched cartoons.*

When it comes to co-sleeping, studies have found that co-sleeping babies cry less. However, studies also have found that both parent and infant sleep more poorly, with more interruptions per unit of time for each.

That's quite a finding. Up until these newer data emerged, co-sleeping was thought to work like a warm, friendly sleeping pill for both parties. To resolve the conflict, researchers decided to eavesdrop on the infant's brain using polysomnographic assessments when bed sharing. Polysomnography is a general term for physiological overnight tests generally employed to evaluate human sleep. The assessments can include EEGs (measuring surface electricity at the scalp), airflow measurements through the patient's nose and mouth, blood pressure, heart rate, and gross motor movement.

When such technology was used to evaluate infant brain activity during bed sharing, researchers uncovered why their sleep was more unsettled. Baby's sojourns through the "quiet phase" of sleep was shorter than for infants who were not co-sleeping. They also woke up more often during that phase than their independently sleeping controls, so even the quality of the quiet phase they got was disturbed.

An evolutionary argument

Still, the practice of co-sleeping is still alive and well. In indigenous cultures, such as the Efé tribe of the Democratic Republic of Congo, families typically sleep together in a small hut. The population regularly includes adults, children, babies, pet dogs, and visitors. Co-sleeping also is the dominant arrangement in crowded urban settings, where living space is at a premium. Nearly 60 percent of Japanese families practice co-sleeping. The US figure is much lower (around 15 percent, though this is in dispute).

From an evolutionary perspective, co-sleeping was probably the typical nighttime behavior, for millions of years. As hunter-gatherers, we kept our babies in close physical contact day and night. Infants didn't evolve in that harsh world to sleep by themselves—or live in isolation for any length of time—because they would be lunch. Surely optimal brain development occurs under any model that seeks to replicate this history. That's what NAP advocates argue: It's supposed to be this way.

Though I am deeply sympathetic with evolutionary arguments, we no longer live in a hunter-gatherer society. While the system may have been optimized for roaming around the Serengeti, you should deploy it mainly if you choose to parent while also roaming around the Serengeti. Or if your living arrangements otherwise require it. If not, it makes sense to explore alternatives relevant to contemporary life and times.

Which method causes baby less stress?

NAP advocates make a developmental argument for their side, having to do with something we call object permanence. Object permanence is the ability to understand that something will still exist even if it is covered up. Babies are not born with this insight. They think if an object has been removed from their visual field, it also has permanently disappeared. NAP advocates argue that since object permanence is not available at first, leaving an infant alone at night can be a truly catastrophic experience. If Dad leaves the room, will Dad ever return? If Mom goes away now, will she ever come back? True in the daytime, true at nighttime, true at all times. Infants should be around their parents as much as possible.

We used to think object permanence was not established until after baby's first birthday. There is now convincing evidence for its formation in the first eight months of life, and maybe even the first three or four months of life. Since most professionals do not advocate any sleep interventions until after 6 months of age, object permanence may not be an issue by the time you have to decide whether you are in the NAP or CIO corner of the ring.

NAP advocates also say their style produces less-stressed children. They cite studies that have examined nighttime levels of infant cortisol. As you recall, cortisol is a stress hormone; elevated levels are usually a reliable sign of stress. In one UK study, infants who experienced NAP styles of nighttime parenting did indeed experience lower levels of cortisol compared to matched controls. You could still see these lowered levels as the kids turned 5. However, this doesn't prove NAP caused the lower stress.

Just as importantly, we have no idea what the typical cortisol values should be for a Western infant. Cortisol levels are heavily modulated throughout the day if you are an adult, but in children they take a while to reach their mature circadian form. To date, infant regulation is mostly a mystery. Until we have a better baseline, we can't start to make sense of the cortisol findings.

Finally, NAP advocates argue that kids are at risk for real and permanent psychological harm with exposure to CIO. Specifically, they point to the fact that crying is a behavior designed to bond the parent to the child. The child is in distress, they say, and the parental response of comfort provides the relational adhesive necessary for proper attachment to occur. CIO advocates point to the fact that attachment is a slow, gradual process. It takes years to develop—or to destroy.

The little attachment work that has been done suggests that kids turn out just fine whether you co-sleep with them or practice some form of crying it out. Leading researchers on the subject of sleep and infant development noted this in 2010:

> *Concerns have been raised that behavioral intervention involving infant protest and crying may compromise infant-parent attachment relationships. However, to date, there are no published studies demonstrating such adverse effects, and ... sleep intervention studies that have measured proxies of attachment found no evidence of derived infant problem behavior or parenting difficulty, which are linked to insecure infant attachment.*

Can I stick with it?

One of the most consistent research findings about CIO, besides the fact that it works, is that CIO is very hard on parents. Responding to a child's cry is something we may have been built to do. The fact that it is superimposed on an asymmetric cultural schedule where parents need to sleep at night so that they can go to work the next day does not change these feelings.

To which proponents over in the NAP-style corner respond, "Hello. Of *course* CIO is hard on parents. It's as unnatural as a punching bag, and you were never supposed to do it!" One parent commenting on a blog post summed up the sentiment:

> *I never understood [Ferber's] method. Why would you sit in a chair near your child and watch them cry. How horrible! How could you do that to your baby? Clayton started sleeping through the night at one year old. I could not imagine listening to him cry and not doing anything.*

Smack! Like I said, it's a prizefight.

On the other side, some parents find that accommodating baby's every want is unsustainable, as this mom's *TruuConfessions.com* post illustrates.

> *Dear son is 11 months and still wakes up 1-2 times during the night. I'm still nursing him, so I always wake up with him. He screams if husband walks in instead. I am one exhausted mom, and as much as I hate to do it, I see sleep training … in his near future.*

So misery isn't uncommon in either corner of the canvas.

What to do?

It may seem that the evidence points in favor of CIO, but I am not ready to put my full weight on CIO methodology. There isn't enough science to be conclusive in either direction. So on which side of the ring are you ultimately going to find yourself? The most confusing part of this prizefight is that both ideas seem to have merit.

I love the idea advocated by the Sears family of parenting consistently across the day, spending truckloads of time with your baby. Not only will it allow you to get to know your baby, it will allow you to spend more time with him on a developmental journey that goes way too fast as it is.

And I love the idea that graduated extinction methods have been evaluated and found to have worked very well, and in multiple cultures. Since you have picked up this book with the idea that you wanted clear science to guide your decisions, CIO methodologies have been the ones most rigorously tested. Not only do they work well, they work better than the NAP approach, if your goal is to get junior to quit disrupting your sleep.

Is it possible to hold two contradictory pieces of information in one's head at the same time? F. Scott Fitzgerald thought so. He wrote:

The test of a first-rate intelligence is the ability to hold two opposed ideas in mind at the same time and still retain the ability to function. One should, for example, be able to see things as hopeless and yet be determined to make them otherwise.

If Mr. Fitzgerald is on to something, then parents with newborns must be geniuses.

Kidding aside, there may actually be a way out of this dilemma. I have constructed a to-do list that I propose you follow, a protocol with five steps. The protocol is especially useful if you have a child still struggling with sleep issues at the half-year mark. It is based on everything we have talked about in these previous paragraphs.

John Medina's plan: Test before you invest

Step 1. Choose a side before baby comes into the world

Professor Medina has some philosophy homework for you to complete prior to the big day. I am asking you to tentatively commit to which side of the ring you enter the boxing match, because you need a rational starting point. So choose A or B:

A) Do you agree with Sears that the wants and the needs of a baby are the same thing in the first year of life? That when baby wants your attention at night, it is because he needs your attention at night?

B) Do you agree with CIO advocates that they can be split? That just because baby wants your attention at night does not a priori mean baby needs your attention; she may need just to go to sleep?

Since science does not know which one you should choose, I have nothing to say to you regarding your choice. Nobody else does, either. That's as it should be, because your child is your child, and nobody else's. You are allowed to be the captain of this choice. Your decision will determine how you proceed in the next four steps.

Step 2. Start with a modified NAP style

When baby comes into your home, on-demand and nighttime visits will be a normal, regular part of your routine for the first three months. Whether you also co-sleep during the night and wear a sling during the day depends on what you decided in Step 1. If you have decided that needs and wants are the same thing for the first year, engage the NAP model full tilt. Share both your shoulder and your bed.

Step 3. At 3 months old, record your baby's sleep habits

Why three months? By this time, you should see real signs of the sleep pattern your little one is developing. For the first three months, you are practicing on-demand parenting, but that doesn't have to be your permanent reaction. For the next three months, make notes about the changes you see in your baby, and get ready to adapt.

Step 4. At 6 months old, make a decision

The behavioral tracking you have done the previous three months may reveal a pattern that fits your lifestyle just fine. Or it may reveal a pattern that does not fit your lifestyle at all. Note that I am asking you to wait six months before you judge. Why? The answer is biological. Sleep interventions are mostly useless until baby's brain is ready. If you try to intervene before that time, you may end up fighting biological forces over which you have very little control.

At the six-month mark, go down one of two paths:

A) Take Sears seriously

If you and your baby have settled into sleep habits that fit your lifestyle and family needs well, fully embrace the Sears methodology. This might be an easy transition, for you have been doing a modified version of his on-demand counsel for the past six months. Sears explains what to do in greater detail in *The Baby Book: Everything You Need to Know about Your Baby from Birth to Age Two*. Buy it, read it, and implement his recommendations in earnest.

B) Take Ferber seriously

If you and your baby have settled into a sleep pattern that does not fit your lifestyle and family needs well, it is time for a change—especially if you have decided that baby's wants and needs are not necessarily the same thing. Consider one of the CIO methodologies, either camping out or the graduated extinction. (As stated earlier, researchers do not advocate for the unmodified extinction model under any circumstances. I am one of them).

Two important caveats: As we have discussed, it is quite normal for newborns to awaken many times during the night. Sometimes, however, the arousals occur (or continue past the newborn stage) because of a medical condition. Problems range from acid reflux to lactose intolerance to undetected infections. Babies can even suffer from obstructive sleep apnea. So ask your pediatrician to rule out any physical problem before you implement a CIO strategy. Graduated extinction should be deployed only if baby is crying because he wants attention. If by the seventh day you see no improvement, or things have gotten substantially worse, you are supposed to stop the program and consider alternative solutions.

The book with the most detailed protocol is Ferber's book *Solve Your Child's Sleep Problems.* Buy it, read it, and get started on your journey.

Step 5. Deploy, evaluate, and adjust

Continue to write down what you are doing and how baby is reacting so that you can remember what is occurring (the first thing to go with sleep deprivation is your memory). NAP styles take longer to assess, if assessment is even the right word, but you can know if graduated extinction is working after only a week's application. If what you do is working, then congratulations, you are done with my protocol.

If your baby is still not sleeping through the night, change strategies. There are many dialects of NAP styles, and many CIO styles, too. *Consider this adaptation to change normal.* Parenting is an amateur sport, filled with trial and error. Even simple pediatric projects are usually error filled, and getting baby to sleep through the night is hardly a simple project. Your decision about wants vs. needs may determine your starting point, but it by no means determines where you end up. Keep experimenting until you find the secret sauce that works for your child.

Reassurance for this flexible counsel comes from an unlikely source, Richard Ferber, whose reputation for being hard-nosed is completely undeserved. He writes:

> Over the more than twenty-five years I've spent working with families and children with sleep problems, I've come to the conclusion that children can sleep quite well under a surprisingly wide range of conditions.... The techniques may vary somewhat, but most problems can be solved regardless of the philosophical approach chosen. No choice is irreversible; parents are free to try one approach, and then change their minds if they find it did not work as well as they had hoped.

Because every brain is wired differently, you may have to try several methods before you find the one that works. A method that worked with Baby No. 1 isn't guaranteed to work with Baby No. 2.

Baby is trying

Remember, baby is not your enemy in his struggle to learn to sleep independently, just a very inexperienced ally. Your goals are naturally aligned, after all. From an evolutionary perspective, it is in his brain's best interest to learn how to stay awake during the day, then learn to sleep through the night. Though it is as much a struggle for him to get it right as it is for you to teach him, you can't give up.

After all, that's the heart and soul of parenting. The constant theme of this book is that babies are people, but they are not adults.

You have to teach them everything. At least at first, you have to be willing to be the professor 24 hours a day.

I once saw a video of a little boy who illustrates nicely a previous night's struggle to stay awake. The clip starts with the child in a high chair, slowly chewing food. But he's sleepy. His eyes are closed, head perilously cocked 90 degrees to the chair. It becomes obvious he is simultaneously trying to eat and stay awake—and he is not able to do much of either. It is funny, and touching. The little guy nods off, starts to chew, swallows, then nods off again, slowly listing to one side as if he were a ship taking on water. He catches himself, tries to right his body, puts more food in his mouth (eyes still closed!), loses the battle, and face-plants into the high-chair tray. He is sound asleep!

Yes, sleep is a challenging proposition for little ones. And they are trying to get it right. It's hard on parents, too, who are also trying to get it right. The good news is that all babies eventually find a way to sleep through the night. The bad news is that they almost never do it on an adult's schedule. You should be used to this by now. It is the largest lesson of Parenting 101: The instant you decide to bring a child into the world, you give up absolute control over the rest of your life. Welcome to the world of parenting.

Key points

- The central fact of newborn sleep is that it is *nothing* like adult sleep. Newborns only have two speeds: "active sleep" and "quiet sleep." They ride the Tower of Terror.
- There is no one-size-fits-all answer for sleep issues.
- Do you think baby's wants and the needs are the same thing during the first year of life? Or not? It's up to you. Science does not know which one you should choose.
- Once baby is 6 months old, choose a plan for better sleep, evaluate your efforts, and then get ready to change your plan.

conclusion

Voltaire once said, "Every man is guilty of all the good he did not do." When I look at and think about and pray for my children, I have this nagging question: What if I'm not doing all I could be doing? Then Voltaire comes to mind, and I am sure of it.

Whenever I lecture to groups about pediatric brain development, parents consistently make this comment: "I wish I had known that earlier." Perhaps you occasionally felt that way when reading this book. I share the same feeling. It's especially acute for me when research findings extend, confirm, or sometimes refute our understanding of how children's brains work. Then I sound just like my audience: "Geez. I wish I had known that earlier!"

Something a friend once told me is quite helpful at these times. He said, "You need to remember that parenting is an amateur sport." When you have your first child, you are automatically inducted into the league of rookie parenting. It is also helpful to know that your child is a rookie human. Rookie coach, rookie player. You are going to make mistakes. Everyone does.

The real-world experience of parenting ranges from waves of exhaustion to oceans of love to ripples of laughter ("No, poop will never come out of your penis" is a sentence I have actually uttered). And it almost never cooperates with our expectations. My wife loves the way comedian Carol Burnett blasted the fantasy of an easy labor: "Giving birth is like taking your lower lip and forcing it over your head." Forever after, kids tend to do the darnedest, most frustrating, kid-like things.

I told my kids today that they were acting like children. They promptly reminded me that they were children. Whoops!

The real world of moms and dads is a much richer, much more amazing experience than the two-dimensional world of data, including all the stuff in this book. It's easy to feel like the exasperated new father in the comic strip *Baby Blues*, who says, "The only time I ever felt qualified to be a parent was before I had kids." How can we summarize the science but still live in the nine-to-five, three-dimensional world of real life? The solution is to simplify. This book has two central themes, and they act in concert with each other. Understanding them may be the best way to remember all of the information that otherwise floods these pages.

Start with empathy

The first theme is empathy. Empathy is enabled by the ability to understand someone else's motivations and behaviors, as this little girl did:

My preschooler was harassed by a class "mean girl." We explained that the mean girl was jealous of a pretty craft project that we had made at home that others were praising. Our dear daughter made another one at home and gave it to mean girl, who was so so so happy. I don't know that I have ever been prouder.

The parents asked their daughter to make an effort to understand the psychological interiors of the bully. This compelled the girl to do a difficult thing: temporarily remove herself from her own experience and jump into somebody else's. Powerful idea. *Hard* idea. This skill, Theory of Mind, is the first step to empathy. It is a consistent willingness to turn down the volume of one's own priorities and experiences in favor of hearing another's. Theory of Mind is not the same thing as empathy. You can use your secret knowledge of someone else's motivations to be a dictator if you like. You need to add a certain measure of kindness to Theory of Mind skills to get empathy, as this child illustrates:

> *Dear daughter was so cute today. My husband was watching football and when his team made a touchdown he got all excited and pretended to head butt me … except I didn't expect it and moved so he ended up doing it for real. It hurt. While my husband was apologizing profusely, daughter brought me her special blanket she never lets go of and her pacifier and shoved it into my mouth and made me lay down on her blanket to make me feel better. LOL!*

In the Relationship chapter, we discussed empathy's role in stabilizing marriages by creating bridges between extrospective and introspective points of view. Remember: What is obvious to you is obvious to you.

In Happy Baby: Soil, we outlined the value of empathy in forming friendships, one of the greatest predictors of a child's future happiness.

In the Smart chapters, we discovered that it takes years of high-quality face time and practice with interpersonal interaction to build a child's ability to decode faces and other nonverbal cues. These skills enable a child to accurately forecast another person's behavior and, in turn, empathize with it. Though empathy skills are unevenly granted by genes, they can be improved with practice. Soil nurtures seed. Open-ended learning environments—with plenty of inter-active, imaginative play—help provide the face time that develops these skills. Television, video games, and text messages, by defini-tion, do not. Empathy has neuroscientific scaffolding behind it, including mirror neurons, which is why it belongs in a *Brain Rules* book.

Focus on emotions

If it is imperative to get inside another person's experience, what should you pay attention to once you arrive? After all, scientists can tease out at least eight different aspects of even our simplest behaviors, as we found in the Introduction with the mom who was dreaming of mai tais. Which aspect is most worthy of your attention? The answer is the second central theme of this book. What you should pay attention to are your child's emotions.

Here's an example from one of the most painful rites of passage in childhood: the impromptu drafting of backyard sports teams. Five-year-old Jacob came home early from playing with the neigh-borhood boys. "Nobody picked me," he said dejectedly to his mom, throwing his baseball mitt on the kitchen floor and turning toward his room. His mother looked thoughtful. "It seems like your feelings really got hurt, Jake. True?" Jacob paused, glaring at the floor. "You look angry, too," Mom continued. "It's no fun when you feel sad and angry, is it, honey?" Jacob now responded with force: "I was really mad! They picked Greg, and he told them not to pick me." Mom asked, "Do you think it would help if you talked to Greg about it?" "No, I just don't think Greg likes me today. Maybe I'll try tomorrow," Jacob said. Mom gave Jacob a hug and later whipped up a batch of terrific chocolate-chip cookies. Which Jacob did not share with Greg.

The mother chose in that instant to pay close attention to her son's emotions. She penetrated her son's psychological space and empathized with him—that's the first theme—but what she chose to focus on once she got there was his emotional life. She empathized with his obvious feelings of rejection. Mom did not try to hide them, neutralize them, or throw stones at them. This consistent choice separates the superstar parents from the rest.

In the Pregnancy and Relationship chapters, we discovered how important emotional health is to both prenatal and postnatal baby brain development. In Smart Baby: Soil, we talked about how strong emotional regulation actually improves a child's academic performance. That's because it improves executive-function behaviors such as impulse control and planning for the future, which in turn affects grades. But emotions don't just influence GPAs. Emotional regulation also predicts a child's future happiness, a notion developed in the Happy chapters. This leads to the astonishing conclusion that a happier baby is a smarter baby, too. In the Moral chapter, we discovered that emotions are the heart and soul behind most of our decisions, from making the right friends to making the right moral decisions. Throughout, we discussed how parents who focus on emotions help create emotional stability in their children.

At the most basic level, these themes can be boiled down to a single sentence: *Be willing to enter into your child's world on a regular basis and to empathize with what your child is feeling.* Simple as a song. Complex as a symphony. The behaviors of good parenting follow from this attitude. If you also create a set of rules and enforce them with consistency and warmth, you have virtually everything you need to start your parenting journey.

Giving, but also getting

Along the way, you'll find something interesting: As you enter your child's emotional world, your own becomes deeper. After my sons were born, it was not long before I noticed a large change had come over me—one that continues to this day. Every time I chose to put my children's priorities ahead of my own, even when I didn't feel like it, I found I was learning to love more honestly. As they became toddlers, then preschoolers, these choices allowed me to become a more patient person. With my students. With my colleagues. With my amazing wife. I became more sensitive in my decision making, too, now that I had to take into consideration not only the feelings of my wife but those of two little people as well. I was becoming more thoughtful despite myself. I also began to care greatly about the future, the world in which my boys will raise their children.

My boys are still small. But their presence in my mind is as large as the day they were born. And their influence on my life looms ever larger as they mature. Or maybe I am the one maturing. I don't mean to say that parenting is one big self-help program. But in the messy world of child rearing, it's startling how profoundly a two-way street the social contract actually is. You may think that grown-ups create children. The reality is that children create grown-ups. They become their own person, and so do you. Children give so much more than they take.

This struck me one night when my wife and I were snuggling with our younger preschooler, putting him to bed. My wife hugged him and thought he felt like soft bread dough. She said to him, "Oh, Noah, you're just so squeezable and soft and delicious! I could almost take a bite out of you. You're so yummy!" Noah responded, "I know, Mommy. I've really got to lower my carbs."

We laughed 'til we cried. Seeing his personality blossom was truly a gift. This is the message I want to leave you with as we part ways. As a new parent, you may feel sometimes that all children do is take from you, but it is just a form of giving in disguise. Kids present you with an ear infection, but what they are really giving you is patience. They present you with a tantrum, but they are really giving you the honor of witnessing a developing personality. Before you know it, you've raised up another human being. You realize what a great privilege it is to be a steward of another life.

I said that parenting is all about developing human brains, but my aim was inches too high. Parenting is all about developing human hearts. There is no idea in this book more important for new parents than that one.

brain rules

pregnancy
Healthy mom, healthy baby

relationship
Start with empathy

smart baby
Feeling safe enables learning
Face time, not screen time

happy baby
Make new friends but keep the old
Labeling emotions calms big feelings

moral baby
Firm discipline with a warm heart

sleepy baby
Test before you invest

practical tips

Throughout *Brain Rules for Baby*, I've offered practical ways to apply the research to the real world of parenting. I want to compile them in one place, along with a few examples from my own parenting experience. These are things that worked for my family. I'm happy to share them, but I can't guarantee that they will work for yours.

Pregnancy

Leave the baby alone at first

The best advice neuroscience can give a mother-to-be about how to optimize her baby's brain development in the first half of pregnancy can be summarized by a single sentence: Do *nothing*. You don't need to speak French or play Mozart to your embryo at this stage. Your baby's brain is not yet hooked up to her ears anyway. Neurogenesis, the major preoccupation of a baby's brain at these early stages, proceeds in a mostly automatic fashion. Just find a calm place where you can throw up on a regular basis, and take your doctor's recommended amount of folic acid, which prevents neural tube defects.

Eat an extra 300 calories a day

Weight gain is normal, and pregnant women should plan on ballooning up. Malnourished moms tend to produce smaller, malnourished babies, and brain size is roughly associated with brain power. Most women need to add about 300 calories per day during pregnancy. Your physician can tell you how many and at what rate.

Eat fruits and veggies

The oldest advice is still the best: a balanced diet of fruits and vegetables. This is simply replicating the nutritional experiences forged over our inescapable evolutionary history. Along with enough folic acid, pediatricians suggest eating foods rich in iron, iodine, vitamin B12, and omega-3. Remember flavor programming, where mothers who drank carrot juice had babies who liked carrot cereal? This notion requires more research, but it is very possible that helping a child start a lifelong love affair with vegetables (or, more probably, a lifelong "I don't hate all vegetables" affair) may start with you eating lots of fruits and vegetables in the last trimester of pregnancy.

Get 30 minutes of aerobic exercise each day

My wife and I would take long walks together during both pregnancies. We often retrace these routes today, and we still remember how we felt about those pregnancies each time we do. Exercise has provided a lot of nostalgia for us.

Exercise is a known stress reducer, good for keeping marauding glucocorticoids away from baby's vulnerable neurons—and mom's, too. It produces lots of brain-friendly chemicals and reduces the risk of clinical depression and anxiety disorders. Consult your physician first; only your doctor knows exactly what you should be doing and how long you should be doing it. It changes with the stages of pregnancy.

Reduce the stress in your life

Pregnancy is stressful, and the body is equipped to handle that. But excess stress can do damage to you and the baby. An overabundance of cortisol targets a baby's developing neurons, interfering with proper brain development. Remove as much toxic stress as possible—for you and for baby.

List the areas where you feel out of control

Make a "Things that really bother me" list. Now mark the ones where you feel out of control. Toxic stress comes from feelings of helplessness. These are your enemy.

Take back control

Exerting control may mean exiting the stressful situations you just marked. If that's not an option, think about ways to reduce the stress that arises from them. Aerobic exercise is a must; you'll find more of the best stress-reducing techniques at *www.brainrules.net*.

Husbands, cherish your pregnant wives

Treat your wife like a queen. Do the dishes. Bring her flowers. Find out about her day. Developing those patterns while your wife is pregnant is one of the greatest gifts dads can give to their kids. That's because one of the four significant sources of stress we discussed comes from a woman's relationship with her significant other. When the man creates a backstop of unrelenting support, the woman has one less thing to worry about.

Relationship

Reconstitute the tribe

For evolutionary reasons, human babies were never meant to be born and raised in isolation from a group. Psychotherapist Ruthellen Josselson believes it is especially important for young mothers to create and maintain an active social tribe after giving birth. There are two big problems with this suggestion: (1) Most of us don't live in tribes, and (2) we move around so much that most of us don't even live near our own families, our natural first tribal experience. The result is that many new parents live on the margins of their social lives. They don't have a relative or trusted friend who can watch their kids while they take a shower, get some sleep, or make out with their spouses.

The solution is obvious: Reconstitute a vigorous social structure using whatever tools you have at hand.

Start forming one *now*, before the baby comes. There are many options. At the formal level, there are local parenting groups (here in Seattle, we have PEPS, Program for Early Parent Support), churches and synagogues, all possessing built-in notions of community. Informally, you can host social get-togethers with your friends. Go out with other pregnant couples in Tribe Lamaze. Throw cooking parties, where you and your friends make a bunch of freezer meals. Having a 50-day meal supply all ready to eat before baby comes home is one of the best gifts you can give any prospective parent. Doing another 50 after baby arrives is a great way to cement your community.

Work on your marriage

Even if you see no trouble on the marital horizon and you have lots of friends, there is no guarantee that this will remain true after baby comes. A few ideas:

Start morning and afternoon inquiries

Begin regular "check-in" times with each other. Check in twice a day, once in the morning and once in the afternoon, easy as a quick phone call, email, or text message. Why twice? The morning allows you to see how the day is beginning to progress. The afternoon helps you prepare for the evening. New parents have only about one-third the time alone together that they had when they were childless. That's just another form of social isolation. Starting now, while you have energy, gives you space to develop the habit before baby comes, when you won't have the energy.

Schedule sex regularly

Yes, the great joy in physical intimacy includes a healthy helping of spontaneity. Problem is, you can kiss spontaneity out the window when you bring baby home. Sexual activity usually plummets after the birth of a child, and the loss of associated emotional intimacy can be devastating for couples. Scheduling sex—however often is right for you—can buffer against this tendency. It also gives each partner time to mentally decompress and get into the mood. Try incorporating two types of sex into your lives: spontaneous sex and maintenance sex.

Develop the empathy reflex with your partner

A woman in one of our research projects had recently been exposed to training in the empathy reflex. She was shopping at Costco after a long day at work when she discovered at the checkout counter that only stubs were left in the checkbook. She called hubby requesting assistance. She instead got a lecture about personal responsibility: Why didn't she look in the checkbook before taking it? Where was her reserve of cash? "That's not what you're supposed to say," she reminded him. "You're supposed to say, 'You sound tired, honey, and frustrated and mad. And you're angry because calling me was the last thing on your mind after a hard day at work and you are probably humiliated right now and you just want to go home!'" She faced the phone. "That's what you're supposed to say, dummy!" Then she hung up. Well, that last bit isn't part of the training. But everyone needs practice in the two-step of reading emotions and guessing the cause. The most common source of conflicts is the gap between a person's unknowable intentions and observable behavior. That gap can be bridged by empathy.

Reconcile deliberately

If you have a fight in front of your children, reconcile in front of your children. This allows your child to model how to fight fair *and* how to make up.

Balance the housework load

Guys, start helping around the house *now*. Make a list of what your wife does. Make a list of what you do. If your list displays the toxic inequality typical in the United States—you know, the one predictive of *divorce rates*—then change the list. Balance it until you both are satisfied with what equality means. Once the list has been renegotiated, get started on these changes immediately. Before you are sleep deprived. Before you are socially isolated. Before you start fighting. There is even empirical support that you will get more sex if you do. No kidding. Somebody actually studied it.

Address your sticking points

No marriage is perfect, for sure, but some marriages will survive parenthood much better than others. Do you know into which category your marriage falls? Marital intervention programs can tell you. Two of the most well-regarded programs in the United States were developed in the laboratories of Philip and Carolyn Cowan, and John and Julie Gottman. Their websites are chock-full of diagnostic tools, practice sessions, books they have written on the subject, and sign-up forms for workshops. Links to these programs, their literature, and the peer-reviewed references are at *www.brainrules.net*.

Find a mental-health professional now

A new parent's first exposure to child-based medical professionals is usually a pediatrician. I am advocating that you add another to the list: a mental-health professional. Someone affordable with whom you can check in as questions come up, just like a pediatrician. There are many reasons to get started on this journey, beginning with the fact that most pediatricians do not have advanced training in mental-health issues. Here are three more:

Mental-health issues will arise for many children. I am not just talking about the usual behavioral suspects, like autism and ADHD. The average age of onset of ANY mental-health issue, from mood disorders to thought disorders, is 14.

Delay is your enemy. The earlier a mental-health issue is detected, the easier it is to treat. It can take a while to find a mental-health professional who fits with your family, so it's good to get started now. I am aware that this advice will be a waste of time for some. For others, it will be the most important thing they will ever do for their kids.

Depression affects as many as one in five new parents. Having a mental-health professional can act like an insurance policy for you, too. If there are no issues, there will be no need to visit, but if one crops up, you will already know where to turn.

Smart baby

Breast-feed for one year

Longer is better. You'll get a smarter baby, a healthier baby, a happier baby. Breast-feeding is one of the most practical, brain-boosting behaviors we know. The benefits are extremely well established.

Describe everything you see

Talk to your baby a lot. This is as simple as saying, "It's a beautiful day" when you look outside and see the sun. Just talk. During infancy, do so in "parentese," those clusters of exaggerated vowel sounds at high frequencies. A rate of 2,100 words per hour is the gold standard.

Create a Chocolate Factory

There may be as many different types of playrooms as there are families, but every one of them should have the following design element: lots of choices. A place for drawing. A place for painting. Musical instruments. A wardrobe hanging with costumes. Blocks. Picture books. Tubes and gears. Anything where a child can be safely let loose, joyously free to explore whatever catches her fancy. Did you see the movie *Willy Wonka & the Chocolate Factory*? If so, you may have been filled with wonder at the chocolate plant, complete with trees, lawns, and waterfalls—a totally explorable, nonlinear ecology. That's what I mean. I am focusing on artistic pursuits because kids who are trained in the arts tend to resist distractions better, stay focused better, and have better scores on fluid intelligence tests.

My wife and I devoted nearly 600 square feet in our house to creating such an environment, filled with music stations, reading and drawing and painting and crafting areas, lots of Legos, and lots of cardboard boxes. There was a math and science station, including a toy microscope. We changed the contents of these stations on a regular basis, and we eventually turned the space into our kids' classroom.

Play "opposite day"

After my children turned 3, I employed some fun activities to improve executive function, roughly based on the canonical work of Adele Diamond. I would tell them that today was "opposite day." When I held up a drawn picture of the night, an inky black background sprinkled with stars, they were supposed to say "day." When I held up a picture with a big blue sky inhabited by a big yellow sun, they were supposed to say "night." I would alternate the pictures with increasing rapidity and check for their responses.

They had a blast with this; for some reason we always ended up rolling on the floor laughing.

I did a kinetic form of this exercise with my elder son, who was a natural drummer, when he was 4. We each had a spoon and a pan.

The rule was that when I struck a pan with a spoon once, he had to do it twice. When I hit a pan twice, he had to strike it three times. Or once. (I changed it up quite a bit.)

The idea for both exercises was to (a) give the boys a rule and (b) help them inhibit what they would do automatically in the face of this rule—a hallmark of executive function. We had a certain place in our Chocolate Factory for these types of play. There are a ton of exercises like these you can do with your kids. For a list of nearly 20 great ones, check out Ellen Galinsky's *Mind in the Making*.

Make play plans

See if elements of the Tools of the Mind program will fit in with your lifestyle. Here's one way this worked at my house: Our boys might decide that they wanted to make a construction site. (They had a favorite video that featured various construction machines, which we watched ad nauseam. We still take it out for birthdays, as a funny nostalgia piece.) We would sit down together and plan the elements of what would go into the construction site, what might occur there once it was built, and how cleanup should best be handled once finished. Our imaginations ran wild, but a linear list of goals would be created from the exercise. Then the boys would play.

A full description of the Tools program is available here: *www.mscd.edu/extendedcampus/toolsofthemind*

Do not hyper-parent

These playroom designs and games have a non-pressured, open-ended quality to them. That's no accident. The more strangled children feel emotionally, the more stress hormones swarm their brains, and the less likely they are to succeed intellectually. Teaching your children to focus, then letting them loose inside a Chocolate Factory, allows them to exercise their gifts far better than kids who can't focus and who aren't allowed choices. Note that what is missing in these ideas is Mandarin lessons and algebra classes and reading Rousseau by age 3.

Take a critical look at (gulp) your behavior

One of the most familiar forms of parental guidance is direct instruction, which parents deploy in earnest as their child becomes verbal. "Please come with me." "Stay away from strangers." "Eat your broccoli." But direct instruction is not the only way kids learn from their parents, and it may not be the most efficient. They also learn through observation. And your kids are observing you like a hawk. Here's a three-step suggestion:

Step 1: Make a list of all the behaviors—the actions and words— you regularly broadcast to the world. Do you laugh a lot? Swear on a regular basis? Exercise? Do you cry easily or have a hair-trigger temper? Do you spend hours on the Internet? Make this list. Have your spouse do this, too, and compare.

Step 2: Rate them. There are probably things on this list of which you are justifiably proud. Others, not so much. Whether good or bad, these are the behaviors your children will encounter on a regular basis in your household. And they will imitate them, whether you want them to or not. Decide which behaviors you want your children to emulate and circle them. Decide which behaviors you'd rather have them not imitate at all and put an X through them.

Step 3: Do something about this list. Engage regularly in the behaviors you love. It's as easy as telling your spouse on a regular basis how much you love her. Put on an extinction schedule the ones you don't want to have around. It's as easy (and as hard) as turning off the television.

Say, "Wow, you really worked hard"

Get into the habit of rewarding the intellectual exertion your child puts into a given task rather than his or her native intellectual resources. Begin by practicing on your spouse and even your friends. If they do something well, say, "You must have put a lot of effort into that" rather than, "Wow, you are really talented." When children praised for their effort fail, they are much more likely to try harder.

Trade for digital time

Knowing full well the need for our kids to be digitally conversant, yet fully aware of the dangers, my wife and I came up with a few rules as our boys became preschoolers. First, we divided digital experiences into categories. Two of the categories involved things necessary for schoolwork or for learning about computers: word processing and graphics programs, web-based research projects, programming, and so on. The boys were allowed to do these as homework required.

Recreational experiences—digital games, certain types of web surfing, and our Wii gaming system—we called Category I. They were off-limits except under one condition. Our sons could "buy" a certain amount of Category I time. The currency? The time spent reading an actual book. Every hour spent reading could purchase a certain amount of Category I time. This was added up and could be "spent" on weekends after homework was done. This worked for us. The kids picked up a reading habit, could do the digital work necessary for their futures, and were not completely locked out of the fun stuff.

Happy baby

Chart your child's emotional landscape

Most infants have a limit to how much stimulation they can take at any one time. Make a list of your baby's "can we stop now?" cues, which can be as subtle as head turning or as obvious as bawling. Then get into a rhythm based on that, interacting in response to your baby's cues and withdrawing when she's had enough.

Continue to monitor your child's emotions as he or she gets older. Jot down a few sentences describing your child's likes and dislikes. Update it continuously as various emotional responses develop. Making a list gets you in the habit of paying attention, and it provides a baseline, allowing you to notice any changes in behavior.

Help your child make friends of the same age

Learning to make friends takes years of practice. Kids consistently exposed to the delightful rough-and-tumble of other children get experience with personalities who are as innocent as they are, as selfish as they are, as desirous of peer interactions as they are. So arrange plenty of playdates. Let your children interact with multiple age groups, too, and a variety of people. But pay attention to how much your child can handle at one time. Social experiences must be tailored to individual temperaments.

Speculate on another's point of view

In front of your children, verbally speculate about other people's perspectives in everyday situations. You can wonder why the person behind you in line at a grocery is so impatient or what the joke is when a stranger talking on a cell phone laughs. It's a natural way to practice seeing other people's points of view—the basis of empathy.

Read together

My wife and I turned this into a family tradition. At the end of each day just before lights out, we got into our pajamas and prepared for bed, then snuggled down together. My wife got out a book and, for the next half hour, read it aloud. Though the boys are a bit too old for snuggling now, we still do this just-before-sleep public reading. It exposes the boys to a broader vocabulary of words in a different "voice," it brings all four of us together as a family, and it compels our brains to get out of our own experiences, imagining different worlds populated by people who don't react as we do.

Develop an empathy reflex with your children

When faced with a strong emotion, turn to empathy first:

1. Describe the emotion you think you see.
2. Make a guess as to where it came from.

Remember, understanding someone's behavior is not the same thing as agreeing with it. It is just your opening response to any situation when intense emotions are involved. If you want to have empathic children, they will need to see it modeled on a regular basis. Empathy comes from being empathized with.

Determine your meta-emotion style

What are your emotions about emotions? One particularly insightful test can be found in John Gottman's book *Raising an Emotionally Intelligent Child: The Heart of Parenting*. Another, more technical book is Volume 4 of the *Handbook of Child Psychology*. Look in the chapter titled "Socialization in the Context of the Family: Parent-Child Interaction," by E. E. Maccoby and J. A. Martin.

Practice verbalizing your feelings

You can do this by yourself, with your spouse, or with close friends. When you experience a feeling, simply state that feeling out loud. Verbalizing emotions gives you a better command over your emotional life, allowing for more insightful self-regulation. It is also a great model for children. I remember trying in vain to open a jar of pickles. My 4-year-old walked in, glanced up at me, and said, "Daddy, you look mad. Are you mad?" "Yep," I replied. "I can't get the pickle jar open." Later that day, I noticed he was getting frustrated building a Lego model. "You look angry, son," I said. "Are you angry?" He looked at me and said, "Yes. I'm mad. This is my jar of pickles!" If your children are surrounded by people who can talk about feelings, they will be able to verbalize their feelings, too—invaluable to you when they reach puberty.

Save up for 10 years of music lessons

Instruments, singing, whatever—make music a consistent part of your child's experience. Long-term musical exposure has been shown to greatly aid a child's perception of others' emotions. This skill in turn predicts your child's ability to establish and maintain friendships.

Guide your child toward a $50,000-a-year career

People who earn six- and seven-figure incomes, studies show, are not substantially happier than those who earn five figures. The cutoff is about $50,000, in 2010 dollars.

Moral baby

CAP your rules.

Rules delivered with certain characteristics have the best shot at instilling moral awareness in children. You can remember them with "CAP."

"C" stands for Clarity. The rules are clear, reasonable, and unambiguous. It often helps to write them down. Chore charts are good examples. Many families simply shout out a rule as a reaction to a frustrating experience: "From now on, you are going to bed by eight!" But what happens to the rule when the emotions die out?

Write down important rules, and post them in a public place for the whole family to see. They can serve as a point of negotiation and a source of humor—as anyone who has read the *Harry Potter* series and the edicts of Dolores Umbridge can attest.

"A" stands for Accepting. The rules are delivered in a consistently warm and accepting environment.

"P" stands for Praise. Every time a child follows a rule, reinforce the behavior. This includes praising the absence of a behavior, such as when a child doesn't yell in a restaurant.

Explain the rationale behind the rule

Explain verbally to your children the reasons for your rules. This allows kids to generalize the lessons to other situations, which leads to moral internalization. If all they have is "Because I said so," only a primitive form of behavior modification takes place.

Effective punishment FIRST

"F" stands for firm. The punishment must mean something. It has to be firm and aversive to be effective.

"I" stands for immediate. The closer the punishment is delivered to the point of infraction, the more effective it is.

"R" stands for reliable. The punishment must be consistently applied whenever the noxious behavior is displayed. Inconsistently applied rules are confusing and lead to uneven moral development.

"S" stands for safe. The rules must be supplied in an atmosphere of emotional safety. Children have a hard time internalizing moral behavior under conditions of constant threat.

"T" stands for tolerant. Actually, this is a call for patience, something we addressed only obliquely. Children rarely internalize rules on the first try and sometimes not on the 10th.

Videotape yourself parenting

Most parents keep a running documentary about the early lives of their children. Indeed, the generation coming will be the most filmed in history. What if you tape yourself parenting your little one, especially during the tough times, and try to analyze what you're doing? It may give you a clearer idea of your effectiveness as parents.

Sleepy baby

Wait for quiet sleep

Once you detect signs of sleep, don't disrupt the process. If you are holding baby, continue to hold baby. Baby is still in active sleep mode and easily aroused. When she reaches quiet sleep, *then* place her in bed.

Enjoy the journey

Parenting is *so* on the right side of worth it!

references

Extensive, notated references
and illustrations are online at
www.brainrules.net/references

thanks

The birth of this book was assisted by many doulas, and I am deeply indebted to all of them. I am grateful for the sunny optimism and tireless work of my publisher, Mark Pearson. And for the instructive, incisive, and caring comments of my editor, Tracy Cutchlow. I still owe you a beer.

I am also indebted to Jessica Sommerville, for supplying the essential oxygen of peer review. And to Carolyn Webster-Stratton, for kind words and encouragement. To Dan Leach, for his curiosity, enthusiasm, and countless inspiring conversations. To Bruce Hosford, for deep friendship, hard work, and endless support. To Earl Palmer, for inspiration, and to John Ratey, for the same. To Rick Stevenson, for visual possibilities and love of narrative. To Alice and Chris Canlis, for creating one of the closest-knit families I know—truly a role model for the world to follow. And to Alden Jones, without whose never-ending concern and unceasing devotion to detail this book and its many moving parts would not be possible.

Lastly, I am indebted to my family. To our two dear children, Josh and Noah, for showing me that true love can exist between fathers and sons, even when you were smaller than the period at the end of this sentence. And to my wife, Kari, simply the most amazing person I have ever met.